Word
2007

BEYOND
THE **MANUAL**

Word
2007

Connie Morrison

Apress®

Word 2007: Beyond the Manual

Copyright © 2007 by Connie Morrison

ISBN-13 (pbk): 978-1-59059-799-6

ISBN-10 (pbk): 1-59059-799-0

Printed and bound in the United States of America 9 8 7 6 5 4 3 2 1

Lead Editors: Jonathan Hassell, James Huddleston

Technical Reviewer: Karla Browning

Editorial Board: Steve Anglin, Ewan Buckingham, Gary Cornell, Jason Gilmore, Jonathan Gennick, Jonathan Hassell, James Huddleston, Chris Mills, Matthew Moodie, Dominic Shakeshaft, Jim Sumser, Matt Wade

Project Manager: Richard Dal Porto

Copy Edit Manager: Nicole Flores

Copy Editor: Ami Knox

Assistant Production Director: Kari Brooks-Copony

Production Editor: Kelly Winquist

Compositor: Susan Glinert

Proofreader: Nancy Riddiough

Indexer: Valerie Haynes Perry

Artist: April Milne

Cover Designer: Kurt Krames

Manufacturing Director: Tom Debolski

Distributed to the book trade worldwide by Springer-Verlag New York, Inc., 233 Spring Street, 6th Floor, New York, NY 10013. Phone 1-800-SPRINGER, fax 201-348-4505, e-mail orders-ny@springer-sbm.com, or visit http://www.springeronline.com.

For information on translations, please contact Apress directly at 2560 Ninth Street, Suite 219, Berkeley, CA 94710. Phone 510-549-5930, fax 510-549-5939, e-mail info@apress.com, or visit http://www.apress.com.

Contents at a Glance

About the Author. xvii

About the Technical Reviewer xix

Acknowledgments. xxi

Introduction xxiii

CHAPTER 1   **Word 2007 Overview**. 1

CHAPTER 2   **Getting Started with the New User Interface** 15

CHAPTER 3   **Viewing Documents** 33

CHAPTER 4   **Formatting and Editing**. 49

CHAPTER 5   **Creating Documents More Efficiently** 71

CHAPTER 6   **Designing Page Layouts**. 127

CHAPTER 7   **Using Reference Features** 155

CHAPTER 8   **Creating Envelopes, Labels, and
Merge Documents** 181

CHAPTER 9   **Working with Others** 199

CHAPTER 10   **Creating and Using Macros**. 225

CHAPTER 11   **Using Templates, Form Controls, and XML**. 241

CHAPTER 12   **Publishing Documents**. 259

Index 277

Contents

About the Author. xvii

About the Technical Reviewer xix

Acknowledgments. xxi

Introduction xxiii

CHAPTER 1

Word 2007 Overview 1

  A Whole New Look. 1

    The Quick Access Toolbar 2

    The Ribbon 2

  Quick Formatting 4

    The Mini Toolbar 4

    Quick Styles 4

    Live Preview 5

    Templates 5

    Themes 7

    SmartArt Graphics 8

    Building Blocks 8

    Equation Builder 9

    Reference Builder 11

  Improved File Format 11

  Document Protection 12

  Compatibility 13

  Collaboration 14

CHAPTER 2

Getting Started with the New User Interface 15

The Ribbon. 15

    Tabs, Groups, and Commands 16

    Using the Mouse to Navigate the Ribbon 17

    Using the Keyboard to Navigate the Ribbon .18

    Minimizing the Ribbon 19

Accessing Common Microsoft Word Features. 19

    Using the Quick Access Toolbar 20

    Choosing from the Microsoft Office Button Options 21

    Creating a New Document 22

    Opening a Document 22

    Converting a Document 22

    Saving a Document 23

    Printing a Document 23

    Preparing a Document for Distribution 23

    Sending E-Mail 28

    Publishing a Document 28

    Accessing Recent Documents 28

Locating Word Settings. 29

Using the New File Formats. 30

Getting Help. 30

CHAPTER 3

Viewing Documents 33

Changing Views 33

    Working in Full Screen Reading View 34

    Working in Outline View 37

    Creating Master Documents and Subdocuments 39

    Working in Draft View 40

    Displaying Helpful Tools 40

    Showing and Hiding Nonprinting Characters 42

    Showing and Hiding ScreenTips 42

    Changing the Zoom 43

    Arranging Documents in Windows 44

    Viewing Macros 45

Using Print Preview 45

Hiding White Space 47

CHAPTER 4

Formatting and Editing 49

Selecting Text and Objects 49

Selecting with Command Buttons 49

Selecting with the Click-Shift-Click Method 50

Selecting with the Keyboard 50

Using the Clipboard 51

Setting Options for the Clipboard Task Pane 51

Repositioning and Resizing the Clipboard Task Pane 52

Using the Format Painter 53

Formatting Fonts 55

Using the Mini Toolbar 55

Previewing Formats 56

Changing Case 57

Applying Subscript and Superscript Formats 58

Shrinking and Growing Fonts 58

Clearing Formats 58

Underlining Text 59

Formatting Strikethrough Marks 59

Adding Text Formats to the Quick Access Toolbar 59

Animating Text 60

Formatting Paragraphs 60

Adding Bullets and Numbering 60

Creating Multilevel Lists 61

Changing Line Spacing 62

Formatting with Styles. 63

Using Quick Styles 63

Creating Your Own Styles 64

Formatting Styles Manually 65

Formatting Automatically As You Type 66

Saving Time Editing 67

Specifying the Spacing Between Sentences 67

Using the Repeat Command 67

Finding and Replacing Text 68

Working in Overtype Mode 69

CHAPTER 5

Creating Documents More Efficiently 71

Working with Building Blocks 71

    Inserting a Building Block 72

    Adding a Building Block 72

    Changing the Content of a Building Block 73

    Changing the Properties of a Building Block .73

    Sharing Building Blocks 73

Creating Cover Pages 74

Creating Tables. 76

    Using Quick Tables 76

    Using the Table Grid 77

    Drawing the Table Borders 78

    Converting Text to a Table 79

    Nesting Tables 80

    Inserting an Excel Spreadsheet 80

Formatting Table Styles. 81

Formatting Table Layouts 83

    Adding and Deleting Rows and Columns 85

    Merging and Splitting Cells and Tables 86

    Changing the Cell Size 87

    Aligning Text Within Cells 89

    Wrapping Text Around a Table 91

Managing Table Data 92

    Sorting Table Data 93

    Repeating Header Rows 93

    Converting a Table to Text 94

    Using Formulas in Tables 95

    Numbering Table Rows 96

Working with Illustrations. 97

    Inserting Pictures 97

    Inserting Clip Art 100

    Inserting Shapes 100

    Inserting SmartArt 107

    Inserting Charts 111

Using Links. 113

    Creating Hyperlinks 113

    Inserting Bookmarks 114

    Inserting Cross-References 115

Formatting Headers, Footers, and Page Numbers. 116

    Adding Building Blocks 117

    Creating Different Headers and Footers in Each Section 117

    Creating Different Headers and Footers for the First Page and
    Odd and Even Pages 118

Using Graphics to Enhance Text 119

Adding a Signature Line 121

Creating Equations. 122

    Saving Documents with Equations 126

    Using Symbols 126

CHAPTER 6

Designing Page Layouts 127

Using Themes. 127

    Applying a Theme 128

    Modifying a Theme 129

    Saving Customized Themes 132

Generating Filler Text 133

Changing Page Orientation and Paper Size 133

Setting Page Margins 134

    Changing Margins for the Entire Document 135

    Changing Default Margin Settings 136

    Setting Margins for a Section in the Document 136

    Setting Margins for a Portion of the Document 137

    Adding a Gutter Setting 137

    Formatting Mirror Margins 138

    Formatting Margins for Printing Two Pages on One Sheet 140

    Formatting Margins for a Booklet 140

Formatting Text in Columns 141

Automatically Hyphenating Text 141

Working with Document Sections. 142

    Creating a New Section 142

    Editing a Section Break 142

    Deleting a Section 143

Changing Vertical Text Alignment 143

Using Watermarks. 144

    Adding a Predesigned Watermark 144

    Creating a Custom Watermark 145

    Creating a Watermark with a Clipart Image 145

    Assigning a Watermark to Specific Pages .146

    Removing a Watermark 146

Adding Background Color to Pages 146

Adding Borders to Pages. 147

Indenting Paragraphs 147

    Formatting a First Line Indent 148

    Formatting a Full-Paragraph Indent 148

    Formatting a Hanging Indent 149

    Formatting a Negative Indent 150

Setting Tabs 150

    Setting Tabs Using the Ruler 150

    Setting Tab Stops Precisely 151

Adjusting Paragraph and Line Spacing 152

CHAPTER 7

Using Reference Features 155

Creating a Table of Contents 155

    Creating a TOC Using Built-In Heading Styles 156

    Adding More Entries to the TOC 159

    Creating a TOC Using Custom Styles 159

    Marking TOC Entries Manually 160

    Displaying TOC Field Codes 161

    Editing Field Codes 162

    Updating a TOC 162

    Removing a TOC 162

Creating Multiple TOCs in the Same Document 162

    Using TC Fields to Create Multiple TOCs 163

    Using Bookmarks to Create Multiple TOCs .163

Creating Footnotes and Endnotes 164

    Inserting and Deleting a Footnote or an Endnote 164

    Changing the Reference Mark Format 165

    Restarting Reference Mark Numbering 165

    Navigating Among Footnotes and Endnotes 165

    Creating a Footnote or Endnote Continuation Notice 166

    Converting Selected Notes to Footnotes or Endnotes 166

    Converting All Notes to Footnotes or Endnotes 166

Creating Citations and Bibliographies 167

    Choosing a Documentation Style 167

    Inserting a Citation 167

    Managing Sources 169

    Generating a Bibliography 170

    Displaying Bibliography Field Codes 171

Formatting Captions 171

Creating a Table of Figures 172

Formatting Cross-References 173

    Creating a Cross-Reference 174

    Displaying Cross-Reference Field Codes 175

    Editing Cross-References 176

Creating an Index 176

    Marking Text for an Index Entry 176

    Marking an Index Entry for a Range of Pages 177

    Generating an Index 177

    Updating an Index 178

Creating a Table of Authorities 179

    Marking Citations for a Table of Authorities 179

    Generating a Table of Authorities 180

    Updating a Table of Authorities 180

CHAPTER 8

Creating Envelopes, Labels, and Merge Documents 181

Creating Envelopes and Labels 181

    Printing an Address on an Envelope 182

    Creating a Single Address Label 183

    Creating a Full Page of the Same Label 185

Creating Mail Merge Documents 186
   Starting the Mail Merge Process 187
   Writing and Inserting Fields 188
   Previewing Results 193
   Completing the Merge 195
Merging to E-Mail 196

CHAPTER 9

Working with Others

Working with Others 199
Proofing Documents 199
   Checking Spelling and Grammar 200
   Setting AutoFormat and AutoCorrect Options 200
   Searching Local and Internet Services 201
   Translating Text 203
   Using Translation ScreenTips 206
   Setting a Language for Proofing 206
   Suppressing the Spelling and Grammar Check 207
   Counting Words 207
Making Comments 208
   Adding Comments 208
   Editing and Deleting Comments 210
Tracking Changes 210
   Displaying Tracked Changes and Comments 211
   Displaying the Reviewing Pane 213
   Printing Documents with Tracked Changes 214
   Accepting and Rejecting Changes 214
Comparing and Merging Documents 215
   Comparing Documents 215
   Combining Documents 217
Protecting Documents 218
   Restricting Access to Modify Documents 218
   Restricting Formatting and Editing 219
   Removing Protection 220
   Restricting Access for Opening or E-Mailing Documents 221
Sharing Documents 221
   Removing Properties and Personal Information 222
   Converting to PDF or XPS Format 222
   Sending a PDF or XPS Attachment in an E-Mail 223

CHAPTER 10

Creating and Using Macros

Creating and Using Macros 225
Displaying the Developer Tab 225
Creating Macros 226
Starting the Recording Process 227
Naming and Storing a Macro 227
Assigning a Shortcut to a Macro 228
Completing the Recording Process 229
Creating and Editing a Shortcut for an Existing Macro 230
Running a Macro 230
Editing a Macro 231
Renaming a Macro 232
Undoing a Macro 233
Deleting a Macro 233
Organizing Macros 233
Renaming a Macro Module 233
Copying a Macro Module 234
Deleting a Macro Module 235
Locking a Macro Project 235
Digitally Signing a Macro Project 236
Creating a Self-Signed Certificate 236
Signing a Macro Project 236
Obtaining a Digital Certificate 237
Setting Macro Security Options 237
Changing the Trust Center Settings 238
Adding Signatures to the Trusted Publishers List 238

CHAPTER 11

Using Templates, Form Controls, and XML

Using Templates, Form Controls, and XML 241
Displaying the Developer Tab 241
Using Templates 242
Creating a New Document Based on a Template 242
Attaching a Template to a Document 242
Making a Template Global 243
Using a Document As a Template 244

Using Form Controls 244

    Creating a Form with Content Controls 245

    Inserting Content Controls 246

    Setting the Properties for Content Controls 247

    Adding Instructional Text 248

    Grouping Content Controls 249

Using Legacy Tools 250

Converting Controls to Word 2007 250

Restricting Users from Editing the Document 251

Understanding XML 252

    Using Schemas 253

    Displaying XML Structure 254

    Setting XML Options 257

CHAPTER 12

Publishing Documents 259

Printing a Document 259

    Using Duplex Printing 259

    Printing a Booklet 260

    Using Other Print Options 260

Preparing Documents for Electronic Distribution 263

    Saving a Documents As a Template 263

    Saving a Document in PDF or XPS Format 264

    Saving a Document As a Web Page 265

    Updating the Information in the Document Information Panel 266

    Inspecting a Document 266

    Encrypting a Document 267

    Adding a Digital Signature to a Document 267

    Marking a Document As Final 268

    Running the Compatibility Checker 268

Publishing to a Blog 269

Publishing on a Document Management Server 271

Creating a Document Workspace 273

Creating a Web Page 274

Index 277

About the Author

CONNIE MORRISON has more than 30 years of combined experience in education and educational publishing. Connie began her career teaching business education at the high school and college levels. Seven years later, she worked as an education consultant in the publishing industry.

Connie's work experience in the classroom and in the publishing industry helped her establish a good foundation for developing content for instructional use. Connie became interested in technology when the Radio Shack TRS80 was introduced, and that's when she began writing her own material and training others to use computers. For more than 17 years, Connie has worked as an author and a freelance technical writer. She has authored numerous educational textbooks, many of which are tutorials for Microsoft Office applications.

Currently, Connie works as a consultant for Encore Training, Inc., providing staff training and professional development to help end users develop their computer skills, become more productive, and use technology to its fullest potential.

About the Technical Reviewer

KARLA BROWNING has a master's degree in educational technology from Michigan State University and over 10 years of experience in technical writing, editing, and instruction. She has written numerous titles, including *Word 2000 MOUS Study Guide* and *Mastering Microsoft Office XP*, and has served as technical reviewer on many others.

Karla was a technology trainer and project manager for TRIAD Consulting, LLC, in Flint, Michigan, from 1996 through 2001. She has a state of Michigan K-12 teaching certificate with endorsements in science and technology. She currently serves as director of science instruction for the Midwest region with Mosaica Education, Inc.

Acknowledgments

Prior to this book, the targeted audience for my work has always been classroom students. The template for the textbooks included detailed, step-by-step instructions. When I was asked to contribute to the *Beyond the Manual* series, I was excited about the opportunity to present the information in a new format, skipping over the obvious and basic steps and addressing only that which the end user needs to know to learn what's new and how to be proficient. I am grateful to Apress for giving me this opportunity. It was great working with the Apress team.

I owe special thanks to the following individuals:

Jim Sumser, for his enthusiasm for the *Beyond the Manual* series, bringing me on board, and making this book possible.

Richard Dal Porto, for coordinating the flow of documents and keeping me on schedule throughout the project.

Ami Knox, for her meticulous copyediting to fine-tune the content, and especially for her kindness and encouragement.

Kelly Winquist, for pulling the whole book together and for providing cheerful support.

Karla Browning, for her critical review to verify the accuracy of the content and for contributing her expertise.

Jonathan Hassell and Jim Huddleston, for their feedback, insights, and guidance for developing the contents of this book and shaping the direction of the *Beyond the Manual* series.

My husband, Gene, and our children, Al, Amy, and Chris, for their love, support, and patience with me as I have worked on this project and several other projects over the years.

Introduction

Word 2007: Beyond the Manual is not for beginners. It's for experienced users of Microsoft Word who are interested in learning about what's new in Word 2007. If you already know word processing basics, and if you are familiar with the main features in previous versions of Microsoft Word, you don't need to start at the beginning. You're ready to dive in, and you can learn what you need to know without reviewing the basics.

Word 2007: Beyond the Manual introduces the changes and the new features in Word 2007, and it also addresses topics for advanced word processing tasks. Practical examples of how and why you would use these features in everyday applications are incorporated. Furthermore, you will find plenty of tips and notes for using shortcuts to complete both new and familiar tasks.

How This Book Is Structured

The intent of the book structure is to make it easy for you to become familiar with the new user interface, the Ribbon, and learn about the new features at the same time. For the most part, the sequence of the content in the book parallels the organization of the Word features on the Ribbon. A synopsis of each chapter follows.

Chapter 1, "Word 2007 Overview," provides an overview of the new look, the changes, and the new features in Word 2007. This will give you some insight about what to look for in the new software.

Chapter 2, "Getting Started with the New User Interface," explains the structure and defines the parts of the Ribbon. You'll learn to navigate the Ribbon using both the mouse and the keyboard. This chapter also provides information about the new file formats in Word 2007. You won't want to skip this chapter, because this is where you'll learn how to access the common Word commands such as open, save, and print.

Chapter 3, "Viewing Documents," covers document views and arranging windows—options that are all available on the View tab. Even though the View tab is not the first tab you see on the Ribbon, this content is intentionally introduced early in the text to give you a foundation for viewing documents as you work with them. For example, here you'll find information about setting the zoom for a document, displaying nonprinting characters, viewing documents side by side, synchronous scrolling, and more.

Chapter 4, "Formatting and Editing," focuses on the commands and features available on the Home tab, which is the first tab displayed on the left side of the Ribbon. This tab includes the basic editing tools for cut, copy, and paste; and it also includes tools for applying character and paragraph formats. After learning how to access these basic formatting tools, you can explore the new gallery of styles that you can use to simplify formatting tasks and produce professional-looking documents.

Chapter 5, "Creating Documents More Efficiently," addresses the commands and tools available on the Insert tab, which is the second tab on the Ribbon. You'll find many familiar features on the Insert tab, such as tools for inserting page breaks, tables, hyperlinks, charts, headers, footers, and more. Be sure to take a closer look, though, because there are many new formatting options. There are also some new features here you won't want to miss reading about. Word 2007 offers new SmartArt graphics and new tools for creating mathematical equations. You'll also find preformatted table formats and new table styles.

Chapter 6, "Designing Page Layouts," presents the new themes available on the Page Layout tab, which is the third tab on the Ribbon. The Page Layout tab also provides new command buttons and features for formatting margins, line spacing, and paragraph indents.

Chapter 7, "Using Reference Features," introduces new features on the References tab. The chapter could be subtitled "Citations and Bibliographies Made Easy." Word 2007 offers new tools for creating and formatting citations and bibliographies and managing reference information. The chapter also includes information about creating tables of contents, indexes, cross-references, captions, and tables of authority.

Chapter 8, "Creating Envelopes, Labels, and Merge Documents," describes the tools and options available on the Mailings tab. There are some new merge features including the Highlight Merge Fields option and the new Rules command. Here you'll also find details about personalizing an e-mail message directed to several recipients.

Chapter 9, "Working with Others," is about collaborating and sharing documents. The main focus of the chapter is on the features and tools found on the Review tab. But the chapter is not limited to comments, tracking changes, and comparing and merging documents. The chapter also addresses how to change autocorrect and auto-format options, how to use research features and language and translation tools, how to compare and merge documents, how to protect documents and restrict formatting and editing, and how to share documents in PDF and XPS format.

Chapter 10, "Creating and Using Macros," covers some of the more advanced features that can be accessed on the Developer tab. By default, the Developer tab does not display, but it is easy to access. Don't be intimidated by the term "developer." This chapter explains the process for creating and editing macros. You will also learn how to digitally sign and set security options for macros.

Chapter 11, "Using Templates, Form Controls, and XML," also covers some of the advanced features available on the Developer tab. If you want to create online forms, you'll find information about working with templates and using content controls, many of which are new and much easier to use. You'll also find some basic information about working with XML documents and using schemas.

Chapter 12, "Publishing Documents," is about the final stages before distributing a document. Several printing options are described, and this information can be quite useful if you plan to prepare hard copies of documents. If you plan to distribute documents electronically, you'll want to know more about the new feature for converting to PDF and XPS formats. If you typically share documents electronically, the new Document Inspector feature can be very useful. You can also learn about encrypting documents, adding digital signatures, publishing to a blog, publishing on a document management server, creating a document workspace, and creating a web page.

Contacting the Author

To contact the author, send an e-mail to CMorrison@Encore-Training.us.

CHAPTER 1

Word 2007 Overview

Over the years, Word features have evolved gradually, and if you're an experienced Word user, you're probably comfortable with the way things are. Now the software has changed once again, and this time Microsoft has definitely done a massive makeover. Radical changes make Word 2007 more intuitive and more powerful. Layout tools organize both the new and legacy features more logically so commands and options are much easier to find and access. Word 2007 really is easier to use, and it really does give you more power and usability. To realize productivity gains, though, you must make a successful transition to Word 2007. Here's quick tour of what's new. Be prepared to get hooked on the new Word 2007!

A Whole New Look

When you launch a new version of software, the first changes you usually notice are different options in menus or new buttons on the toolbars. Word 2007 does offer many new menu options, but that's not the first thing you'll notice. The new Word 2007 has a whole new look and feel. The familiar commands and options are still available, but they are presented with a new visual design. This visual design is often referred to as a *new user interface* (see Figure 1-1).

At first glance, you'll notice many visual tools, and initially this can be overwhelming for both new and experienced users. If you've used earlier versions of Word, you'll recognize most of the commands and options, but it may take you longer to find specific commands and features. Be patient, and don't allow your frustration to inhibit you from exploring the new software. In the end, it will be worth the effort!

Figure 1-1 *The new user interface presents a new visual design.*

The Quick Access Toolbar

The Quick Access Toolbar (see Figure 1-2) at the top-left corner of the screen is where you'll find the Microsoft Office button and the Save, Undo, and Repeat commands. You can customize the Quick Access Toolbar so it displays the commands you use most often.

Microsoft
Office
Button

Figure 1-2 *Customize the Quick Access Toolbar to display your most commonly used commands.*

The Microsoft Office button replaces the legacy File menu. When you click the Microsoft Office button, you have access to common Word commands such as New, Open, Save, Print, and Close. This menu also gives you quick access to Word options. In previous versions of Word, the settings for spellchecking, editing, saving, and printing can only be accessed in dialog boxes that are scattered throughout the menus. In Word 2007, you can quickly find all those settings in one place by choosing the Word Options command in the Microsoft Office button menu. Information about how to customize the Quick Access Toolbar is provided in Chapter 2.

The Ribbon

Just below the Quick Access Toolbar is the Ribbon (see Figure 1-3). The Ribbon replaces the menu bar and toolbars and streamlines the way you choose commands.

Once you become familiar with the new user interface, working with Word 2007 will actually save you time, because the new Ribbon makes it easier and quicker to access commands. The Ribbon displays several tabs, beginning with the Home tab at the left. On each tab, related options are all grouped together in one place, so the commands are easier to find. For example, all the commands and buttons you need to format characters can be found in the Font group on the Ribbon (see Figure 1-4).

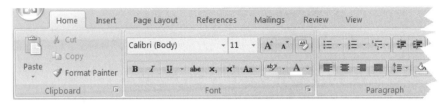

Figure 1-3 *The new Ribbon makes it easier and quicker to access commands.*

Figure 1-4 *The Font group on the Home tab organizes all the text format options in one place.*

Some options are contextual, which means when you choose a command, several new options will automatically display. These options are readily available when you need them, but they also automatically disappear from the screen when you move on to a new task. For example, when you insert a table, two new Table Tools tabs display in the Ribbon. These two tabs offer groups of commands for table designs and layouts (see Figure 1-5).

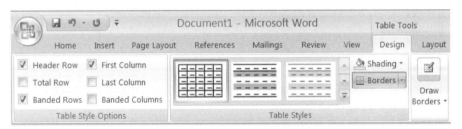

Figure 1-5 *Contextual tabs like this one display only when you need them.*

When the table in the document is selected, the Table Tools tabs are displayed, giving you quick access to all the related table commands. However, when you are no longer working with the table and you reposition the insertion point elsewhere, the Table Tools tabs no longer display. Hence, the screen does not become cluttered. Chapter 2 describes the new user interface in detail and explains how to navigate the Ribbon using both the mouse and the keyboard. Chapter 2 also presents how to access common Word features.

Quick Formatting

If you're an experienced Word user, you may already be very proficient with many of the formatting features, so you are capable of creating professional-looking documents. However, knowing how to do it and having the time to do it are two different issues. It can be very time-consuming displaying all the toolbars, showing all the menu options, and opening all the dialog boxes to find and apply multiple formats. Word 2007 simplifies the task not only by organizing the formatting options on the Ribbon, but also by providing several new features. Many of these new formatting features are introduced in the following text. You can learn more about them in Chapters 4, 5, and 6.

The Mini Toolbar

As the versions have evolved, the Word software has become much more intuitive. Now when you select text, Word presumes you will want to format the selected text. To make these commands quickly accessible, Word displays the new Mini toolbar just above the selection. The Mini toolbar displays buttons for changing the font and paragraph formats (see Figure 1-6).

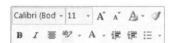

Figure 1-6 *The Mini toolbar provides quick access to character and paragraph formats.*

When you first select text, the display of the Mini toolbar is transparent. If you want to access the formats on the toolbar, simply position the mouse pointer over the toolbar. The toolbar will become active, and the display will brighten. However, if you don't want to apply text formats, you can ignore the toolbar. Your next action (such as cut, copy, or delete) will turn off the transparent display of the toolbar. The Mini toolbar is described in more detail in Chapter 4.

Quick Styles

Word 2007 also provides a gallery with sets of Quick Styles that will help you format documents easily. The styles include several formats that you can apply at the same time. The Quick Styles are available in the Styles group on the Home tab. You can, of course, add some of your own styles to the gallery and delete any of the built-in styles that you don't use (see Figure 1-7). You can learn more about how to modify built-in styles and create your own styles in Chapter 4.

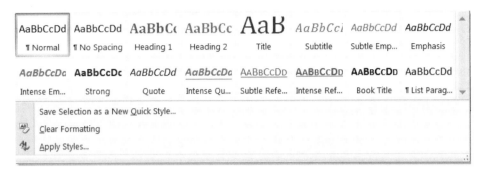

Figure 1-7 *Use Quick Styles to create professional-looking documents quickly.*

Live Preview

The Live Preview feature displays format results before you apply the format. Figure 1-8 illustrates a live preview for a Quick Style format. The first sentence in the paragraph shown below the box of styles is selected, and it is currently formatted with the Normal style. When you move the mouse pointer to a different style, the background shading that shows the selection disappears, and the selected text reflects the change in style (the text font style and color change). The Live Preview feature reduces the number of times you need to choose the Undo command when you're choosing formats! You can learn more about the Live Preview feature in Chapter 4.

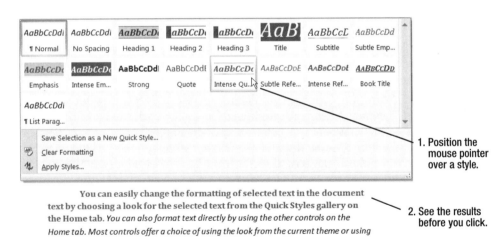

1. Position the mouse pointer over a style.

2. See the results before you click.

Figure 1-8 *The new Live Preview feature lets you see format results before you click.*

Templates

The new design elements include new galleries with a variety of new installed templates (see Figure 1-9). And there are more new templates that are easily accessible at Microsoft Office Online. Information about accessing these new templates is given in Chapter 2.

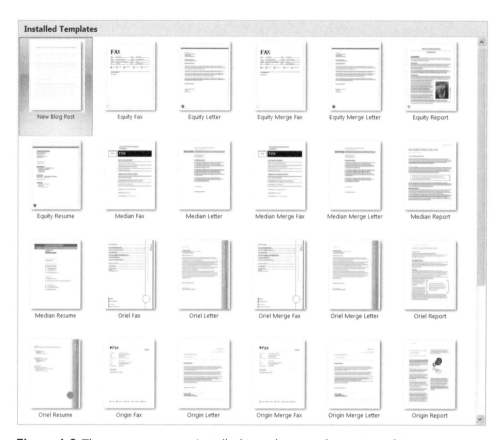

Figure 1-9 *There are many new installed templates, and more templates are available online.*

Along with the Normal blank document, Word 2007 provides a template for a blog post. The new blogging feature enables you to create blogs with images, tables, and text formats. When you create a new document based on the new blog post template, the Blog Post tab displays all the commands you need to link directly to your blog site and publish the blog directly from Word (see Figure 1-10). You can learn about publishing a blog post in Chapter 12.

Figure 1-10 *You can create blog posts in Word and publish them directly to your blog site.*

Themes

Word 2007 also offers many new themes, which can be accessed in the Themes group on the Page Layout tab (see Figure 1-11). You can apply themes to Word documents, web pages, and e-mails. The themes enable you to apply custom formats for fonts, color schemes, backgrounds, and other effects. A theme applies to the entire document, and it can change the overall appearance of the document. If you aren't satisfied with the new built-in themes, you can customize them, or you can find more themes at Microsoft Office Online. You can learn how to apply and modify themes in Chapter 6.

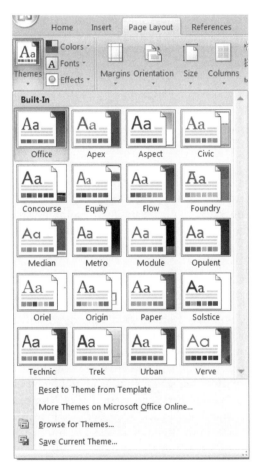

Figure 1-11 *There are 20 new built-in themes, and more themes are available online.*

SmartArt Graphics

When you need to share data, visuals can help to make your communication more effective. The new SmartArt graphics enable you to create professional-looking illustrations to display your data by illustrating relationships, charts, and matrixes. The SmartArt graphic shown in Figure 1-12 illustrates a process of three steps.

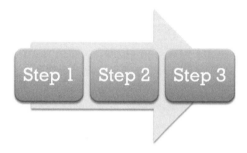

Figure 1-12 *The new SmartArt graphics make it easy for you to create professional-looking illustrations.*

You can create a SmartArt graphic in three easy steps. Choose the type of illustration (list, process, cycle, hierarchy, etc.), select a layout, and enter the text or data in the predesigned art. With just a few clicks, you can create an awesome illustration of designer quality. You'll learn more about SmartArt graphics in Chapter 5.

Building Blocks

Building blocks are document parts (text and/or graphics) that are saved in galleries so they can be used again. For example, you may want to save a paragraph of text that provides a privacy statement at the end of your e-mails so that you can quickly add the paragraph to e-mails in the future. You may think that building blocks are the same as AutoText. There are some similarities, but building blocks are more functional because the content is also preformatted. Word 2007 has several built-in building blocks, such as cover pages, headers and footers, page numbers, and watermarks. You can access these building blocks by displaying the Building Blocks Organizer (see Figure 1-13).

You can save your own building blocks in the Building Blocks Organizer. Chapter 5 discusses building blocks and the Quick Parts command in more detail, as well as the galleries for building tables, headers, footers, and equations. Chapter 6 covers the gallery of watermark building blocks.

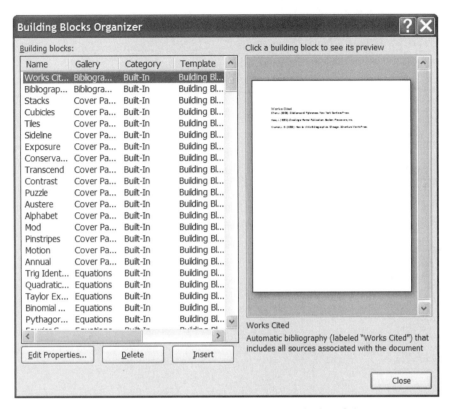

Figure 1-13 *The Building Blocks Organizer stores blocks of document content that you can reuse.*

Equation Builder

In previous versions of Word, you may have used the Microsoft Equation 3.0 or Math Type add-ins. To edit equations created with either of those programs, you had to install the add-in. To create an equation in Word 2007, you no longer need the add-in programs. Word 2007 includes new tools for building equations. You can create an equation by inserting symbols or by choosing from preformatted equations. Some of the built-in preformatted equations are illustrated in Figure 1-14.

You can easily switch between Professional (two-dimensional) and Linear (one-dimensional) views. It is much easier to create and edit equations in Linear view (see Figure 1-15). Chapter 5 provides more in-depth discussion about creating, editing, and converting equations.

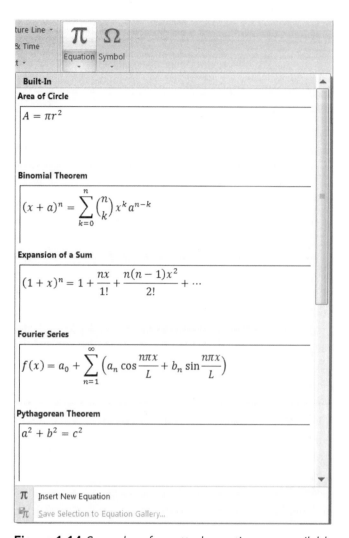

Figure 1-14 *Several preformatted equations are available.*

$$x = \frac{-b \pm \sqrt{b^2 - 4ac}}{2a}$$

$$x = (-b \pm \sqrt{(b^2 - 4ac)})/2a$$

Professional View

Linear View

Figure 1-15 *You can easily convert to Linear view, which makes editing much easier.*

Reference Builder

Students and other individuals who are involved in research will definitely appreciate the new reference builder features. The References tab includes all the tools and commands you need for creating tables of contents, footnotes and endnotes, citations, bibliographies, captions, cross references, indexes, and tables of authorities.

The new tools for creating citations and bibliographies save users lots of time (see Figure 1-16). Using the Source Manager, you can create and maintain a library of sources. You need to enter the data for each source only once. The data is stored in the Source Manager and is available not only for the current project, but also for future projects. When you cite one of your sources, the information is readily available, and Word creates and automatically formats the citation for you. When the project is complete, you simply choose the Bibliography command, and Word automatically creates and formats a Bibliography page or Works Cited page. It's that easy! You'll learn much more about the new reference features in Chapter 7.

Figure 1-16 *Creating citations and bibliographies is so easy now.*

Improved File Format

Word 2007 uses a new file format that significantly decreases the document file size. The new file format also makes the files more secure. Files that contain scripts or macros are separated from basic documents and templates. There are two new file extensions that enable you to quickly distinguish documents created in the new version of Word. These new extensions also enable you to determine whether a file contains codes or macros. To illustrate, file names for earlier versions of Word display the extensions .doc and .dot (see Figure 1-17). Basic documents created in Word 2007 display a file extension ending with the letter "x" (for example, .docx or .dotx). However, if a Word 2007 document contains codes or macros, the file extension for the document will end in the letter "m" (for example, .docm or .dotm).

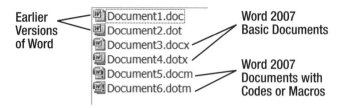

Figure 1-17 *The new file extensions help you distinquish documents that contain codes or macros.*

Also, with the new file format, the data is stored differently, which provides improved corruption recovery. If a document closes abnormally and is damaged, you are more likely to recover the data. Chapter 2 provides information about the new file formats and their compatibility with other Word versions.

Document Protection

When you create new documents or edit existing documents, the new Document Information Panel makes it easy for you to add and/or change the document's properties (see Figure 1-18).

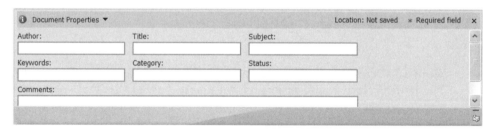

Figure 1-18 *You can view and edit document properties in the new Document Information Panel.*

The fields displayed in Figure 1-18 are for standard document properties. You can, of course, choose the Advanced Properties option to display more field options to include statistics, contents, and custom information. The Document Information Panel is discussed in more detail in Chapter 12.

However, when you share documents with others, you may not want the readers to see information about the document properties, such as author name, creation date, and editing time. The new feature Document Inspector enables you to remove this sensitive information from documents (see Figure 1-19). The Document Inspector feature is covered in more detail in Chapter 12.

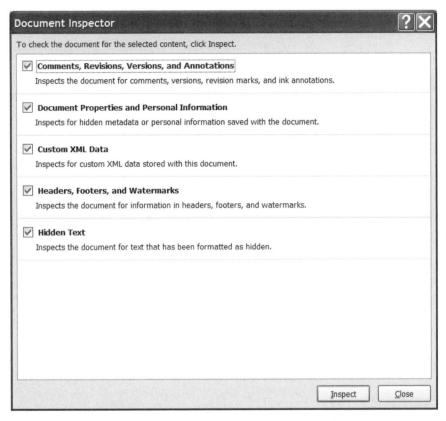

Figure 1-19 *Use the Document Inspector to check for sensitive information before you share a document with others.*

Compatibility

You can open documents created in earlier versions of Word and then convert the documents to the new file formats .docx, .dotx, and .dotm. On the other hand, if you want others to be able to open and edit the document in older versions of Word, you can edit the document in compatibility mode and then save the document using the older file format. When working in compatibility mode, the new features and enhancements are not available. If users of earlier versions of Word attempt to open Word 2007 files, an alert may display indicating the format has been converted, some features have been removed, and/or the ability to edit some features has changed.

The Compatibility Checker, shown in Figure 1-20, also helps you identify how elements in your document will convert from Word 2007 to earlier versions of Word. For example, some formats and graphics will become static, and you won't be able to edit them. In other cases, such as AutoText entries, you may lose some information.

Knowing this in advance may be critical, so the Compatibility Checker is very helpful. Chapter 2 discusses how to use the Compatibility Checker.

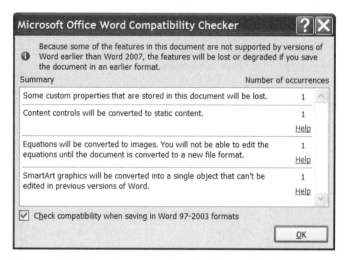

Figure 1-20 *The Compatibility Checker will help you identify compatibility issues should you choose to convert the document to an earlier version of Word.*

Collaboration

If you plan to share your documents with others, Word 2007 offers an add-in feature that enables you to save the documents in XPS or PDF format. These formats are especially useful when you want others to view your documents but not edit them. You'll see more information about these add-ins in Chapters 9 and 12. Open XML formats enable you to integrate XML information with other document content. XML formats also enable you to link data in a Word document to an external data source. An explanation of XML compatibility is given in Chapter 2, and a description of how to use XML features is provided in Chapter 11.

CHAPTER 2

Getting Started with the New User Interface

When you first launch Word 2007, you might find the screen to be a bit overwhelming. There's lots to see, and it may appear cluttered, but don't make any quick judgments. Once you know where to find the features you use every day, you'll get comfortable with the new look. And it won't take long. Let's get started!

The Ribbon

The *Ribbon* is a blue banner that stretches across the top of the screen. It shows the most commonly used commands and displays numerous Word options in a visual format. When looking for options, you no longer need to open and close as many as 30 or more toolbars or open countless menus and dialog boxes. The options are now organized within the Ribbon and are very visible and convenient to access. Obviously, you can't see all the Word options at once, but as you begin working with a document, the Ribbon will adapt by displaying contextual tools. For example, if you insert a picture in your document, commands for formatting the picture will appear in the Ribbon. When you deselect the picture, the Ribbon responds to your action and the commands for the picture disappear.

The Ribbon is similar in other Office applications, so once you learn how to use the Ribbon in Word 2007, you'll find it easy to use in other programs, too. Figure 2-1 shows the Ribbon.

Figure 2-1 *The Ribbon is a blue banner that stretches across the top of the screen.*

Tabs, Groups, and Commands

The Ribbon has three parts: tabs, groups, and commands. The three parts are illustrated in Figure 2-2. The tabs identify core tasks such as Insert and Page Layout. The groups show related items for each of the tasks such as Font and Paragraph formats. The commands are pulled together for each group and can be executed by clicking buttons, entering information in dialog boxes, or selecting options from menus.

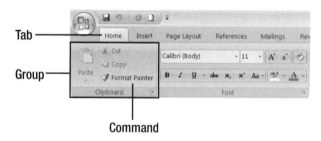

Figure 2-2 *Commands are organized on the Ribbon within groups on several different tabs.*

TIP For the Ribbon to display as in Figure 2-2, your screen must be set to a high resolution (such as 1024×786), and the program window must be maximized. If your screen is set to a low resolution, a few groups on the Ribbon will display only the group name, and the commands in those groups will not display. You will need to click the arrow on the group button to display the commands. Generally, the groups that display only the group name at a lower resolution are those with less frequently used commands.

When working on a Tablet PC with a smaller screen, Word 2007 adjusts the Ribbon to show smaller versions of tabs and groups. The larger the monitor, the larger the display of tabs and groups on the Ribbon will be.

Using the Mouse to Navigate the Ribbon

Even though most of the menus and toolbars have been eliminated, you can still use the mouse to move around and view your options. Simply click one of the tabs. Each tab displays related groups.

Some of the groups include the More button ▾, as displayed in the Styles group on the Home tab (see Figure 2-3).

More button

Figure 2-3 *The More button is positioned at the bottom of the scroll bar.*

When you click the More button, further options within the group display as shown in Figure 2-4.

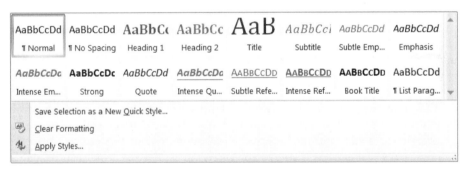

Figure 2-4 *More options display after clicking the More button.*

To display more options in the group:

1. Click the More button in the Styles group (just to the left of Change Styles). A menu with a list of all the styles is displayed, along with some options at the bottom of the menu.

2. Click anywhere in the document window to close the menu.

Many of the groups also display the Dialog Box Launcher ▣ at the bottom-right corner of the group. When you click this button, a traditional dialog box will display. Figure 2-5 illustrates the Dialog Box Launcher in the Font group on the Home tab.

Figure 2-5 *The Dialog Box Launcher is in the lower-right corner of many of the groups.*

To open the dialog box:

1. Point to the Dialog Box Launcher in the Font group. A ScreenTip displays an image and describes the button.

2. Click the Dialog Box Launcher to open the Font dialog box.

3. Close the dialog box.

Using the Keyboard to Navigate the Ribbon

The Ribbon also offers new and easier ways to use the keyboard. If you have proficient keyboarding skills, you may be able to work faster and more efficiently using keyboard shortcuts.

Each tab and each group option on the Ribbon has a keyboard shortcut. These shortcuts are called *Access keys*. In order to use these keyboard shortcuts, you must first switch from *Text Entry mode* (the default mode) to *Command mode*, which activates the Access keys. You use the Alt key to toggle between Text Entry mode and Command mode.

Upon switching to Command mode, the *key tips* (the required key strokes) are visible in *badges* on all the tabs. Each tab has a badge with a key tip. You use these key tips to access the various tabs and the options within the groups. Sometimes the keystrokes will execute a command. Other times, the keystroke will display a dialog box or open a menu.

> **NOTE** In previous versions of Word, there were underscored letters on many of the menu items. The underscored letters have been replaced with these key tips.

To practice using keystrokes to access commands:

1. Press Alt to switch to Command mode.

2. Press R to display the Review tab.

3. Press G to display the Track Changes command.

4. Press O to open the Track Changes Options dialog box.

5. Close the dialog box.

Word automatically returns to Text Entry mode.

> **TIP** You can also use the Tab key to move from one option to another within a group. After selecting the last option in a group, pressing the Tab key again will select the first option on the next group.

In addition to using the Access keys to execute commands, you can use key combinations. For example, Ctrl+C will copy selected text. When you point to a command or option on the Ribbon, the key combinations are displayed in a ScreenTip. Using key combinations can save you a lot of time and keep you on the fast track. Throughout this book, you will see tips and reminders about using key combinations.

> **NOTE** Most of the old key combinations from earlier versions of Word still work, and the key combinations are similar in all Office applications.

Minimizing the Ribbon

The Ribbon does take up a lot space. If you want to maximize your document screen space, you can minimize the Ribbon.

To minimize the Ribbon:

1. Double-click a Ribbon tab or use the key combination Ctrl+F1. The groups will disappear, but the tab labels will still display.
2. To maximize the Ribbon, click a Ribbon tab or use the key combination Ctrl+F1. The entire Ribbon displays.

> **NOTE** If you prefer to keep the Ribbon minimized, click the Customize Quick Access Toolbar button on the Quick Access Toolbar (see the upcoming section "Using the Quick Access Toolbar"). Select Minimize the Ribbon. Then to access the Ribbon as you are working, click the desired tab, and all the groups for that tab will display. When you have completed the command, the Ribbon will automatically minimize.

Accessing Common Microsoft Word Features

The most commonly used Word features include the Save command and the Undo and Redo commands. Because they are used so frequently, Microsoft created a special toolbar so they can be accessed quickly. Just to the left of the new toolbar, you will see the new Microsoft Office button. This button displays a menu with additional commonly used commands such as Open, Print, and Close.

Using the Quick Access Toolbar

The Quick Access Toolbar is positioned in the top-left corner as shown in Figure 2-6. This toolbar includes the most commonly used Word commands. By clicking the Customize Quick Access Toolbar button ▼ (on the right side of the toolbar), you can customize the toolbar by adding other icons you frequently use.

Customize Quick
Access Toolbar

Figure 2-6 *The Quick Access Toolbar hosts the most commonly used Word commands. Click the Customize Quick Access Toolbar button to customize the toolbar.*

To add a toolbar button to the Quick Access Toolbar:

1. Click the Customize Quick Access Toolbar button at the right side of the toolbar. A list of commands appears, and the commands currently displayed on the Quick Access Toolbar are identified with checkmarks.

2. Select More Commands.

3. Under Choose commands from, click the down arrow and select an option to help you locate the command. Then, scroll through the list you have chosen and select the desired command.

4. Click Add. The feature is added to the list at the right.

5. Use the up and down arrows at the far right to change the order in which the buttons will display on the toolbar. Buttons for each of the added features should all display on the Quick Access Toolbar. You can adjust the order of the buttons on the toolbar by using the Move Up and Move Down buttons in the Word Options dialog box.

You can add multiple commands to the Quick Access Toolbar, and the width of the toolbar will grow as the number of buttons increases. Keep in mind, though, that the intent of the toolbar is to organize commands that you use most frequently. Quick access will cease to exist if you must choose from a multitude of buttons. If you find your Quick Access Toolbar has become too cluttered, you can easily remove one or more buttons.

To remove a toolbar button from the Quick Access Toolbar:

1. Click the Customize Quick Access Toolbar button on the toolbar.

2. Deselect the option you wish to remove from the toolbar.

> **NOTE** If you don't like the location of the Quick Access Toolbar, you have the option of moving it to display below the Ribbon. You can make this change by clicking the down arrow at the right side of the toolbar and selecting Show Below the Ribbon.

Choosing from the Microsoft Office Button Options

The File menu is one of the most familiar menus in all software, so you're probably wondering where it is. At the left side of the toolbar is the Microsoft Office button. When you point to this button, a ScreenTip displays "Office Button" and includes a description.

When you click the Microsoft Office button, a menu with options similar to the old File menu displays. The menu is shown in Figure 2-7. At first it may seem that there aren't that many changes, but when you take a closer look, you'll see that there are in fact several new options. Many of the commands you commonly use are now contained in this menu so they are quicker to access. Furthermore, the new features available in this menu will make your work easier and more efficient.

Figure 2-7 *The File menu can be accessed by clicking the Microsoft Office button.*

NOTE As has always been true in earlier versions, when you see the ellipsis (...) in a menu or dialog box option, more choices will display when you click the option. This creates a safe zone if you're not familiar with the command, because when you select the option, no command will be executed. Instead, you will have some more options.

Creating a New Document

The first command in the menu is the New command, which opens the New Document dialog box. The options include a blank document as well as several document templates. Dozens of templates have already been installed, and you can review those by clicking the link Installed Templates at the left side of the New Document dialog box.

If you don't find what you're looking for in the installed templates, many more templates are available by clicking the links for online templates. There are several categories from which you can choose, and these links will take you directly to the Microsoft web site where you can view and select dozens of templates from a variety of categories.

Another new template in the New Document dialog box is the new blog entry document. When you first use this feature, you must register your blog account. If you're new at blogging, you can click the link for Office Marketplace to learn more about blog providers as well as how to create and manage blog entries hosted within the Windows SharePoint Services environment.

Opening a Document

The Open command reveals the Open dialog box, and a new option is the Trusted Templates folder. You can add your own selection of templates in this folder so that they are quick and easy to access.

Converting a Document

If you open a document created in an earlier version of Word, you will see the Convert command. When you choose this command, the document is converted to the new file format, which enables you to use all the new Word 2007 features. Because you converted the document, when you save the document, by default the document will be saved as a .docx document (see the section "Using the New File Formats" later in this chapter).

Saving a Document

Just to the right of the Save As command, you'll notice a right arrow. When you point to this arrow, options for saving the document in another format display. For example, you can save the document for an older version of Word, dating back to Word 97.

You also have the option of saving the document in a PDF or XPS file format. These formats are useful when you want to share a document that is to be read and printed, but not edited. For example, if you save a resume in one of these formats, you can be confident that when the document is opened and/or printed, it will have the same format that you intended. To save a document as a PDF or XPS file, you may need to install a PDF or XPS add-in, which is free for Word 2007 users, or you can install a third-party solution.

Printing a Document

If you click the Print command, the usual Print dialog box will display. If you want to skip the dialog box and go right to Print Preview or send the document to the printer, point to the arrow next to the Print command and choose Quick Print or Print Preview. See Chapter 12 for more in-depth coverage.

Preparing a Document for Distribution

The next new command you'll see in the File menu is the Prepare command. The Prepare command provides options for preparing the document for distribution. See Chapter 12 for more in-depth coverage of all the distribution options.

Setting Document Properties

When you choose the Properties option, the Document Information Panel displays across the top of the screen showing the document properties (see Figure 2-8). This form replaces the Properties dialog box. You can enter or edit text in each of the form fields. To display more options, click the down arrow in the top-left corner next to Document Properties and then choose Advanced Properties. To close the form, click the Close box in the top-right corner of the form.

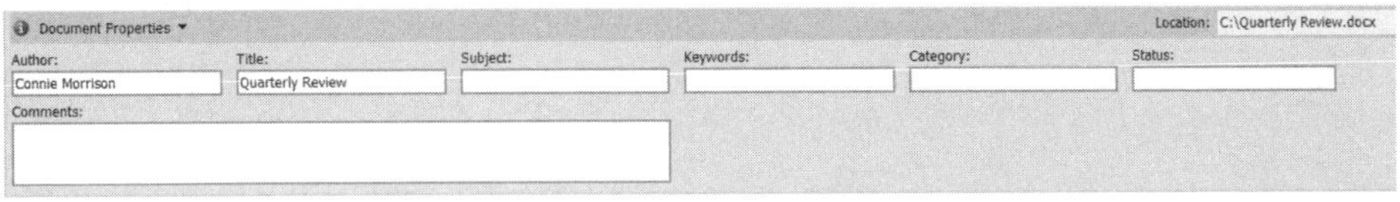

Figure 2-8 *The new Document Information Panel replaces the Properties dialog box.*

> **NOTE** When you use the Document Information Panel to edit the properties for a document that is saved to a document management server, the updated properties are saved directly to the server.

Inspecting a Document

It's always good to do one last proofreading of your document. And though you may always look over your document before you make it available to others, there may be several things you missed—especially if you're planning to share the document electronically. For example, if you tracked changes in your document, the document might still contain revision marks and comments or ink annotations. These features make it possible for those who receive the document to see who worked on the document. They can even read the comments!

The document may also contain hidden metadata or personal information. Most of this information can be found in the properties of the document. When the recipients access the document properties, they can see the author, the subject, and the title of the document as well as any comments related to the document. Furthermore, information about the date the document was created, the amount of editing time spent on the document, the number of revisions, and the last date the document was either modified or accessed is also available.

If you intentionally format parts of the document as hidden text, that text will not print. However, recipients who review the document electronically can still see the "hidden text." Recipients can also see routing slips, printer paths, and file paths. If you make the document available on a document management server, recipients can see the server location. The document may also contain custom XML data.

Thus, if you make the document available to others electronically, you want to make sure the recipients will not have access to sensitive information. Sometimes private information appears in headers, footers, and watermarks. The Inspect Document command provides several options for helping you block this type of information in your documents. The options are shown in Figure 2-9. When you select the Inspect Document command, you can choose the features you want to check for and then Word will alert you if they exist. You can then choose to leave them as is or remove them. It is definitely worth your time to explore and use this new feature.

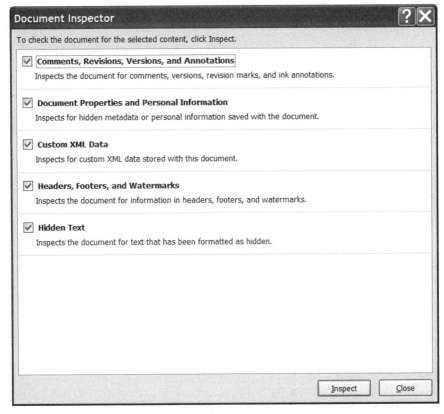

Figure 2-9 *The Document Inspector enables you to remove sensitive and private information before you share a document electronically.*

Encrypting a Document

If you want to prevent others from accessing your document, you can use the encryption technology. You can encrypt only files and folders stored on NTFS volumes. The Open XML formats in Word 2007 provide stronger encryption than previous versions of Word.

When you choose the Encrypt Document option, you are prompted to supply a password (two times). Once you have encrypted the document, you can continue to work with the file. The encryption is transparent, but if others attempt to open, copy, move, or rename the encrypted file, they must first enter the password.

To decrypt the document:

1. Use Windows Explorer to locate the document.
2. Right-click the file name.
3. Select Properties.
4. On the General tab, select Advanced.
5. Turn off the option Encrypt contents to secure data.

You will still need to enter the password to access the document.

> **NOTE** The encryption feature is only valid in an NTFS system. NTFS (New Technology File System) is the standard file system for Windows NT, Windows 2000, Windows XP, Windows Server 2003, and Windows Vista. NTFS replaced FAT (File Allocation Table), which was the file system used in DOS and earlier versions of Windows. NFTS includes security features and supports data access control. Therefore, files and folders saved in the system can include permissions. However, if you copy a file or folder from the NTFS file system to a FAT system, the file or folder will be decrypted.

Adding a Digital Signature

Adding a digital signature assures the reader that the author of the document is authentic and that the document has not been altered. Once a digital signature is added to a document, the document becomes read-only. The signer of the document can use the keyboard to enter a signature, select an image of his or her signature, or use a tablet PC to write the signature.

To sign a document, you must have a digital ID. You can purchase a digital certificate from third-party authorities. You can also create your own digital ID, but this ID can only be validated on your own computer.

Marking a Document As Final

The Mark as Final option will designate the document as read-only. As in previous versions of Word, this means the document can be opened and reviewed, but changes cannot be saved using the current document file name. The "read-only" feature is beneficial when you share documents with others. The receivers of the document will not be able to alter the document before passing it on to others. To edit and save changes, the user will need to save the document using a new file name.

Running the Compatibility Checker

The Compatibility Checker identifies features that are not supported by earlier versions of Word. This command is obviously very useful when you are sharing documents with others who may not be opening the document using Word 2007. When you save a document in a format for an earlier version of Word (see the section "Saving a Document" earlier), the Compatibility Checker will alert you of any new features added to the file that may be disabled in the version of Word you have chosen. For example, if you added some SmartArt to the document, a message will display indicating that the text, graphics, and effects will be combined as one object and you will not be able to edit them (see Figure 2-10).

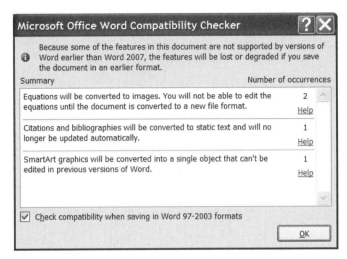

Figure 2-10 *The Compatibility Checker will warn you of features that are not supported in previous versions of Word.*

When you open a document created in a previous version of Microsoft Word, the words "Compatibility Mode" will display next to the file name in the document title bar at the top of the screen. The options available on the Ribbon tabs will be limited to the options available in that version of Word. Essentially what happens is some of the new Word 2007 features are either turned off or modified to parallel what is available in the older version of Word. Obviously you will want to remain in Compatibility mode if you plan to continue sharing the document with users who have older versions of Word. To access all the options available in Word 2007, you must convert the document (see the section "Converting a Document" earlier in the chapter).

When users of an older version of Word open a Word 2007 document, a dialog box will display asking to download a converter that will enable them to open the document from the newer version of Word. Users of Word 2003, Word 2002, or Word 2000 can, however, install a compatibility pack for Microsoft Office 2007 system file formats.

The document will not necessarily look the same in the older version, but the document can be edited and shared. The converter works only with documents created in the applications listed in Table 3-1.

This compatibility pack will enable users to open Word 2007 documents in their earlier version of Word and then edit some items and save the document in the Word 2007 format. There are, though, many elements in Word 2007 that will change when the document is opened in an older version of Word. These elements will be identified when they are introduced in later chapters.

Table 3-1. Convertible Document Applications

Office Application	Operating System
Office 2000 SP3	Windows 2000 SP4
Office XP SP3	Windows XP SP1
Office 2003 SP1	Windows Server 2003

Sending E-Mail

It's simple to e-mail a document. Instead of using the Email toolbar button, you select the Send option; Word then opens a new document with an e-mail header. The document file name is already displayed as an attachment for the e-mail. Enter your e-mail message, click Send, and the document is distributed.

Publishing a Document

When you're ready to distribute the document, you are ready to publish it for others. Your options include posting the document as a blog, sharing the document by saving it to a document management server, or creating a document workspace. By creating a document workspace, your local copy of the document will be synchronized with the server. This enables you to share your document with others. All the versions, changes, and comments will be in one place. You are able to see your changes and at the same time work on the document with others.

To create a document workspace:

1. Open the File menu and point to the Publish command.

2. Select the option Create Document Workspace. A task pane will display at the right.

3. Enter a document workspace name and the URL to identify the location for the new workspace.

4. Click Create.

Accessing Recent Documents

Another very useful feature in Word 2007 that may also save you a lot of time is the list for most recently accessed documents. In previous versions of Word, you can customize your settings for the File menu to show up to 9 of the most recently accessed documents. Now the bar has been raised, and you can display up to 50 documents.

To change the number of most recently accessed documents you want to display, open the File menu and choose Word Options at the bottom of the menu. Click Advanced, and then scroll down to Display.

You can also "pin" the document by displaying the Recent Documents list and then clicking the pin icon ⊷ to the right of the document name. This pin pegs the document so that the document is permanently in the list and will display at the top of the list. In other words, if you have 10 pegged documents in your list, those 10 documents will be listed first and then an additional 40 documents will appear below in the order in which those 40 documents were opened.

Locating Word Settings

It seems that no matter what task you are doing, there's always a "behind the scenes" setting that impacts the outcome. For example, there are several settings for checking spelling and grammar, and users have the option to customize those settings. In previous versions of Word, you could access the settings by choosing the Options command in the Tools menu. However, you could also access settings through other menus and even sometimes in dialog boxes. To make it quicker and easier to find and customize all of Word's settings, the options for changing the settings are now all organized in the Word Options dialog box, which you access through the Microsoft Office button. The Word Options dialog box is illustrated in Figure 2-11.

In subsequent chapters, you will have many opportunities to open the Word Options dialog box and explore possibilities for customizing the settings that control so many of the Word commands.

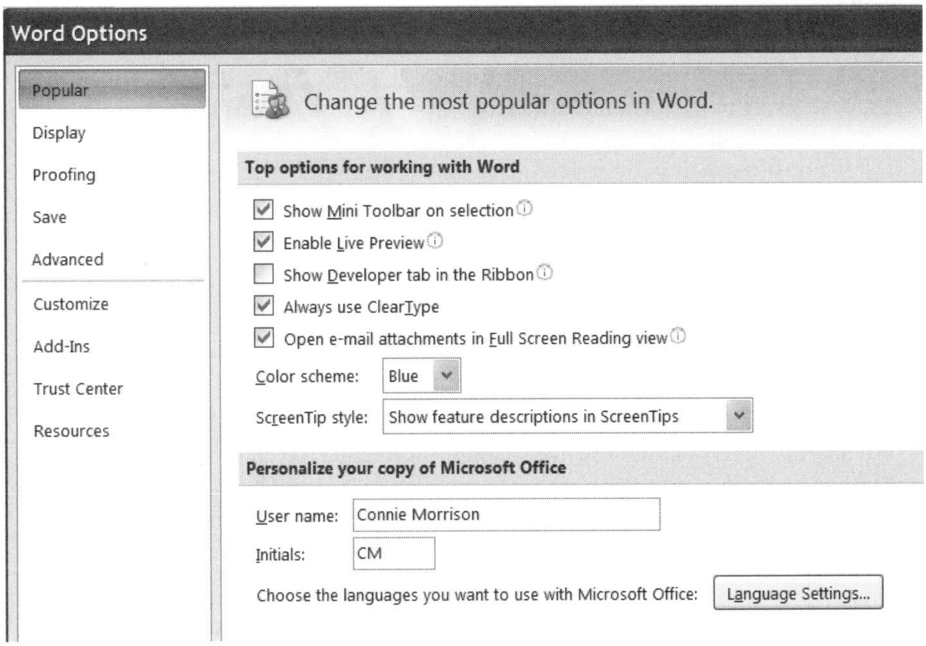

Figure 2-11 *All the Word settings can be found in the Word Options dialog box.*

Using the New File Formats

Previous versions of Word use the .doc file extension for standard documents and the .dot file extension for templates. Word 2007 offers four new file extensions that help you identify documents with XML code and macros. Word 2007 saves a standard Word document with the file extension .docx. A template is saved with the file extension .dotx. The "x" means XML. When you save a standard document with an embedded macro or code, Word 2007 automatically saves the file with the extension .docm. When you save a document template with an embedded macro or code, Word 2007 automatically saves the file with the extension .dotm. The "m" means macro.

The Word XML format is improved. The XML format is compressed and thereby reduces the file size. XML format offers more security because it blocks scripts and macros so you can block unwanted codes or macros. XML also ensures that corrupted files can be recovered. The benefit of Word 2007 using the XML format is that it provides the opportunity to link the data in a Word document with external systems and live data sources.

Getting Help

With each version of Office, the support features improve. There are a variety of resources available, including Help screens, tours, training, videos, and communication with Microsoft support personnel. The first step to getting answers to your questions is to click the Help button in the upper-right corner of the screen. Your success in getting an answer to your question depends on your ability to identify the keywords regarding the matter. The more you search, the better you get at recognizing and identifying the keywords for your search.

> **TIP** The button names often include keywords for searches. Also, keywords are often included in the ScreenTips.

So, what's new in the Help feature? Well, the Office Assistant is gone. And, the Type a Question for Help Box is also gone. And, there's no Search pane. All the Help features are now in one window called the Help Viewer, which you access by clicking the Help button in the top-right corner of the screen. The options previously provided in all of these features are still available; they're just all in one place.

> **TIP** You can also open the Help Viewer by pressing F1.

Word remembers the keywords you've searched for in the Help window. If you want to revisit some of the Help windows, click the down arrow in the search box to display the keywords you previously entered (see Figure 2-12).

There are also numerous slide shows, training videos, tutorials, downloads, and articles available online. These resources will provide an overview of the new software and guide you in using some of the new features. When you display the Help Viewer, a status will display at the bottom-right corner of the Viewer indicating whether you are connected to Office Online. If you are not connected, the status will show "Offline."

To connect to Office Online:

1. Click the Help button or press F1 to open the Help Viewer.

2. Click Offline at the bottom of the Help Viewer.

3. Choose Show content from Office Online. (Once you choose this option, it remains turned on.)

You can also seek help from Microsoft support professionals via phone, chat, or e-mail.

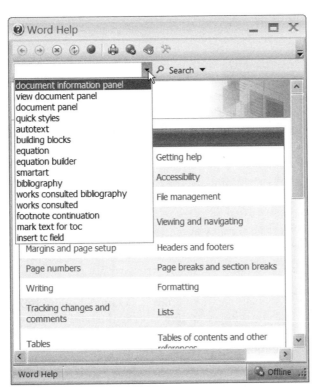

Figure 2-12 *You can easily revisit previously viewed Help windows by choosing from the list in the Search box.*

To contact Microsoft support professionals:

1. Click the Microsoft Office button.

2. Select Word Options at the bottom of the menu.

3. Select Resources and then click Contact Us. A dialog box displays information and URLs for online support information. Telephone numbers are also provided for TTY users.

In the Help window, you can access an interactive reference guide to help you quickly locate commands in the new software. When you open the guide, the screen shows the default window for Word 2003, with the main menu, the Standard toolbar, and the Formatting toolbar visible. When you point to a command or button illustrated on these three toolbars, a ScreenTip displays describing where you can find that command in Word 2007. If you click one of the commands or button, an animation will appear to show you the location of the command or button in the new Word 2007. (To access the interactive reference guide, open the Help window and search for "interactive reference guide.")

> **NOTE** Did you ever notice that searching the Help windows is similar to surfing the Web? Navigating the Help windows is like browsing the Internet. You use links to navigate and locate information, and you enter keywords to search for information.

You can change the size of the Help window by dragging one of the four borders. You can also reposition the Help window by dragging the title bar. Upon closing the Help window, Word will remember the new settings. Then, when you open a Help window again, the window will be the same size and in the same position on the screen. Changing the size and position of the Help window in Word does not affect the Help windows in any of the other Office applications.

> **TIP** Each time you open the Help window, the Help home page will display. If you have located information in the Help screens and you want to continue accessing information in the Help window, minimize the window instead of closing it. This will allow you to return to the Help window at the same place you left it.

Another feature to take advantage of is the option to always display the Help window on top. This is useful because it enables you to keep the Help window visible and accessible as you work. For example, if you have a document open and you need to get Help, you can open the Help window to find information and continue working in your document at the same time. Click the Keep on Top/Not on Top button in the Help window toolbar to toggle the option on and off.

When a dialog box is open, you can click the Help button in the title bar. If information related to the dialog box is available, the information will be displayed. If there is no Help information regarding the dialog box information, the home page for the Help feature is displayed.

CHAPTER 3

Viewing Documents

Not only does Word 2007 have a new look, but the way you look at your documents has also changed. Microsoft has moved the view options to some new locations, and you'll find some brand-new features along with many enhanced ones.

The View tab displays several related groups, offering some new options for how you can view your documents. As you can see in Figure 3-1, the toolbar organizes all the commands you need for changing document views, showing and hiding nonprinting text and symbols, changing zoom settings, and arranging windows.

Figure 3-1 *The View Tab organizes commands and options for viewing documents.*

Changing Views

Changing the way Word displays a document can make the task easier. The options in the Document Views group are similar to view options in previous versions of Word (see Figure 3-2). Print Layout is still the default view. Print Layout view and Web Layout view have not changed, but there are new ways to access features in Full Screen Reading view and in Outline view. Also, Normal view has been replaced with Draft view.

Figure 3-2 *The Document Views group includes commands for changing the way the document displays.*

You can also change the document view by clicking the buttons in the status bar at the lower-right corner of the screen (see Figure 3-3). When a document is reopened, it is opened in the same view it was displayed in when the document was saved.

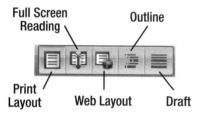

Figure 3-3 *You can also change views using buttons in the status bar at the bottom-right corner of the screen.*

Working in Full Screen Reading View

The Reading Layout view was first introduced in Word 2003 to maximize the space available for viewing a document. This feature is now called the Full Screen Reading view.
Let's take a closer look:

1. Open a multipage document.
2. Select the View tab.
3. Position the mouse pointer over the Full Screen Reading command in the Document Views group. A ScreenTip displays, describing the view.
4. Select the Full Screen Reading command. Notice that when the document is displayed in Full Screen Reading view, the Ribbon is no longer visible.
5. To navigate through the document, click the Next Screen and Previous Screen buttons at the top of the window (see Figure 3-4).

Figure 3-4 *Use the buttons at the top of the screen to navigate in Full Screen Reading view.*

There are several shortcuts to help you navigate through the document in Full Screen Reading view.

- To move one screen at a time, press Page Down and Page Up or press the spacebar and Backspace. Or, click the arrow keys at the bottom corners of the screen. Or, press the right arrow or left arrow keys.

- To jump to the end of the document, press End.

- To jump to the beginning of the document, press Home.

- To jump to a particular page or section in the document, click the down arrow in the screen box at the top center of the window and choose from the options available.

The default settings for Full Screen Reading view display two pages side by side, just like pages in a book. You can change these settings by clicking the View Options button at the top-right corner of the screen. The menu of options shown in Figure 3-5 will display.

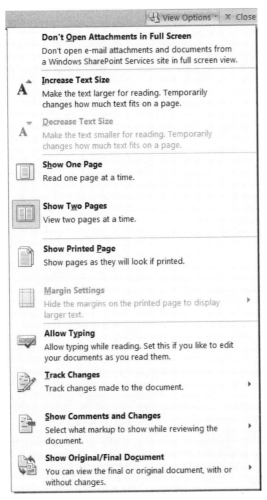

Figure 3-5 *You can change Full Screen Reading settings in the View Options menu.*

Full Screen Reading view offers several editing features, most of which can be accessed in the View Options menu. For example, you can turn on the option Allow Typing, which enables you to add new text and edit the existing text. As you edit in Full Screen Reading view, you can track and review changes, show comments and changes, and you can even choose to display the original or the final document with the changes. After reviewing and editing, you can save the changes to the document—all in Full Screen Reading view.

And there are even more editing and formatting features for Full Screen Reading view in the Mini toolbar that displays at the top-left corner of the screen. The Mini toolbar, shown in Figure 3-6, includes buttons for saving, printing, highlighting text, and inserting comments.

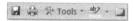

Figure 3-6 *The Mini toolbar for Full Screen Reading view*

The Mini toolbar also includes a Tools button, which displays the menu shown in Figure 3-7.

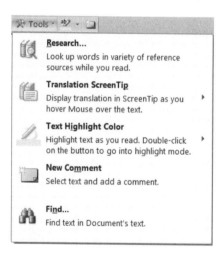

Figure 3-7 *The Tools menu provides additonal options for Full Screen Reading view.*

The Research option displays a task pane that enables you to access several reference sources including dictionaries, encyclopedias, a thesaurus, research web sites, and business and financial web sites. The Tools menu also includes an option to display text translations in ScreenTips. To use this feature, you must first choose a language. When you point to a word in the document, the translation will display in a ScreenTip (see Figure 3-8). To turn this option off, open the Tools menu, select Translation ScreenTip, and then choose Turn Off Translation ScreenTip.

The document must be submitted no later

Figure 3-8 *Choose a language and then point to a word to display a translation.*

To use the highlighter feature, choose the Text Highlight Color option from the Tools menu, or click the Text Highlight Color button on the Mini toolbar. When the highlighter feature is turned on, the mouse pointer changes to display a marker ✏. To change the highlighter color, click the down arrow to the right of the button and select a new color. The highlighter feature remains on until you click the Text Highlight Color button again or press Esc. The Tools menu also includes the New Comment command and the Find command.

> **TIP** To exit Full Screen Reading view, click the Close button in the top-right corner of the screen or press Esc.

When you open a Word document attached to an e-mail, the document may automatically open in Full Screen Reading view.

To prevent an e-mail document from opening in Full Screen Reading view:

1. Open a document in Full Screen Reading view.

2. Select View Options in the toolbar at the top-right corner.

3. If the first option in the menu, Don't Open Attachments in Full Screen, is displayed with a checkmark to the left of the button, the option is turned off. Select the option to toggle it on or off. When the checkmark does not display, e-mail attachments will open in Full Screen Reading view.

4. Click the Close button in the top-right corner of the screen to exit Full Screen Reading view.

Working in Outline View

When you choose the Outline button in the Document Views group, the Outlining tab automatically displays. As shown in Figure 3-9, all the commands you need for working in Outline view are provided in two groups on the Outlining tab. In previous versions of Word, these commands display on the Outline toolbar.

Working in Outline view enables you to see the structure of a document because the headings in the document can easily be distinguished from the body text (see Figure 3-10). If you're the type of person who likes to create an outline before you begin writing your document, you can begin creating the document in Outline view. At any time, you can switch to the other document views.

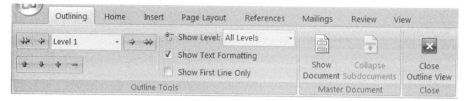

Figure 3-9 *The Outlining tab replaces the Outline toolbar.*

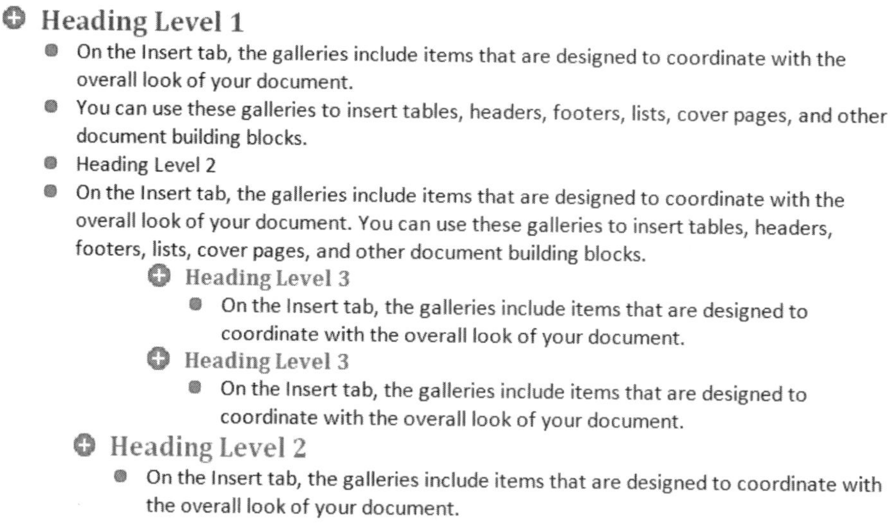

⊕ **Heading Level 1**
- On the Insert tab, the galleries include items that are designed to coordinate with the overall look of your document.
- You can use these galleries to insert tables, headers, footers, lists, cover pages, and other document building blocks.
- Heading Level 2
- On the Insert tab, the galleries include items that are designed to coordinate with the overall look of your document. You can use these galleries to insert tables, headers, footers, lists, cover pages, and other document building blocks.
    ⊕ Heading Level 3
    - On the Insert tab, the galleries include items that are designed to coordinate with the overall look of your document.
    ⊕ Heading Level 3
    - On the Insert tab, the galleries include items that are designed to coordinate with the overall look of your document.
⊕ **Heading Level 2**
- On the Insert tab, the galleries include items that are designed to coordinate with the overall look of your document.

Figure 3-10 *The structure of the document is obvious when it is displayed in Outline view.*

When working with a document in Outline view, you can collapse the body text so that only the headings display. You can even specify which heading levels you want to display. Collapsing the body text allows you to quickly reorganize the content in the document by moving the headings. You can drag and drop the headings, or you can use the buttons in the Outline Tools group to move the headings. When the body text is collapsed before you reposition a heading, the body text is automatically moved with the heading. Figure 3-11 illustrates a document displayed in Outline view with the body text collapsed.

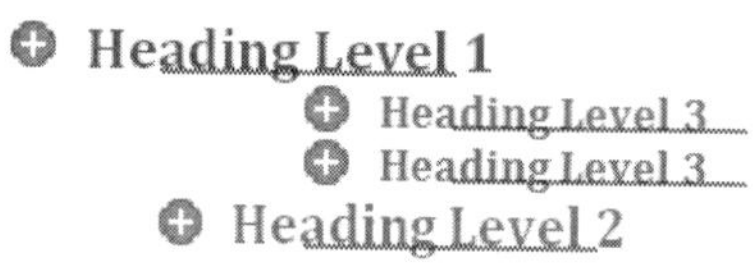

⊕ **Heading Level 1**
    ⊕ Heading Level 3
    ⊕ Heading Level 3
⊕ Heading Level 2

Figure 3-11 *It is easy to reorganize document content when the body text is collapsed.*

> **TIP** To select a heading when a document is displayed in Outline view, point to the left of the paragraph until it changes to a right-pointing arrow, and then click. To select a heading, its subheading, and body text, point to the left of the paragraph. When the pointer changes to a right-pointing arrow, double-click.

> **NOTE** When you select a heading in Outline view that includes collapsed text, the collapsed text is also selected (even though the collapsed text is not visible). If you move, copy, or delete the selected text, the edits also affect the collapsed text.

When you choose the Close Outline View button in the Close group, the document switches to Print Layout view.

Creating Master Documents and Subdocuments

When working with a long document, dividing the document into smaller subdocuments can make organizing and maintaining document content much easier. You can work with the subdocuments independently and then manage the entire document by creating a master document.

Master documents are created in Outline view. When you click the Show Document button in the Master Document group, the group expands to include command buttons for managing subdocuments (see Figure 3-12). If you have not yet created the subdocuments, you can use the current document as the master document. You can designate headings in the current document that you want to become subdocuments. The heading and all body text below the heading will be saved as a separate subdocument.

Figure 3-12 *The Master Document group expands to display more commands when you work with subdocuments.*

To create subdocuments from an existing document:

1. Display the existing document in Outline view.

2. Select a heading in the document.

3. Click the Show Document button in the Master Document group, and then click the Create button. A subdocument icon will display at the left of the heading.

4. Select subsequent headings and format each of them as subdocuments.

5. Save the document. The document becomes the master document. Word will automatically create subdocuments and assign each of them file names based on the outline heading that was selected.

On the other hand, if the subdocuments already exist and you want to combine them into a single document, you can create a master document and add the existing subdocuments to it. You can continue to work with the subdocuments independently, but when you want to access all the information at the same time, you can open the master document.

To combine documents and create a master document:

1. Open a new document and display it in Outline view.

2. Click the Insert button in the Master Document group and locate the first desired document. The document will be inserted into the new document and a Subdocument icon will display at the left of the content.

3. Click the Insert button again and locate the second subdocument.

4. After inserting all the subdocuments, save the master document. Notice that each subdocument is formatted in a separate section in the master document.

Word creates links in the master document for each of the subdocuments. As a result, when you open a master document, the information for each of the subdocuments is always up to date.

> **NOTE** When subdocuments are collapsed in a master document displayed in Outline view, the heading for the subdocuments displays as a hyperlink.

Working in Draft View

Draft view is essentially the same as Normal view. Draft view enables you to edit a document quickly. The zoom is automatically set at 100%, and the focus is on the document text. Many elements such as headers and footers, footnotes, and text boxes do not display. After making the necessary edits and switching back to Print Layout view or Full Screen Reading view, all the nonvisible elements will once again display.

Displaying Helpful Tools

The Show/Hide group, illustrated in Figure 3-13, makes it convenient to choose options for navigating documents and aligning text and graphics within documents.

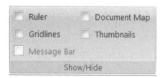

Figure 3-13 *These tools are useful in navigating documents and aligning text and graphics.*

To line up objects, set tabs, and adjust paragraph indents, display the Ruler by turning the option on in the Show/Hide group.

Displaying gridlines in your document is helpful for aligning objects. In earlier versions of Word, the Gridlines option is generally found with the drawing tools; but you may need to display the Drawing toolbar and open a dialog box to turn the setting on. Now in Word 2007, the option to display the gridlines is easier to access. When the option is turned on, each page of the document will display a grid like the one shown in Figure 3-14. The gridlines display only in Print Layout view, and they do not print.

The next event is scheduled for June 18.

Figure 3-14 *Displaying gridlines is useful for aligning objects.*

The Document Map feature has been available in several versions of Word, and the Thumbnails feature was introduced in Word 2003. However, both of these options are now more visible and easier to access. Another new option in the Show/Hide group is the Message Bar. Security alerts, such as a document containing an unsigned macro, will display in the Message Bar.

To disable the Message Bar:

1. Click the Microsoft Office button.

2. Select Word Options at the bottom of the menu.

3. Select Trust Center, and then under Microsoft Office Word Trust Center, select Trust Center Settings.

4. Select Message Bar and turn on the option Never show information about blocked content.

5. Click OK.

Showing and Hiding Nonprinting Characters

The Show/Hide ¶ command offers you an alternative way to view your document by displaying nonprinting characters such as blank spaces, tabs, and hard returns. You will not see it in the Show/Hide group, but it is displayed in the Paragraph group on the Home tab. This feature has been available for many versions of Word, but few users take advantage of it. Many Word users do not like this option because it clutters the text and makes it more difficult to read. Initially, it is awkward to use because you see all these dots and other characters mixed in with the text. However, if you can get over this minor discomfort, you'll learn to appreciate the advantages of displaying nonprinting characters. It definitely helps you edit and proofread your documents. For example, consider this scenario. You open a document someone else created. You're trying to add new text in an existing list, but when you use the Tab key to align the text, your new text doesn't align with the existing text. What's the problem? You display the nonprinting characters and you see that the author of the document created the indents by pressing the spacebar instead of using the Tab key. No wonder the columns are uneven!

By default, the nonprinting characters are not displayed. To view the nonprinting characters, display the Home tab and then click the Show/Hide ¶ button in the Paragraph group. To turn off the display, click the Show/Hide ¶ button again.

If you want to see certain nonprinting characters always display (such as tabs or spaces), you can change the settings so they will automatically display in all documents, regardless of whether Show/Hide ¶ is turned on or off.

To change the settings:

1. Click the Microsoft Office button.

2. Select Word Options.

3. Select Display.

4. Under Always show these formatting marks on the screen, select the marks you want to display.

5. Click OK.

Showing and Hiding ScreenTips

As has already been mentioned, ScreenTips are available for the Ribbon content. Some ScreenTips simply provide the icon name, while other ScreenTips include a description of the command, and sometimes even a link to a Help topic. These are called *enhanced ScreenTips*.

To show or hide enhanced ScreenTips:

1. Click the Microsoft Office button.

2. Click Word Options at the bottom of the menu.

3. Under Top options for working with Word, in the ScreenTip style drop-down list, select your preference.

Changing the Zoom

In previous versions of Word, you use the Zoom button on the Standard toolbar to choose the zoom setting for viewing documents. Among the options in the Zoom drop-down list, you can view two pages at a time and adjust the zoom based on the width of the window in which the document is displayed. All of these options can now be accessed in the Zoom group, which is shown in Figure 3-15.

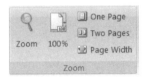

Figure 3-15 *Use the zoom features to get a closer look or to see more of a page.*

To set the zoom at 100 percent, click the 100% button. To manually adjust the zoom in Word 2007, you can select the Zoom command in the Zoom group. The Zoom dialog box will display, and you can change the settings to precise adjustments. If you are viewing several pages in a document, click the down arrow for the Many pages options and choose a layout for multiple pages.

Another way to access the Zoom dialog box is to click the minus and plus buttons on the Zoom Slider positioned on the lower, right-hand corner of the status bar. If you don't need to be exact, you can drag the Zoom Slider (see Figure 3-16) to the left or the right to increase and decrease the zoom percentage. Or hold down the Ctrl key and use the wheel on the mouse to increase and decrease the zoom. Another shortcut to opening the Zoom dialog box is to click the percentage number on the Zoom Slider.

Zoom Slider

Figure 3-16 *Use the Zoom Slider to zoom in and out quickly.*

When you edit a document and save the changes, the zoom setting is saved as well. But, if you open a document and change only the zoom setting, when you save the document, the zoom setting will not be saved. To save the zoom setting, the document must also be edited.

To change the zoom setting and complete a simple edit:

1. Click the Zoom button in the Zoom group (or double-click the percentage in the Zoom Slider) to open the Zoom dialog box.

2. Choose the desired zoom setting.

3. Add and delete a single space anywhere within the document.

4. Save the changes to the document.

Each time you open the document, it should open with the saved zoom settings. To save a new zoom setting, repeat the preceding steps.

> **TIP** To change the options on the status bar, point to the bar and right-click, then select the desired options.

Arranging Documents in Windows

You can also change the view of a document by manipulating the windows on the screen. The options in the Window group, shown in Figure 3-17, parallel those available in the Window menu in previous editions of Word.

Figure 3-17 *The Window options are similar to those found in other versions of Word.*

The New Window button enables you to open the current document in another window. This is a useful feature because it allows you to edit a document while you keep one copy intact and open for display.

An alternative to opening a new window is using the Split button to divide the current window into two separate windows. Click the Split button, position the pointer, and click where you want the split to occur. The same document appears in each window, so you can view different sections of the document at the same time. Click the Remove Split button to view the document in one window again.

The Arrange All button enables you to open multiple documents and display all the windows at the same time. When you display multiple windows in Word 2007, you will probably want to minimize the Ribbon to allow more space to view the document contents.

The View Side by Side option was introduced in Word 2003. This feature enables you to compare two different documents, side by side, at the same time. When two windows are displayed side by side, the Synchronous Scrolling option is available. This option allows you to scroll both documents at the same time. If you don't want the documents to scroll together, you must turn the option off in one of the windows by clicking the Synchronous Scrolling button ⊞ in the Window group. The option is on when the button is enclosed in an orange box. When the option is turned off, the orange box does not display.

You can adjust the width of each of the windows when they are displayed side by side. Simply drag the window border to the left or the right. To make sure both documents share the screen equally, Office Word 2007 offers a new feature, Reset Window Position. When you click the Reset Window Position button ⬛ in one of the documents, both documents become identical in size.

| **TIP** Press Ctrl+F10 to maximize the active window.

Viewing Macros

The Macros button in the Macros group displays the Macros dialog box where you can view, create, edit, and run macros. Working with macros is addressed in Chapter 10.

| **TIP** Press Alt+F8 to display the Macros dialog box.

Using Print Preview

The Print Preview command is now accessed in the Microsoft Office button menu. Open the menu and position the mouse pointer over the Print command, and then choose Print Preview. The document will display in Print Preview, and the Print Preview tab shown in Figure 3-18 will display.

Figure 3-18 *The Print Preview tab provides convenient access to printer options and page setup settings.*

| **NOTE** Be sure to point to the arrow and do not click the Print command. If you click the Print command, the Print dialog box will display.

In the Print group, the Print button opens the Print dialog box. The Options button opens the Display settings in the Word Options dialog box (see Figure 3-19). You can change the print settings under Printing options. This button saves you time because you get to these printing options with a single click. (Otherwise, you must click the Microsoft Office button, select Word Options, and then click Display.)

Word Options

Popular	
Display	
Proofing	
Save	
Advanced	
Customize	
Add-Ins	
Trust Center	
Resources	

Change how document content is displayed on the screen and when printed.

Page display options

☑ Show white space between pages in Print Layout view ⓘ
☑ Show highlighter marks ⓘ
☐ Show document tooltips on hover

Always show these formatting marks on the screen

☐ Tab characters →
☐ Spaces ⋯
☐ Paragraph marks ¶
☐ Hidden text a͟b͟c͟
☐ Optional hyphens ¬
☐ Object anchors ⚓
☐ Show all formatting marks

Printing options

Change printing options here.

☑ Print drawings created in Word ⓘ
☐ Print background colors and images
☐ Print document properties
☐ Print hidden text
☐ Update fields before printing
☐ Update linked data before printing

Figure 3-19 *The Options button in the Print group takes you directly to the Printing options in the Word Options dialog box.*

Notice that the Page Setup group includes options to change margins, orientation, and size. You can make all these changes without closing out of Print Preview. You can also click the Dialog Box Launcher to open the Page Setup dialog box. The Zoom group is also accessible on the Print Preview tab. The buttons and the options are the same. The Preview group, which is illustrated in Figure 3-20, includes an option for displaying the Ruler.

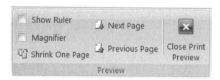

Figure 3-20 *The Preview group provides options so you can edit the document without exiting Print Preview.*

There is also an option to turn on the Magnifier. The Magnifier toggles between Fit Whole Page and 100% zoom levels. This is beneficial when you want to edit the document in Print Preview mode.

To use the Magnifier option:

1. Turn on the Magnifier option. The pointer symbol changes to indicate the Magnifier is on. Click anywhere in the document to change the zoom.
2. Turn off the Magnifier, and you will then be able to edit the document.
3. When you are done editing, turn the Magnifier back on and click anywhere in the document to switch back to desired zoom.

You can navigate the document in Print Preview mode using the Next Page and Previous Page buttons.

The Shrink One Page button is a new feature that gives you the option to reduce the overall size of the document. For example, you preview the document and notice that a few lines of text at the end of the document wrap to a third page. You don't want to waste the paper for just a few lines of text, so you click the Shrink One Page button. Word will automatically adjust the font size and paragraph spacing to reduce the document by one page so that all the text will print on just two pages.

It is always good practice to use the Print Preview feature before you send a document to the printer. To make the feature easier and quicker to access, you can add a button to the Quick Access Toolbar.

To add the Print Preview button to the Quick Access Toolbar:

1. Click the Customize Quick Access Toolbar button. A list of commands will display.
2. Select Print Preview. The button is added to the toolbar.

Hiding White Space

When you're working with multipage documents, you can save screen space and display more text by hiding the white space at the top and bottom of each page. To do this, the document must be displayed in Print Layout view.

To hide white space:

1. Point to the bottom or the top edge of one of the pages in the document.
2. When the double arrows display, double-click (see Figure 3-21).

Figure 3-21 *Double-clicking at the top or bottom edge of the document page will hide white space and enable you to display more text on the screen.*

The white space at the top and bottom of each page is eliminated. As you scroll through the document, you'll see less white space and more text.

3. To show the white space again, point to the bottom or top edge of a page.

4. When you see the double arrows, double-click.

You can also show or hide white space between pages by clicking the Microsoft Office button, selecting Word Options, clicking Display, and choosing the option under Page display options.

4

Formatting and Editing

Word users spend most of their time formatting and editing documents. From changing fonts and colors to finding and replacing text, there are countless options available. The Home tab on the Ribbon, shown in Figure 4-1, helps users see the relationship of various formatting and editing features.

Figure 4-1 *The Home tab displays several formatting and editing tools.*

Selecting Text and Objects

Selecting text and objects is a common task for many software applications, and to format existing text, you must first select it. To select text and objects, you can use commands, the mouse, or the keyboard.

Selecting with Command Buttons

The Select command in the Editing group provides three options, as shown in Figure 4-2. In previous versions of Word, these options are available in the Edit menu or at the top of the Styles and Formatting task pane.

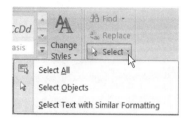

Figure 4-2 *Three selection commands can be accessed in the Editing group.*

- The Select All command will select everything in the document, which includes all text and objects. Headers, footers, and footnotes are not included in the selection. You can also execute the Select All command by pressing Ctrl+A.

- The Select Objects command enables you to select objects that are positioned behind text. When the command is toggled on, the mouse pointer changes to a four-headed arrow whenever you move the mouse over the object. You know the command is toggled on when the option in the drop-down list has an orange background.

- The Select Text with Similar Formatting command enables you to quickly select all text with the same styles or formats with a single click. Select a word or group of words and then click Select Text with Similar Formatting. All text with the same format is highlighted. If you choose to change the format, the change will apply to all of the selected text.

Selecting with the Click-Shift-Click Method

Dragging across text to select is easy, but sometimes it is difficult to get the selection precise. To accurately select text, use the Click-Shift-Click method. Click where you want the selection to begin, hold down the Shift key, and click where you want the selection to end. This method works regardless of the size of the selection. You can select a small group of words, or you can select pages of information. That's the advantage. After the first click, you can use the mouse to scroll to a new location, and then you click again. And, there are no direction restrictions. You can select text from top to bottom, bottom to top, left to right, and right to left.

> **NOTE** The Click-Shift-Click method works on web pages, too!

Selecting with the Keyboard

The EXT option (to toggle extend selection mode on or off) is no longer displayed on the status bar. However, if you want to extend a selected area of text, simply hold down the Shift key and press the arrow keys. Or, hold down the Shift key and click the mouse button where you want the selection to end. You can use this method to extend the selection or to reduce the selection.

Table 4-1 summarizes some keyboard shortcuts for selecting text.

Table 4-1. Keyboard Selection Shortcuts

To Select	Do This
A single word	Point to the word and double-click.
An entire line of text	Point to the left side of the line of text. When the mouse pointer changes to an arrow, click the left mouse button.
An entire paragraph	Point anywhere within the paragraph and triple-click.
An entire document	Point to the margin area on the left side of the document and triple-click. Or, press Ctrl+A.
Nonconsecutive text	Select the first body of text, hold down the Ctrl key, and then begin a new area of selection.

Using the Clipboard

The first group at the left on the Home tab is the Clipboard group (see Figure 4-3). This group includes three of the most frequently used commands: Cut, Copy, and Paste.

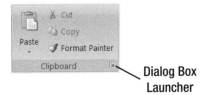

Dialog Box
Launcher

Figure 4-3 *Three of the most frequently used commands can be found in the Clipboard group. The Dialog Box Launcher displays the Clipboard task pane.*

Setting Options for the Clipboard Task Pane

To display the items stored on the Clipboard, click the Dialog Box Launcher at the bottom-right corner of the group. The Clipboard task pane will store up to 24 items.

You can customize when and how the Clipboard task pane displays by clicking the Option button at the bottom of the Clipboard pane. The options are as follows:

- When you turn on the option Show Office Clipboard Automatically, the Clipboard task pane will display when you click the Cut or Copy commands in the Clipboard group.

- When you turn on the option Show Office Clipboard When Ctrl+C Pressed Twice, you can use the keyboard to copy and display the Clipboard contents. Select the content to be copied and then hold down the Ctrl key. The first time you press C, the text is copied to the Clipboard. The second time you press C, the Clipboard task pane will display.

- When you turn on the Collect Without Showing Office Clipboard, the items are copied, but the Clipboard task pane does not display.

- When you turn on the option Show Office Clipboard Icon on Taskbar, the Office Clipboard icon is displayed in the status area of the system taskbar.

- When you turn on the option Show Status Near Taskbar When Copying, a ScreenTip will temporarily display near the system taskbar in the bottom-right corner of the screen when you cut or copy an item to the Clipboard. The ScreenTip will identify the number of the item as it appears in the Clipboard list (for example, 4 of 24).

Repositioning and Resizing the Clipboard Task Pane

The task panes in Word 2007 offer new commands for Move, Size, and Close. You can access these commands in the drop-down menu at the top-right corner of each task pane, as shown in Figure 4-4.

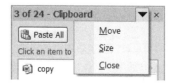

Figure 4-4 *The task panes in Word 2007 have a new drop-down menu.*

To move the task pane:

1. Click the down arrow in the top-right corner of the task pane, and select Move. The mouse pointer changes to a four-headed arrow.

2. Move the mouse, and the task pane will follow.

3. When you have positioned the task pane where you want it, click the mouse button. When you reopen the task pane, it will display in this same position.

4. To reposition the task pane in its original position at the left of the document, double-click the title bar on the task pane.

To resize the task pane:

1. Click the down-arrow in the top-right corner of the task pane, and choose Size.

2. Move the mouse right, left, up, and/or down. The task pane will automatically adjust in size as you move the mouse.

3. When the task pane is the size you want, click the mouse button. When you reopen the task pane, it will display with the same dimensions. To restore the task pane to its original size, you must resize the pane manually.

> **NOTE** You can still reposition task panes by dragging the title bar; and you can resize task panes by dragging one of the pane borders.

Using the Format Painter

Notice that the Format Painter button has also been included in the Clipboard group. The *Format Painter* feature enables you to copy and paste text and paragraph formats. It appears that many Word users are not familiar with the Format Painter feature. If you don't know how to use the Format Painter button, you need to learn now.

The Format Painter is easy to use, and it can save you lots of time with repetitive formatting tasks. For example, you select some text and you try several font styles, sizes, and colors, and finally you've got what you want. But, do you remember what formats you finally settled on? You don't need to know! With a single click, you can simply copy all the formats that are there. When you select one or more words and then choose the Format Painter command, the text formats are copied into the Format Painter, and you can paste the formats to other parts of the same document or other open Word documents.

To copy and paste text formats using the Format Painter:

1. Open a new document. Type your first name and press Enter.

2. Type your last name and press Enter.

3. Type your street address and press Enter.

4. Type your city, state, and ZIP code.

5. Select your first name.

6. Apply several character formats such as bold, italic, font, font size, and font color.

7. If necessary, select your first name again.

8. Click the Format Painter button in the Clipboard group. Notice that when you position the mouse pointer over text, the pointer changes to a paintbrush.

9. Click your last name. All the font formats you applied to your first name are pasted to your last name.

10. Leave the document open.

When you single-click the Format Painter button, you get only one brush stroke. You can click a word or you can drag the pointer over several lines of text to paste the format to a group of words, but after you use the brush stroke once, the Format Painter option is automatically turned off.

> **TIP** The keyboard shortcut for a single brush stroke is Ctrl+Shift+C.

If you need to paste the formats in more than one place in the document, you will need to make multiple brush strokes. When you double-click the Format Painter button, you get unlimited brush strokes. The brush strokes are available until you turn off the Format Painter option. To turn the Format Painter off, click the Format Painter button, press Esc, or choose another command. You can also use the Format Painter to copy and paste paragraph formats. *Paragraph formats* include alignment, line spacing, indents, and spacing before and after paragraphs. When you select all the words in a paragraph and then choose the Format Painter command, both the text formats and the paragraph formats are copied to the Format Painter.

To copy and paste paragraph formats using the Format Painter:

1. Click anywhere within your first name and right-align the line of text. Press Ctrl+2 to change to double line spacing.

2. Select your first name and double-click the Format Painter button.

3. Click your last name. The alignment and paragraph spacing formats are applied to the paragraph, and the pointer still shows a brush stroke.

4. Click the city in your last line of text. Both the text and paragraph formats are pasted. However, the text formats are applied only to the word you clicked.

5. Drag the pointer over all the text in both lines of your address. When you drag the pointer across text, the new format is pasted to all of the words. The new paragraph format is applied to both lines of selected text. Each line is a separate paragraph.

> **NOTE** If all you are pasting is the paragraph formats, all you need to do is to click within a paragraph. To copy paragraph formats, select and copy the entire paragraph of text, or select and copy the nonprinting paragraph mark at the end of the paragraph.

6. Click the Format Painter button or press Esc to turn off the Format Painter.

7. Leave the document open.

> **TIP** To display text formats in a document, press Shift+F1. The Reveal Formatting task pane will display. Click in the text you want to review. The font, paragraph, and section formats applied to the current text and paragraph will display in the task pane.

Formatting Fonts

The Font group shown in Figure 4-5 organizes all the options for changing the appearance of the text. The most frequently used commands are displayed, but you can access all the options by clicking the Dialog Box Launcher to display the Font dialog box.

Dialog Box
Launcher

Figure 4-5 *The Dialog Box Launcher displays the Font dialog box.*

If there's a feature you frequently use, and you don't see it in the Font group (for example, customizing the underline color), you can add the command to the Quick Access Toolbar.

> **TIP** You can quickly open the Font dialog box by pressing Ctrl+Shift+F or Ctrl+Shift+P or Ctrl+D. These shortcut key combinations will work even when the Home tab is not displayed.

Using the Mini Toolbar

If you've done much exploring with this new version of Word, you've probably noticed that when you select text, a floating toolbar displays on the screen. Although it's somewhat transparent, it sometimes gets in the way and blocks your view. That would be the Mini toolbar shown in Figure 4-6. The Mini toolbar is designed to help you work more efficiently by making options available when you need them and where you need them. Here's how it works. You select some text, and Word anticipates that you may want to format the text. The Mini toolbar with many of the Font group options displays in a toolbar just above the selected text. The toolbar, however, is transparent as shown in Figure 4-5.

When you are formatting text

Transparent
Mini Toolbar

Figure 4-6 *When first displayed, the Mini toolbar is transparent.*

If you want to use the Mini toolbar, you can move the mouse pointer on top of it. The toolbar display will be much more vivid as shown in Figure 4-7, and you can choose from the format options. The Mini toolbar will continue to display until you move the mouse pointer away from the selected text.

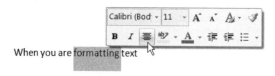

Figure 4-7 *When you point to the Mini toolbar, the display becomes much more vivid.*

> **NOTE** If you right-click selected text, a shortcut menu and the Mini toolbar will both display.

Previewing Formats

Another way to speed up formatting is to use the new Live Preview feature. When this option is enabled, you can preview the results before you apply a format. You select text and then point to a format command. As your mouse pointer hovers over the format command, the selected text in your document will change to show the new format. If you like the change, click the command. If you want to try something different, move the mouse pointer to a new format command and get another live preview. Figure 4-8 shows a live preview of a font change from Times New Roman to Lucida Calligraphy.

To preview the font styles and the font sizes in the Font group:

1. Select your first name.

2. Click the down arrow next to the Font box.

3. Point to a font style in the list. The live preview will display in your document.

> **TIP** If you do not see a live preview of the font styles before you apply them, click the Microsoft Office button, choose Word Options, select Popular, and turn on the option Enable Live Preview. Live Preview will not display the changes when you point to the buttons in the Font group or any of the options on the Mini toolbar.

4. Point to several different font styles and notice the live preview of the first name text in your document.

5. To close the drop-down list, click outside the list.

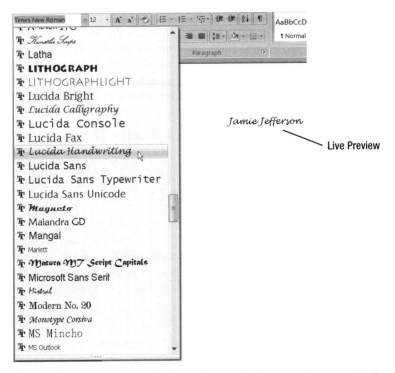

Figure 4-8 *Live Preview displays the results in your document before you apply the format change.*

Changing Case

Now there's a convenient way to change the case of text. For example, after entering text in a document, you decide you want to emphasize one of the words by changing all the letters in the word to all caps. In most earlier versions of Word, you must open the Font dialog box to access the All Caps command. Word 2003 users can choose the Change Case command in the Format menu, or they can customize the Format toolbar and add the Change Case button. However, in Word 2007, the Change Case button Aa▾ is already available by default in the Font group. The Change Case command offers five options: Sentence case, lowercase, UPPERCASE, Capitalize Each Word, or tOGGLE cASE. The tOGGLE cASE option toggles the case from uppercase to lowercase.

To change the case of text:

1. Select the text you want to change.

2. Click the down arrow on the new Change Case button and choose one of the options just described.

> **TIP** You can also change case by selecting the text and pressing Shift+F3. Each time you press the key combination, you will toggle through the lowercase, capitalize each word, and all caps options. To format all selected text in all caps, press Ctrl+Shift+A. To toggle back to the original text format, press Ctrl+Shift+A again.

Applying Subscript and Superscript Formats

There are two new toolbar buttons for formatting text as subscripts or superscripts: the Subscript button ×, and the Superscript button ×˙ . These buttons are available in Word 2003, but only when you customize and add them to the Formatting toolbar. The Subscript and Superscript commands are also available in the Font dialog box.

> **TIP** The shortcut key combination for Subscript is Ctrl+=. The shortcut key combination for Superscript is Ctrl+Shift++.

Shrinking and Growing Fonts

There are also two new toolbar buttons for increasing and decreasing the font size—the Grow Font A˙ and the Shrink Font A˙ buttons. Each time you click the toolbar button, the font size increases or decreases one increment. The increments are preset. Display the drop-down list for the font size to view all of the increments. The Grow Font and Shrink Font buttons are also available in Word 2003, but again, you must add them to the Formatting toolbar.

> **TIP** You can also use shortcut keys to increase and decrease the font sizes. To increase the font size in increments, select the text and press Ctrl+Shift+>. To decrease the font size in increments, select the text and press Ctrl+Shift+<. To increase the font size one point at a time, select the text and press Ctrl+]. To decrease the font size one point at a time, select the text and press Ctrl+[.

To be more precise on the font size, you can select the number in the Font Size box and enter the desired font size. For example, you can enter 12.5 or 12.8.

Clearing Formats

The Clear Formatting button is new. Although the Clear Formatting command is available in Word 2003, there's no toolbar button. In Word 2003, you must first display the Styles and Formatting task pane to display the Clear Formatting command. Now in Word 2007, you can easily clear all formats by just clicking a button. An alternative to using the Clear Formatting button is to click the Dialog Box Launcher in the Styles group and then choose Clear All at the top of the list.

> **TIP** The shortcut for removing all manual formatting is to select the text and/or objects and press Ctrl+spacebar. To remove all paragraph formatting from text, press Ctrl+Shift+N. Think of the N as representing the "Normal" style.

Underlining Text

In previous versions of Word, to customize the underline format, you must open the Font dialog box to change the settings. The new Underline button ⊔ in the Font group enables you to change the underline style and color without opening the dialog box. Click the down arrow on the button to choose a style and color. The style and color will be saved, so the next time you click the button, the underline will be formatted the same. If you want a different underline, click the down arrow and make the changes.

> **TIP** To quickly format a double underline, select the text and press Ctrl+Shift+D.

Formatting Strikethrough Marks

Also new is the Strikethrough button ᵃᵇᶜ for formatting text with strikethrough marks. In earlier versions of Word, you can apply a strikethrough or a double strikethrough format, but you must first open the Font dialog box or customize the Formatting toolbar.

> **NOTE** If you're editing a document and you want to show that some text should be deleted, tracking changes would be the more practical way to go about it. Then the reviewer of the changes can choose to accept or reject the change. See the section on Tracking Changes in Chapter 9.

Adding Text Formats to the Quick Access Toolbar

If there are text formats that you use frequently, and there are no options for those formats on the Ribbon, you may be able to add those formats to the Quick Access Toolbar. For example, if you often format text in small caps, Word already has a button for the small caps format. The button doesn't appear on the Ribbon, but you can add the button to the Quick Access Toolbar.

To customize the Quick Access Toolbar by adding a button not found on the Ribbon:

1. Click the Customize Quick Access Toolbar button at the right side of the Quick Access Toolbar.
2. Choose More Commands.
3. In the list on the left, under Choose commands from, select Commands Not in the Ribbon or All Commands.
4. Scroll through the list and select the command name you want to add to the toolbar.
5. Click the Add button between the two list boxes.
6. Click OK.

| **TIP** The keyboard shortcut for formatting small caps is Ctrl+Shift+K.

Animating Text

The text animation options of earlier versions of Word are not available in Word 2007. However, the effect does work in Word 2007. To animate text in the new version, create and then copy animated text from an earlier version of Word and paste the animated text in your Word 2007 document.

Formatting Paragraphs

The Paragraph group includes commands for bullets, numbering, indents, alignment, line spacing, shading, and borders. It also includes the Sort command and the Show/Hide ¶ command. There's also a new button for multilevel lists (see Figure 4-9).

Multilevel List

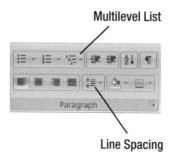

Line Spacing

Figure 4-9 *Among the options in the Paragraph group is a new button for multilevel lists.*

Adding Bullets and Numbering

When you click the down arrow next to the Bullets or Numbering buttons, a drop-down list will display recently used formats and a library of available formats. To create a new bullet or number format, select Define New Bullet at the bottom of the drop-down list. Choose a symbol, picture, or font for the bullet. The new bullet will be added to the gallery. To remove the bullet from the list, point to the bullet, right-click, and choose Remove. If you want to create a new number format, click the Numbering button and choose Define New Number Format at the bottom of the drop-down list. Choose the number style and font, and select an alignment. To remove the numbering format from the list, right-click the format in the list and choose Remove.

Creating Multilevel Lists

The new Multilevel List button makes it easy for you to create a list of items at different levels (similar to an outline form). There are several multilevel list styles from which you can choose. After choosing a style, Word will automatically format the paragraph indents and number each paragraph.

To choose a list style from the gallery:

1. Position the insertion point where you want the list to begin.

2. Click the down arrow on the Multilevel List button.

3. Select a style.

4. Enter your list. Press the Tab key to change to the next lower level; press Shift+Tab to change to a higher level.

If you don't see a multilevel style that meets your needs, you can create your own. Your new style will be automatically added to the gallery so you can use the style again in the future.

To create a new multilevel list style:

1. Position the insertion point where you want the list to begin.

2. Click the down arrow on the Multilevel List button.

3. Choose Define New List Style. The Define New List Style dialog box will display.

4. Name the new style.

5. Choose the number formats, the font settings, and the position for each level.

6. Choose whether you want the list style to be available only in the current document or all new documents based on this template.

7. When you have defined each level, click OK.

The new multilevel list style is automatically added to the gallery. If you choose to make the list style available only in the current document, the style displays under Current List and under List Styles in the Multilevel List drop-down menu when the current document is open. If you choose to make the style available in all new documents based on the template, the new style will appear in the menu under List Styles for future documents.

> **TIP** If you want to manually control a number in the list, right-click the number and choose the Set Numbering Value option.

You also have the option of modifying existing list styles. To modify a list style:

1. Select the list you want to edit so it is displayed in the menu under Current List.

2. Click the down arrow on the Multilevel List button.

3. Choose Define New List Style. The Define New List Style dialog box will display.

4. Choose the level(s) you want to change and make the number format, font, and/or position edits.

5. Click OK. The modified style will be added to the current list.

> **NOTE** Choose the Define New Multilevel List command to make the style available only for the current document. Choose the Define New List Style command if you want to use and even change the style in the future.

Changing Line Spacing

Position the insertion point in the paragraph you wish to format. When you click the down arrow on the Line Spacing button, you'll see several options for line space settings. You'll also see two new options for adding and removing space before or after a paragraph, as shown in Figure 4-10.

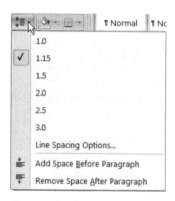

Figure 4-10 *The Line Spacing button also provides options for adding/removing space before and after paragraphs.*

The commands will vary depending on whether the paragraph already has customized spacing above or below. The default settings for space above and after paragraphs is 0, but if you have applied a style to the paragraph, the spacing may be different. When you use one of these line spacing commands to add space, 12 pts. will be added. When you use one of the commands to remove space, the pt. setting will become 0. If the paragraph is already formatted with added space before or after, you will not see a command to add space. Likewise, if no space has been added before or after the paragraph, you will not see a command to remove space. To customize the line spacing for multiple paragraphs, first select all of the paragraphs and then choose the command.

The shortcut keys for single line spacing are Ctrl+1. For double spacing, press Ctrl+2. For 1.5 spacing, press Ctrl+5. Press Ctrl+0 (zero) to toggle between adding or removing space before a paragraph. 12 pts. will be either added or removed each time you press the key combination.

To remove paragraph formats (alignment, bullets and numbering, and line spacing), press Ctrl+Q. To open the Paragraph dialog box, double-click one of the indent markers on the Ruler (Left Indent, Hanging Indent, or Right Indent). If the Ruler is not displayed, click the View tab on the Ribbon and then turn on the Ruler option in the Show/Hide group. You can also access the Paragraph dialog box from the Page Layout tab, where you will find more commands for indents and spacing. There is more information about formatting indents and tabs in Chapter 6.

Formatting with Styles

One of the goals for Microsoft Word 2007 was to enable the user to spend more time writing and less time formatting. This new version of Microsoft Word definitely makes it easy for you to format documents quickly. You can easily change the formatting of selected text in the document text by choosing a Quick Style in the Styles group on the Home tab (see Figure 4-11). *Quick Styles* are sets of styles created to work together. You can apply styles using the new Quick Styles gallery, or you can use the Styles task pane.

The More Button

Figure 4-11 *You can access the new Quick Styles gallery in the Styles group.*

Using Quick Styles

To apply the styles, click in the paragraph or select the text you want to change. Then select a style from the Quick Styles gallery in the Styles group. To view all the styles displayed in the gallery, use the arrows on the right to scroll through the list, or click the More button to expand the list.

> **TIP** To apply the Normal style, press Ctrl+Shift+N. To apply heading styles, press Alt+Ctrl+1 for the Heading 1 style, Alt+Ctrl+2 for the Heading 2 style, and Alt+Ctrl+3 for the Heading 3 style.

The options in the Quick Styles gallery are organized in style sets. The default styles displayed are from the Classic set. To view the style sets, click Change Styles at the right side of the Styles group. Then, select Style Set and choose a style set. If there's a style set you prefer, you can set it as the default. Live Preview is available and especially helpful when choosing a style because you can see the effects of various styles before you choose one. Depending on the text that is selected, some styles may not apply.

You can also view all of the styles in a vertical list by displaying the Styles task pane. To display the Styles task pane, select the Home tab and then click the Dialog Box Launcher in the Styles group. Or, press Alt+Ctrl+Shift+S to display the Styles task pane. It's a lot of keys to press at the same time, but it works!

At the bottom of the Styles task pane, you can turn on Show Preview so that the available styles are illustrated in the list just as they will look like when applied to text in the document. The font, font size, and font color are all previewed as well as paragraph indents. Also at the bottom of the Styles task pane, you will see three buttons, as shown in Figure 4-12. The first button, New Style, opens the Create a New Style from Formatting dialog box. The new style you create will be based on the current style. If you have not applied a style, the new style will be based on the Normal style.

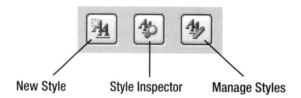

New Style   Style Inspector   Manage Styles

Figure 4-12 *The three buttons at the bottom of the Styles task pane open dialog boxes where you can choose styles settings.*

The second button, Style Inspector, opens the Style Inspector task pane. The information in this pane will help you determine whether the paragraph and text formats were applied using a style or using manual formatting. Any formats displayed in the gray boxes were applied manually. You can also use the buttons in this pane to remove the formats and/or display the Reveal Formatting pane.

The third button, Manage Styles, displays the Manage Styles dialog box. Here you can select and edit styles, determine how the styles are listed, protect formatting changes, and set defaults.

Creating Your Own Styles

Although a Quick Style set likely contains more styles than you need to format a document, you may want to create a new style.

To create a new style:

1. Open a new document and enter your first and last name.

2. Select the text and display the Mini toolbar.

3. Format the text bold and italic, and choose your favorite color for the font color. Then, change the font to your favorite font style.

4. Right-click the selected text, choose Styles in the shortcut menu, and then choose Save Selection as a New Quick Style.

5. In the Create New Style from Formatting dialog box, enter a style name. For example, Name.

6. Click OK.

The new style is saved in the Quick Styles gallery. It will also appear in the Styles task pane. The styles are arranged in alphabetical order. Sometimes styles get deleted from the gallery. To add a style to the Quick Styles gallery, right-click the style name in the Styles task pane and choose Add to Quick Styles gallery.

To remove a style from the Quick Styles gallery, right-click the style name (either in the gallery or in the Styles task pane) and choose Remove from Quick Styles gallery. To permanently remove a style, click the Manage Styles button in the Styles task pane. Display the Edit tab, select the style, and choose Delete.

Formatting Styles Manually

You can override all style formats. For example, after applying a style, you decide to modify the font size. Simply select the text and make the change. If you want to save your changes for future applications of the style, right-click the style, choose Styles in the shortcut menu, and then choose Update *Style Name* to Match Selection.

The Styles task pane keeps track of all the manual formatting. Each time you override a style and change the format, a new style name displays in the Style task pane. For example, if you apply a Heading 1 style and then change the font size to 16 pt., the new style name will display Heading 1 + 16. The character formats are easily identified with "a" icons and the paragraph formats are easily identified with ¶ icons.

To track style formats:

1. Click the Microsoft Office button.

2. Choose Word Options.

3. Choose Advanced.

4. Under Editing options, turn on Keep track of formatting.

Resize the Styles task pane as needed to review the details about the manual formatting. The format tracking list can become quite extensive as you work with a document. To minimize the list, you can turn off several of the format tracking options or choose how the list of changes is sorted.

To turn off some of the tracking options:

1. Click the Dialog Box Launcher in the Styles group.

2. Select Options at the bottom of the task pane. The Style Pane Options dialog box will display.

3. Under Select formatting to show as styles, turn off the checkboxes for one or more of the options for paragraph level, font, and bullet and numbering formatting.

To view the details about the formats, you can display the Reveal Formatting task pane. When the Reveal Formatting task pane is visible, you can click anywhere within the document, and details about the paragraph and font formats for that text will display in the task pane. To display the Review Formatting task pane, press Shift+F1. If you want to modify the formats, click the links in the Review Formatting task pane. The relative dialog boxes will open, and you can make the necessary changes.

You can turn on an option so that Word can help you identify possible formatting errors throughout your document. For example, you format several sections of text using a quote style. While editing the document, you increase the font size for one of the quotations. Word will identify the inconsistency with a blue underline below the edited text. To respond to the alert, right-click to display a shortcut menu. Word will provide a suggestion to correct the inconsistency. You can click the suggestion to make the correction, or you can choose to ignore the notice for this one occurrence, or for all occurrences throughout the document.

To turn on the option to find formatting inconsistencies:

1. Click the Microsoft Office button.

2. Choose Word Options.

3. Click Advanced.

4. Under Editing options, select Mark formatting inconsistencies.

5. Click OK.

Formatting Automatically As You Type

Word's AutoFormat feature uses the built-in paragraph styles to format paragraphs throughout your document. You may find many of the AutoFormat options useful. For example, when entering fractions, Word can automatically format them. Or, when you enter two hyphens, Word will automatically convert the characters to the dash symbol. However, there may be some options that you want to turn off—such as the automatic numbered lists.

To display the options for automatic formatting as you type:

1. Click the Microsoft Office button.

2. Select Word Options.

3. Select Proofing.

4. Select AutoCorrect Options.

5. Select the AutoFormat As You Type tab.

6. Enable the options you want by selecting the option. To disable an option, click the checkbox to remove the green checkmark.

Often, when AutoFormats are applied, a smart tag will display on the screen. When you point to the smart tag and click the down arrow, you have the options to undo the AutoFormat, stop the AutoFormat, or open the AutoCorrect dialog box to control the feature.

Saving Time Editing

Editing involves proofreading and finding and replacing text and data. Following are some valuable shortcuts and tips that can save you both time and effort.

Specifying the Spacing Between Sentences

Most keyboarding classes now teach you to leave one blank space between sentences. However, there are still some "old school" people out there—perhaps your boss or your professor—who go by the old keyboarding rules and mandate that you enter two blank spaces between sentences. Regardless of whether you learned to keyboard with the "old school" rules or the "new school" rules, you know how hard it is to switch back and forth. So, if you know who your reader is, you can change some settings and let Word do all the proofing for you.

1. Click the Microsoft Office button.
2. Select Word Options.
3. Select Proofing.
4. Under Writing style, choose whether you want Word to check Grammar Only or Grammar and Style. (Style refers to writing style.)
5. Under the heading When correcting spelling and grammar in Word, click Settings.
6. Under the heading Require, choose whether or not you want to require a comma before the last list item.
7. Also under Require, determine whether you want all punctuation to appear inside the ending quotation marks.
8. Then, decide whether you want one space or two spaces between sentences.

Word will automatically identify any inconsistencies in your document with green wavy lines below the occurrences. If you choose "don't check" in the Require section, Word will not check for any inconsistencies for the rules.

You can make these changes for a single document, or you can have the settings apply for all documents. At any time, you can restore the original rules by selecting Reset All.

Using the Repeat Command

So often, you make a change somewhere in your document and need to make that same change somewhere else in the same document. For example, you select some text and apply the bold format. Regardless of how you made the change (keyboard or mouse), you can repeat the action with a single keystroke.

The F4 key repeats the last editing action you performed. For example, if you just pasted some text in a document, you can use your mouse to reposition the insertion point and press F4 to paste again. You can repeat the paste command as many times as you want. Instead of moving the mouse to do both (reposition the insertion point and click the Paste command), you can use one hand for the mouse and use your free hand to press F4. Remember, the F4 key repeats your very last action, so if the last thing you did was press the Delete key, when you press F4, Word will delete the next character to the right of the insertion point.

| **TIP** You can also use the keyboard shortcut Ctrl+Y to repeat the last action.

Finding and Replacing Text

The Editing group, shown in Figure 4-13, displays commands for finding and replacing text. The Replace and Select buttons are new. In earlier versions of Word, you can customize the Standard toolbar by adding the Find and Replace buttons. However, the Find button in the Editing group differs slightly in Word 2007 because you can choose to go directly to the Find tab or the Go To tab in the Find and Replace dialog box. The Replace button will take you directly to the Replace tab in the Find and Replace dialog box. (The Select button is discussed earlier in this chapter in the section "Selecting with Command Buttons.")

Figure 4-13 *The Editing group*

These common tasks need little explanation; however, there are some tips that relate to these commands. The down arrow next to the Find command enables you to choose to display either the Find tab or the Go To tab in the Find and Replace dialog box. A shortcut to open the Go To tab is to double-click the page number on the status bar.

You can also use shortcut key combination Ctrl+F5 to find the last location of the insertion point in the document. For example, if you use the Go To tab to move to another page in the document, you can use the shortcut keys to return to the previous location in the document. The shortcut keys will toggle between the last three locations of the insertion point.

Just as you can repeat the last action, you can also repeat the last Find entry. Even though the Find dialog box is closed, Word remembers the last text you searched for. Hold down the Shift key and press F4. Word will search for the same text again. This makes it fast to find multiple locations of the same text throughout a document. You can open the dialog box, enter the criteria for the search, locate the first occurrence, and close the dialog box. Then, you can continue to press Shift+F4 and quickly see all the remaining occurrences without the need to keep the dialog box open.

Working in Overtype Mode

The Overtype mode dates back to the early versions of Word. When enabled, as you enter new text, it replaces the existing text. You've probably accidentally switched to Overtype mode by inadvertently pressing the Insert key. In Word 2007, the Overtype mode status does not display in the status bar, and the Insert key will not toggle the option on unless you change the settings.

To enable the Overtype mode:

1. Click the Microsoft Office button.
2. Choose Word Options.
3. Click Advanced.
4. Under Editing options, turn on the option Use overtype mode.
5. To quickly toggle the Overtype mode on and off, turn on the option Use the Insert key to control Overtype mode.

CHAPTER 5

Creating Documents More Efficiently

Creating a document usually involves much more than entering and formatting body text. Documents often include elements such as cover pages, tables, illustrations, hyperlinks, headers and footers, and equations. Word 2007 provides many new tools for inserting and formatting these elements on the Insert tab (see Figure 5-1). In addition, Word provides new galleries of building blocks, which are reusable document parts. In this chapter, you will learn how to access these building blocks as well as how to add your own building blocks to the galleries.

Figure 5-1 *The Insert tab provides tools for inserting and formatting several document elements.*

Working with Building Blocks

Building blocks provide another means for you to work more efficiently. Building blocks are text and graphics that can be used repeatedly. Word already has many items stored in the Building Blocks Organizer. For example, there are several AutoText entries, including letter closings *Regards, Sincerely*, and *Yours truly*. Building blocks, however, are much more than AutoText entries. Cover pages, equations, headers, footers, page numbers, tables, and text boxes are also considered to be building blocks, and they, too, are included in the Building Blocks Organizer (see Figure 5-2).

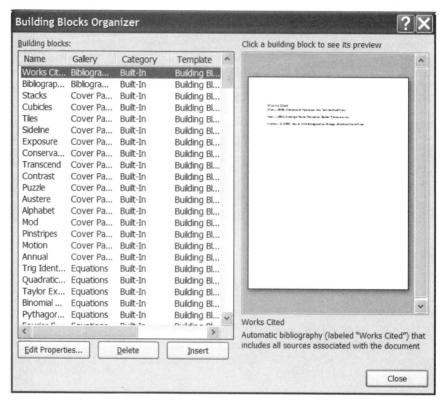

Figure 5-2 *You can access the building blocks at any time using the Quick Parts button.*

Inserting a Building Block

Building blocks appear in different galleries and menus, depending on the gallery identified when they were saved. For example, you may have chosen to save a building block in the Tables gallery. Regardless of where the building block is saved, you can always select it in the Building Blocks Organizer.

To insert a building block from the Building Blocks Organizer:

1. Position the insertion point where you want to insert the content.

2. Click the Quick Parts button in the Text group.

3. Select Building Blocks Organizer.

4. Select the desired building block and click Insert.

Adding a Building Block

You can add your own items to the Building Blocks Organizer. You can add as many entries as you want, and you can access the building blocks at any time as you work with documents by clicking the Quick Parts button.

To add a building block to the Building Blocks Organizer:

1. Select the text or graphic. If you want the paragraph formatting to be stored with the text, be sure to display the nonprinting characters and include the paragraph mark in the selection.
2. Click the Quick Parts button.
3. Select Save Selection to Quick Part Gallery and enter a name for the building block.
4. Choose the gallery where you want the building block to be accessed, and if desired assign a category and include a description.

Changing the Content of a Building Block

Over time, you will likely need to update the content in some building blocks. You can edit the building block content and then save the changes.

To change the content of a building block:

1. Insert the building block content in a document and edit the content.
2. Select the revised content and then click the Quick Parts button.
3. Select Save Selection to Quick Part Gallery. Make sure the gallery, name, and category are exactly the same as the original.
4. When asked if you want to redefine the building block entry, click Yes.

Changing the Properties of a Building Block

There may be times when you want to change the name of the building block or assign the building block to another gallery or category. The properties of a building block can be edited at any time.

To edit the properties of a building block entry:

1. Click the Quick Parts button.
2. Select Building Blocks Organizer and locate the desired building block.
3. Click Edit Properties. The Modify Building Block dialog box will display.
4. Enter a new name in the Modify Building Block dialog box.

Sharing Building Blocks

If you collaborate with others on documents, you may want to share your building blocks. To make building blocks available to others, you can create a template.

To create a template to share building blocks:

1. Open a new document and save the document as a template.
2. With the template open, enter the building block material.

3. Select the content for the first building block. Click the Quick Parts button in the Text group and select Save Selection to Quick Part Gallery.

4. Enter a name and identify the category. Make sure the template is displayed in the Save in box. Click Options, select one of the options, and click OK.

5. Repeat Steps 3 and 4 to save additional building blocks, and then save and close the template.

Share the template with others. When they attach the template to a document, the building blocks will be available.

To attach a template to a document:

1. Open the document, click the Microsoft Office button, select Word Options, and then select Add-ins.

2. At the bottom of the dialog box, select Templates in the Manage box.

3. Click Go, and then click Attach to locate the template. Turn on the option Automatically update document styles, and then click OK.

If you convert a Word 2007 template to a Word 97–2003 format, the content from the Building Block Organizer will become static AutoText entries. Content from tables, headers, footers, page numbers, equations, table of contents, bibliographies, watermarks, and custom galleries will be converted to AutoText. The positioning of text boxes may change. For example, text boxes centered vertically or aligned to the bottom will be permanently aligned to the top. If you convert the template back to the Word 2007 format, the AutoText will remain static.

Creating Cover Pages

The document is finally complete, and you give a sigh of relief because your work is done. Then, you remember you need to create a cover page. It won't take long. Just use the buttons in the Pages group shown in Figure 5-3.

Figure 5-3 *Click the Cover Page button in the Pages group to choose a preformatted cover page.*

The Cover Page button offers 15 different building blocks (templates) for cover page designs. The template includes graphics and styles, and there are also fields formatted with prompts to guide you in adding the necessary information (see Figure 5-4).

Regardless of where the insertion point is positioned, Word automatically inserts the new page at the beginning of the document. Click the fields to enter the custom information for the document. The fields will print just as they appear on your screen, so if you do not add custom information in all the fields, you need to delete the fields you do not use. To remove a field, click anywhere within the field. The field name will display at the top-left corner of the field. If necessary, click the field name to select the entire field and then press Delete. You can change the cover page design after you enter the custom information without reentering the information. Click the Cover Page button and choose a new design. The information will display in the new design.

Figure 5-4 *Enter the custom information in the fields.*

To change the cover page design after entering information in the fields, click the Cover Page button in the Pages group and select a new design. The layout and formats will change, and the custom information you already entered will remain unchanged. To remove the entire cover page, select and delete all the fields and the page break. Sometimes the Page Break line displays above the fields as shown in Figure 5-4.

If you have formatted page numbers in your document, the cover page will become page number 1 in the document. By default, the page number will not print on the cover page, but you probably don't want the cover page to be included in the page count. The easiest way to get around this is to click the Page Number button in the Header & Footer group and select Format Page Numbers in the drop-down menu. The Page Number Format dialog box will display. Under Page numbering, select Start at, change the setting from 1 to 0, and then click OK.

The Blank Page command inserts a new page at the location of the insertion point. Therefore, should you choose to design and create your own cover page, position the insertion point at the beginning of the document, and then click the Blank Page button in the Pages group.

The Page Break command moves text and graphics to the next page. Position the insertion point where you want the new page to begin, and then click the Page Break button. All text and graphics following the insertion point will be moved to the top of the next page in the document. The shortcut key combination to insert a new page is still Ctrl+Enter.

Creating Tables

The tools you use to create a table will likely depend on the data you need to display. You can insert or draw a table, and you can also convert existing text to a table format. If you have experience working with Excel, you may choose to insert a spreadsheet to display your data. Figure 5-5 shows the new menu for Table commands.

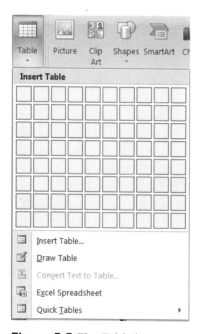

Figure 5-5 *The Table button in the Tables group provides a menu of commands for creating a table.*

Using Quick Tables

Word's Quick Tables feature is useful when you want to create a commonly used table format such as a calendar or a tabular list. You can choose a table style from a gallery of preformatted tables (see Figure 5-6). The advantage to using the Quick Table templates is that your table will already be formatted. All you need to do is select the content in each cell and replace it with your own data. If you need more table cells, you can add additional columns and rows.

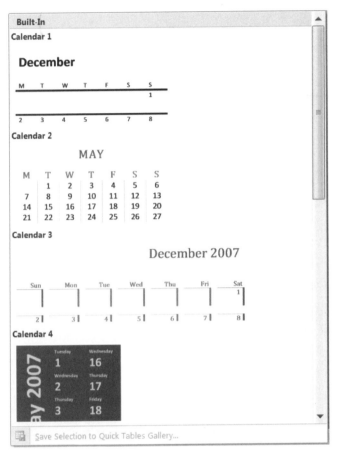

Figure 5-6 *The Quick Tables menu displays nine preformatted, built-in tables.*

Word 2007 provides nine different table styles in the Quick Tables gallery. However, you can add your own table styles to the gallery. Select the table you want to add to the menu, choose the Table command, and select Quick Styles. Click Save Selection to Quick Tables Gallery at the bottom of the Quick Styles menu. In the Create New Building Block dialog box, enter a name and description for the new table style.

Using the Table Grid

If you don't find a table style that meets your needs, you can create a table by choosing the Table Grid command and defining the number of columns and rows. Drag the mouse pointer over the cells to select the desired number of rows and columns (see Figure 5-7). If necessary, you can add/delete columns and rows later.

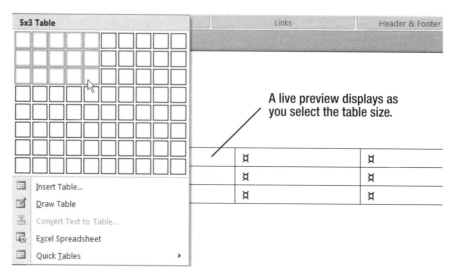

A live preview displays as you select the table size.

Figure 5-7 *Use the table grid to define the table size.*

Drawing the Table Borders

Another way to create a table grid is to use the Draw Table tool. The advantage to drawing a table grid is that you can create cells of varying heights and widths.

To draw the table borders:

1. Click the Draw Table command in the Table menu. The mouse pointer will change to a pencil.

2. Drag the pencil on the screen to create cells. Draw lines within cells to split the cells (see Figure 5-8).

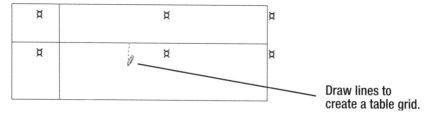

Draw lines to create a table grid.

Figure 5-8 *The Draw Table tool enables you to vary the heights and widths of cells.*

3. After you draw the first cell, the Ribbon will change to display the Table Tools Design tab. The Draw Borders group at the far right side of the Ribbon displays tools for drawing table borders (see Figure 5-9).

Figure 5-9 *The Draw Borders group provides options for table border lines, including design, weight, and color.*

4. To remove lines from the table and merge cells, click the Eraser tool in the Draw Borders group. The mouse pointer will change to an eraser. Click the line(s) you want to remove (see Figure 5-10).

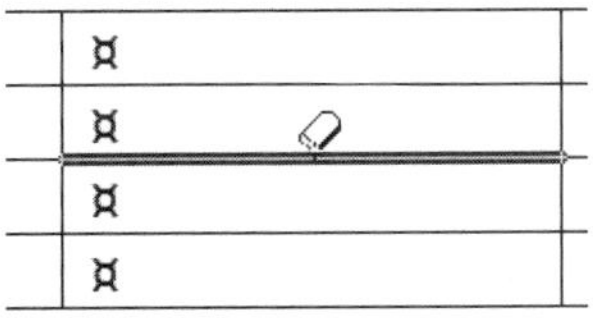

Figure 5-10 *Use the Eraser tool to remove lines from the table.*

5. Press Esc to exit the drawing mode.

> **TIP** To automatically wrap text around a table as you create it, hold down the Ctrl key as you use the Draw Table tool.

Converting Text to a Table

Converting text to a table can save time, because it eliminates the need to reenter data. Furthermore, if you have extensive data to convert, you can avoid the risk of making errors that may occur if you reenter the data. When you select text in your document before clicking the Table button, the option Converting Text to a Table will be enabled in the Table menu. However, before converting text to a table, you must make sure the text is separated by characters such as commas or tabs. These characters will identify where you want to begin a new column in the table. Paragraph marks must be used to indicate when to begin a new row. For example, the list of items illustrated on the left in Figure 5-11 can easily be converted to a table. The separators in this example are the blank spaces between the words. The second name in the list in Figure 5-11 did not include a middle name or initial, so an extra space was added between the first and last name so that the table cell would remain blank.

Joshua·A.··Smith¶

Andrea··Durham¶

Janelle·M.·Hasse¶

Aidan·Jack·Chang¶

Joshua¤	A.¤	Smith¤	¤
Andrea¤	¤	Durham¤¤	
Janelle¤	M.¤	Hasse¤	¤
Aidan¤	Jack¤	Chang¤	¤
¶

Figure 5-11 *Text with separators such as tabs, commas, or spaces can easily be converted to a table.*

Nesting Tables

A nested table is a table inside a table cell (see Figure 5-12). Nested tables are commonly found in web pages because web page layouts are often structured using a table format. Therefore, to display a table on a web page, the table is inserted inside one of the table cells used in the structure. You can create a nested table by inserting a table in a table cell. You can also create a nested table by copying an existing table and then pasting it into a table cell.

A Table Inserted in a Table Cell

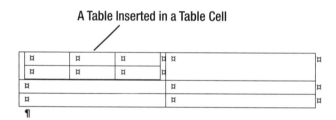

Figure 5-12 *Nested tables are common in web pages.*

Inserting an Excel Spreadsheet

The advantage of using the Excel Spreadsheet command to create a table is that you can utilize many of the Excel features, including merging, centering, conditional formatting, AutoSum, sorting, and filtering. When you insert a spreadsheet in a Word document, the Ribbon will change to display the Home tab from the Excel application (see Figure 5-13). Click outside the spreadsheet object, and the object will display like a normal Word table grid. Double-click inside the table, and the display will revert to the Excel spreadsheet object. When the document is printed, the spreadsheet will look like a Word table. All formats include fonts, borders, and shading must be applied when the table is open in the Excel spreadsheet.

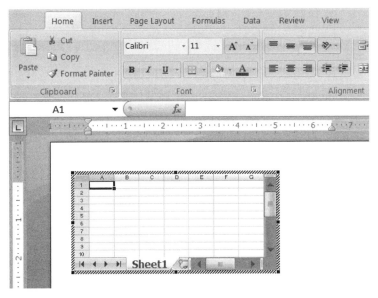

Figure 5-13 *When you use the Excel Spreadsheet command to create a table, you can utilize the Excel features.*

Formatting Table Styles

The options in the Table Style Option group (see Figure 5-14) on the Table Tools Design tab help you format the table so it is easier to read. Selecting an option in this group applies special formatting for elements within the table.

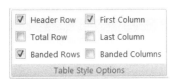

Figure 5-14 *Use the Table Style Options to identify elements in a table that should have special formatting.*

By default, three of the six options are already turned on. You can, of course, turn off one or all of the default settings and turn on one or more of the other options.

- *Header Row*: Indicates that the table will have a header row and that row should be formatted differently.
- *First Column*: Indicates special formatting for the first column.

- *Banded Rows*: Indicates odd rows are to be formatted differently than even rows. For example, all the odd rows have shading.

- *Total Row*: Indicates special formatting for a row that will include a total.

- *Last Column*: Indicates special formatting for the last column in the table.

- *Banded Columns*: Indicates that there should be different formatting for odd and even columns.

Once you've selected the options in the Table Style Options group, you are ready to choose a table style. Use the scroll bar at the right side of the Table Styles group to view the built-in table styles, or click the More button to display all the table styles at once (see Figure 5-15). The styles are customized to comply with the options you select in the Table Style Options group. For example, the styles displayed in Figure 5-15 show shading and/or borders in the first row and the first column because the Header Row and the First Column options are turned on in the Table Style Options group. When these table style options are turned off, the shading and borders are not included in the table styles. When you move the mouse pointer over the thumbnail of the style, Live Preview will show the effects of applying the new style.

When you apply a style, all manual formatting is removed. But, once the style is applied, you can modify the style formats. For example, you can make changes to the shading and borders by using the Shading and Borders commands in the Table Styles group.

You can customize the border lines using the Line Style, Line Weight, and Pen Color tools, which are displayed in the Draw Borders group.

To modify the existing table style, click the More button for Table Styles and select Modify Table Style at the bottom of the menu. The Modify Style dialog box will display; here you can change the font and the font attributes, and you can also change the settings for the border lines and shading colors. It is recommended that you enter a new style name in the Name box so that any changes you make are saved under a new style name.

If you want to use the table style to create a new style for document parts other than a table, choose the New Table Style command at the bottom of the Table Styles menu. The dialog box is very similar to the Modify Style box, but in the Create New Style from Formatting dialog box, you can select other style types: Paragraph, Character, Linked (paragraph and character), or List.

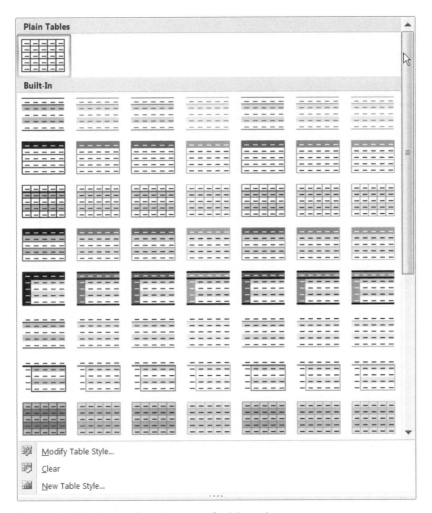

Figure 5-15 *Word offers dozens of table styles.*

Formatting Table Layouts

Notice that the Table Tools Ribbon has a second tab labeled Layout (see Figure 5-16). You will want to display this tab when you are editing and formatting the table contents.

Figure 5-16 *Display the Table Tools Layout tab when you want to change the number of table cells or format the text within the cells.*

The Select button in the Table group, shown in Figure 5-17, lets you select all or part of the table.

Figure 5-17 *The Table group includes a button for selecting all or part of the table.*

Another alternative for selecting the entire table (in Print Layout view) is to click the table move handle that displays at the top-left corner of the table (see Figure 5-18). The handle displays a four-headed arrow, and when you point to the handle, the mouse pointer also changes to a four-headed arrow. When you click, the entire table is selected. Of course, you can also drag the move handle to reposition the table in the document.

Move Handle

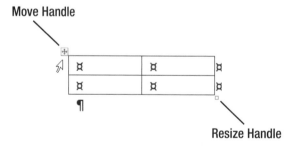

Resize Handle

Figure 5-18 *Click the table move handle to quickly select the entire table.*

The View Gridlines button toggles the display of table gridlines on and off. If the table cells have borders, you will not see the gridlines. However, if you have removed the table borders, you will want to display the gridlines so you know where the cells begin and end.

The Properties button opens the Table Properties dialog box, displaying options for table alignment, row heights, column widths, and the vertical alignment of text within a cell. Many of these settings are also accessible in the other groups on the Table Tools Layout tab.

Adding and Deleting Rows and Columns

When you use the Delete key on the keyboard to remove text within a cell, the text is removed and the cell remains intact. To remove the cell, you must use the Delete command in the Rows & Columns group (see Figure 5-19).

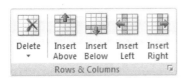

Figure 5-19 *These tools make it easy to add and remove rows and columns.*

To remove a cell, row, or column, first position the insertion point in the cell where you want to make the deletion. Then click the Delete button in the Rows & Columns group and select an option to delete cells, columns, rows, or the entire table. You can also delete a cell by positioning the insertion point in the cell and then right-clicking and choosing Delete Cells in the shortcut menu. When you choose a command to delete a single cell, the Delete Cells dialog box will display so you can indicate whether you want to shift the remaining cells or delete the entire row or column. You can also display the Delete Cells dialog box by clicking the Dialog Box Launcher in the Rows & Columns group.

To insert a new row, position the insertion point in a row within the table and then click the Insert Above or the Insert Below button in the Rows & Columns group. To insert multiple rows, select the number of rows you want to insert and then click the Insert Above or the Insert Below button. (Table 5-1 provides tips for selecting table cells.) You can also insert a new row at the end of the table by positioning the insertion point in the last cell in the table and pressing Tab. When you insert a new row, the row includes all the formats already applied to the adjacent selected row.

Table 5-1. Tips for Selecting Table Cells

To Select	Do This
A cell	Point to the left of the cell and click when the pointer changes to an arrow, or triple-click in the cell.
A row	Point to the left of the row and click when the pointer changes to an arrow.
A column	Point to the top of the column and click when the pointer changes to an arrow.
Adjacent cells	Drag the mouse across the cells, or use the Click-Shift-Click method.
Nonadjacent cells	Select the first cell. Hold down Ctrl and select each of the other cells.
The entire table	Click the table move handle at the top-left corner of the table.

To insert a new column, show the Table Tools Layout tab and click the Insert Left or Insert Right button in the Rows & Columns group. To insert multiple columns, select the number of columns you want to insert and then click the Insert Left or the Insert Right button. When you insert a new column, the new column includes all the formats already applied to the adjacent selected column.

Merging and Splitting Cells and Tables

The Merge Cells command in the Merge group (see Figure 5-20) is useful when you want to combine cells so you can create a heading that spans across multiple columns.

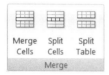

Figure 5-20 *The Merge group options enable you to customize the layout of the table cells.*

If you change your mind and want to revert the merged cell back to separate cells, use the Split Cells command. You can also use the Split Cells command when you want to add additional cells, but not for the entire column. Figure 5-21 shows a table with both merged and split cells.

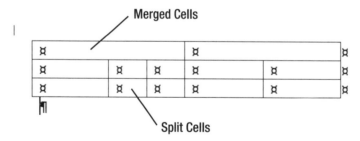

Figure 5-21 *Use the Merge Cells and Split Cells commands to create headings and special sections within a table.*

When you use the Split Table command, the table is divided into two separate tables as shown in Figure 5-22. The second table begins with the row where the insertion point is positioned.

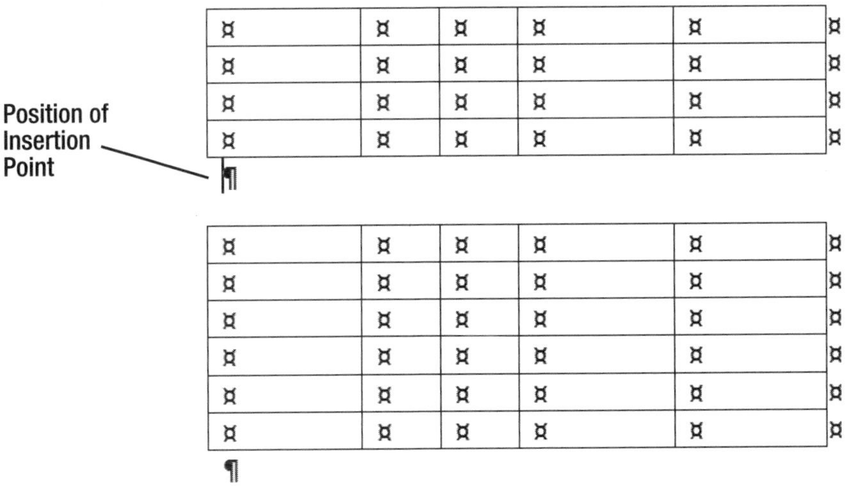

Position of
Insertion
Point

Figure 5-22 *When you split a table, the table is separated at the position of the insertion point in the table.*

Changing the Cell Size

You can change the height and width of cells by dragging the borders. However, if you want the sizes to be more exact, you can use the options in the Cell Size group (see Figure 5-23). For example, you may want to decrease the cell sizes to minimize the size of the table. Or, you may want to increase the cell sizes so there is plenty of white space in each cell so that more information can be added later. When you use these options to adjust the cell height and/or the column width, all the cells in the row/column are adjusted. To format multiple rows or columns, select the rows or columns before you apply the format.

Figure 5-23 *You can enter specific cell measurements quickly in the Cell Size group.*

When you choose the option AutoFit Contents, Word will automatically adjust the width of all the cells in the table based on the contents in the cells, and any new cells added will include the AutoFit format. Figure 5-24 shows a comparison of a table before and after automatically fitting the cell contents. When the AutoFit Contents option is applied to one or more columns, you can still manually adjust the widths of the columns. To adjust a column width manually, position the insertion point in the column and enter a number in the Width box in the Cells Size group. Or, click the arrows in the Width box to increase or decrease the column width in increments.

Qty.¤	Price¤	Total¤	¤
110¤	$.99¤	$108.90¤	¤
552¤	$1.19¤	$656.88¤	¤
125¤	$2.10¤	$262.50¤	¤

¶

Qty.¤	Price¤	Total¤	¤
110¤	$.99¤	$108.90¤¤	¤
552¤	$1.19¤	$656.88¤¤	¤
125¤	$2.10¤	$262.50¤¤	¤

¶

Before AutoFit   After AutoFit

Figure 5-24 *Minimize the table size by automatically sizing the cells to fit the table contents.*

If you have rows or columns with varying heights and widths, you can distribute the space equally among them so all the cells are the same size. First select the rows or columns that you want to adjust and then click the Distribute Rows or the Distribute Columns button. Figure 5-25 shows examples of a table before and after the spacing in the rows has been distributed.

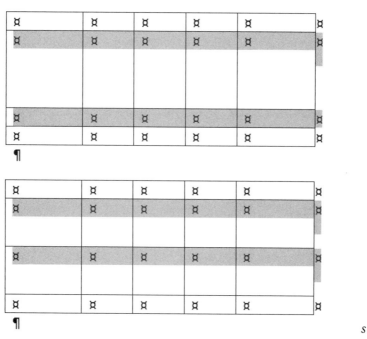

Figure 5-25 *The table on the top shows a table with two selected rows of varying height. The table on the bottom shows the same two rows after the space for rows has been distributed equally.*

Aligning Text Within Cells

While you can access some alignment options in the Table Properties dialog box, there are many more to choose from in the Alignment group (see Figure 5-26).

Figure 5-26 *Select options from the Alignment group to format the position of text within a cell.*

The nine buttons on the left in the Alignment group align text both horizontally and vertically within the cell. These alignment options are especially useful when the table cells contain numbers with commas and/or decimals. Applying a right alignment makes the data easier to read. The center alignment options are useful when a cell has a lot of white space because you can center the text to appear in the middle of the cell.

The Text Direction button rotates between three text orientations. Changing the text orientation can be useful when your column headings are much longer than the content in the column below the heading. Figure 5-27 illustrates the three text directions. If you want to format the same text direction for multiple cells, select the cells first and then click the Text Direction button.

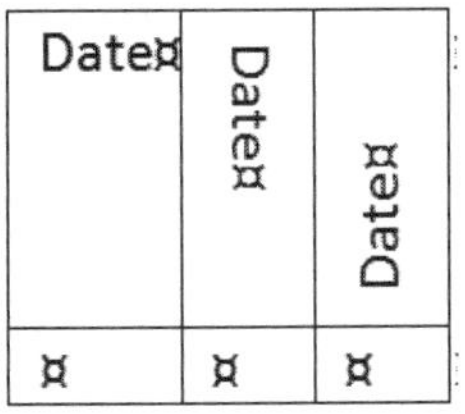

Figure 5-27 *The Text Direction button rotates between three text orientations.*

The cell margins determine the amount of white space surrounding the text in each cell. To control the amount of white space that displays in the cells, you can adjust the cell margins. This is sometimes referred to as *cell padding*. You can adjust the cell margins for a single cell or for all the cells in the table. Also, you can choose to add extra space between cells. Figure 5-28 compares three tables to show the effect of adjusting cell margins and adding extra space between the cells.

Qty.	Item #	Price
55	501203	$3.50
112	501339	$4.25
34	501338	$1.19

Default Cell Margin Settings

Qty.	Item #	Price
55	501203	$3.50
112	501339	$4.25
34	501338	$1.19

Increased Top and Bottom Margin Settings

Qty.	Item #	Price
55	501203	$3.50
112	501339	$4.25
34	501338	$1.19

Added Space Between Cells

Figure 5-28 *The cell margin settings control the amount of white space in table cells.*

To adjust the cell margins for the entire table:

1. Position the insertion point anywhere within the table.

2. Display the Table Tools Layout tab.

3. Click the Cell Margins button in the Alignment group. The Table Options dialog box will display.

4. Change the settings for one or more of the cell margins and click OK.

The settings in the Table Options dialog box apply to all the cells in the table. To adjust the cell settings for a single table cell, you must display the Cell Options dialog box. Figure 5-29 illustrates a table with cell margins formatted differently in a single cell.

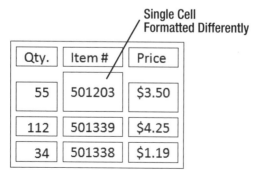

Single Cell
Formatted Differently

Qty.	Item #	Price
55	501203	$3.50
112	501339	$4.25
34	501338	$1.19

Figure 5-29 *You can format the cell margins for a single cell in a table.*

To change the margin settings for a single cell:

1. Position the insertion point in the cell you want to change.
2. Display the Table Tools Layout tab.
3. Click the Properties button in the Table group. The Table Properties dialog box will display. Display the Cell tab.
4. Click Options to display the Cell Options dialog box.
5. Turn off the option Same as the whole table.
6. Change the cell margin settings and click OK twice.

> **TIP** You can also change table settings by right-clicking a table and choosing commands from the shortcut menu.

Wrapping Text Around a Table

To maximize space in a document, you can wrap text around a table, just like you can wrap text around a picture or other object (see Figure 5-30). When you choose to wrap text around a table, you also can choose the horizontal and vertical position of the table. For example, you can align the table horizontally at the right side of the paragraph relative to margin, and you can align the table vertically 0" relative to the paragraph. These settings would position the table as shown in Figure 5-30. If desired, you can also change the amount of white space between the table and the surrounding text.

On the Insert tab, the galleries include items that are designed to coordinate with the overall look of your document. You can use these galleries to insert tables, headers, footers, lists, cover pages, and other document building blocks. When you create pictures, charts, or diagrams, they also coordinate

Qty.	Item#	Price
55	501203	$3.50
112	501339	$4.25
34	501338	$1.19

with your current document look. You can easily change the formatting of selected text in the document text by choosing a look for the selected text from the Quick Styles gallery on the Home tab. You can also format text directly by using the other controls on the Home tab. Most controls offer a choice of using

Figure 5-30 *The options for positioning a table and wrapping text around the table can be found in the Table Properties dialog box.*

To wrap text around a table:

1. If the table already exists, drag and drop or copy and paste the table inside the paragraph where you want it positioned. If the table does not exist, position the insertion point in the paragraph where you want the table to display, and create the table.
2. Click anywhere within the table.
3. Display the Table Tools Layout tab and select Properties in the Table group. The Table Properties dialog box will display. Display the Table tab.

4. Under Text Wrapping, select the Around option.

5. Click the Positioning button to display the Table Positioning dialog box.

6. Enter specific spacing for aligning the table both horizontally and vertically.

7. To increase the white space between the table and the surrounding text, edit the settings under Distance from surrounding text.

8. To anchor the text to the surrounding text, turn on the option Move with text. If you turn this option off, the table will be anchored to the page and will not move with the text.

> **NOTE** You can reposition the table in a different paragraph by using the table move handle to drag and drop the table. The text wrapping and position formats will remain intact, but they will apply to the new paragraph.

9. When the Move with text option is turned off and the Allow overlap option is turned on, the table will remain positioned on the page with the wrap-around format enabled. When new text is added to the page, the table will stay where it is, and if necessary, the new text will wrap around the table.

10. Click OK twice.

Managing Table Data

When text is organized in a table, you have several options for managing the data. For example, you can sort the data and perform calculations. The commands for managing the data in a table are accessed in the Data group (see Figure 5-31).

Figure 5-31 *The commands for sorting and calculating table data are in the Data group.*

Sorting Table Data

To sort a group of cells in a table, select the cells, and then click the Sort button in the Data group. The Sort dialog box will display. The default settings for the Sort command will sort table data based on the selected column. With this setting, all the data in the table is rearranged based on the selected column. If you want to sort only the data in the selected column, click Options in the Sort dialog box and turn on the option Sort column only.

| **NOTE** You cannot sort a table that contains merged or split cells.

Repeating Header Rows

One of the default table settings allows rows to break across pages. This means that a table can be split at the bottom of a page with some of the table rows wrapping to the top of the next page. If you don't want a table to be split between two pages, you can turn this option off.

To turn the option off so table rows will not break across pages:

1. Position the insertion point anywhere within the table.
2. Click the Properties button in the Table group on the Table Tools Layout tab.
3. Display the Row tab in the Table Properties dialog box.
4. Turn off the option Allow table to break across pages.
5. Click OK. If the table does not fit on the page, the entire table will wrap to the next page.

Another alternative is to allow rows to break across pages, and repeat the header row at the top of each page. By default, this option is not turned on. The Repeat Header Rows button in the Data group toggles on and off. When the Repeat Header Rows feature is turned on, the button is orange, and Word will automatically insert the header row at the top of each page if the table is split and continues at the top of the next page. Figure 5-32 shows a document displayed in Print Layout view before and after the table split between two pages. In the example, when the table rows wrapped to the next page, the header row was repeated in the first row on the second page. To toggle the option on and off, you must first position the insertion point within the header row, and then click the Repeat Header Rows button.

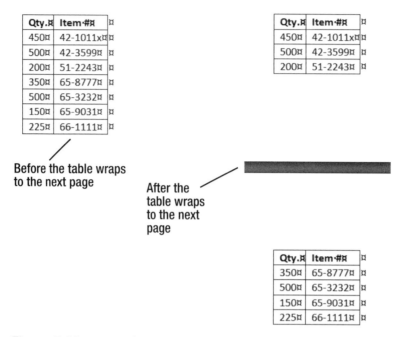

Figure 5-32 *Turn on the Repeat Header Rows feature so the header row is automatically inserted when the table rows wrap to the next page.*

Converting a Table to Text

Just as you can convert text to a table, you can convert a table to text. When you choose the Convert to Text command, the Convert Table To Text dialog box will display, and you must choose how you want to separate the text. You can choose paragraph marks, tabs, or commas. Or, in the Other box, you can enter a character or a symbol, such as a blank space or a forward slash. Figure 5-33 shows two examples of converting a table to text. The first example uses tabs to separate the text. The second example uses a forward slash.

Qty. → Item #¶		Qty./Item #¶
▪ 450 → 42-1011x¶		▪ 450/42-1011x¶
▪ 500 → 42-3599¶		▪ 500/42-3599¶
▪ 200 → 51-2243¶		▪ 200/51-2243¶
▪ 350 → 65-8777¶		▪ 350/65-8777¶
▪ 500 → 65-3232¶		▪ 500/65-3232¶
▪ 150 → 65-9031¶		▪ 150/65-9031¶
▪ 225 → 66-1111¶		▪ 225/66-1111¶

Figure 5-33 *When converting a table to text, you must specify how to separate the text (with tabs, commas, forward slashes, etc.).*

Using Formulas in Tables

Word provides some basic math functions that you can use to perform calculations in tables. For example, you can create formulas to calculate sums, averages, and counts. Although not as sophisticated and powerful as Excel formulas, the Word formulas are similar. Figure 5-34 shows examples of formulas you can use in a Word table.

=SUM(A1:A7)

=(A1+A5+A6)

=(B2+B4)/2

=SUM(ABOVE)

=SUM(LEFT)

AVERAGE(A1:A12)

COUNT(C10:C22)

Figure 5-34 *Word formulas are similar to those used in Excel.*

As you can see, the symbols for the operators are the same as those used in Excel. Although Word doesn't label the table cells, Word table cells have the same names as Excel spreadsheet cells. Because Word doesn't label the cells, though, you must count across and down to determine the cell name. The first cell in the table is A1, just like it is in Excel. Unlike Excel, though, you cannot enter the formula directly in the table cell. To create a formula in Word, you must use the Formula command.

To insert a formula in a table cell:

1. Position the insertion point in the cell where you want to perform the calculation.

2. Click the Formula button in the Data group. The Formula dialog box will display. Depending on where the insertion point is positioned in the table, the default formula =SUM(ABOVE) may display in the Formula box. If the default formula is what you need, go to Step 4.

3. Edit the default formula if it displays, or enter a new formula. Click the down arrow in the Paste function box to select a function, and the function you select will be added to the Formula box.

4. Choose a format in the Number format box, and then click OK. The results of the formula are displayed.

5. To edit a formula, click in the cell where the formula was inserted, and then click the Formula button to display the Formula dialog box.

Numbering Table Rows

If your table of data requires numbered rows, you can use the Numbering button to quickly add numbers to all of the rows. The number formats are stored in the paragraphs within each cell. You can apply the number format to empty cells, or you can apply the format to cells with content. When you add or delete rows, the numbers will automatically be updated.

To number table rows:

1. Select the cells you want to number. The cells don't even need to be consecutive. For example, you can select the first two cells in column A, and then select the fourth, fifth, and sixth cells in the same column.

2. Display the Home tab and click the Numbering button in the Paragraph group. (Click the down arrow next to the Numbering button to choose a style from the Numbering Library.)

If text or objects are entered in the selected cells, the numbers will be inserted to the left of the text or object. Figure 5-35 compares two tables—one with the numbers inserted in a separate column, and one with the numbers inserted to the left of text. If you don't see the numbers, the column may not be wide enough. Drag the column border to widen the column.

1.	Joshua¤	A.¤	Smith¤	¤
2.	Andrea¤	¤	Durham¤¤	
3.	Janelle¤	M.¤	Hasse¤	¤
4.	Aidan¤	Jack¤	Chang¤	¤

¶

1. → Joshua¤	A.¤	Smith¤	¤
2. → Andrea¤	¤	Durham¤¤	
3. → Janelle¤	M.¤	Hasse¤	¤
4. → Aidan¤	Jack¤	Chang¤	¤

¶

Figure 5-35 *You can use the Numbering feature to automatically number table rows.*

Working with Illustrations

Pictures, charts, clip art, and drawings all help to capture a reader's attention. All of these features can be found in the Illustrations group (see Figure 5-36) on the Insert tab. Word 2007 also provides a new feature called *SmartArt*.

Figure 5-36 *Tools for adding visuals to a document can be accessed in the Illustrations group.*

Inserting Pictures

When you click the Picture button in the Illustrations group, the Insert Picture dialog box is displayed, and you must choose a picture from a file. When the picture in your document is selected, the Picture Tools Format tab is also displayed. All the options you need for formatting the picture are right there when you need them (see Figure 5-37).

Figure 5-37 *When a picture in your document is selected, the Picture Tools Format contextual tab will display.*

Making Adjustments for Picture Settings

The Adjust group includes many of the options for changing the picture settings. In earlier versions of Word, these settings are found in the Format Picture dialog box, but you have to view several folder tabs to find them all. Now, the Adjust group (see Figure 5-38) makes these settings quicker to access.

Figure 5-38 *The Adjust group provides quick access to picture settings.*

Applying Picture Styles

The Picture Styles group (see Figure 5-39) offers a new feature providing several preformatted picture shapes with shadows or 3-D effects already applied. Shadows and 3-D effects are background formats that add more depth to an image. You can change the direction and color of a shadow. You can use 3-D effects to change the color and the angle of an image. You can also use 3-D effects to change the surface reflection and the direction of lighting.

Figure 5-39 *Picture styles are preformatted picture shapes with shadows or 3-D effects.*

When choosing a picture style, you can use Live Preview to save time. There are several styles to choose from. Consider the shape that will work best with the picture. For example, a square picture will fit well in a circle shape, and a rectangular picture will fit well in an oval shape (see Figure 5-40). Also, your picture may fit in the shape better if you first crop the sides, top, or bottom of the picture. If you don't see the shape you are looking for in the Picture Styles gallery, select Picture Shape at the right in the Picture Styles group. You can choose from any of the Word AutoShapes.

Figure 5-40 *Choose a shape that fits your picture.*

After you apply a picture style, you can also customize it by changing the border and adding picture effects. To add or edit shadow or 3-D effects, click the Picture Effects button in the Picture Styles group. If you add shadow effects to a picture, you cannot add 3-D effects, and vice versa. For example, if you have already applied a shadow option and then you add a 3-D effect, the shadow format will be removed. Keep in mind that when shadow effects are applied, the picture may not be positioned inline with text. Depending on the shadow effect applied, the picture may float above or below the text, and you will need to select another text wrapping option.

After formatting the picture style, you can resize the picture as needed (see the upcoming section "Resizing Pictures and Objects"). If you turn on the Lock aspect ration in the Size dialog box, the size of the picture will change proportionately to the size of the shape.

Positioning and Aligning Pictures and Objects

In earlier versions of Word, options for positioning and aligning pictures and objects are scattered throughout the Picture toolbar and the Drawing toolbar and in the Format Picture dialog box. Now the commands are organized in one place and easier to find in the Arrange group (see Figure 5-41).

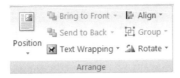

Figure 5-41 *When the picture or object is selected, these options automatically display.*

When you click the Position button, a menu of options for only square text wrapping will display, and you can use Live Preview to see the results before you choose one of the options. If instead you click the Text Wrapping button, a menu with all text wrapping options will display, but Live Preview is not available. The Align options enable you to position objects relative to the margins or the page. When you use these settings, you can be sure the position of the object will be adjusted relative to the margin or page adjustments. More options for positioning the object are available by clicking the Position button or the Text Wrapping button and choosing More Layout Options at the bottom of the menu.

Resizing Pictures and Objects

The easiest way to resize a picture or object is to drag the sizing handles, but if you want to format using specific sizes, you can enter the height and width measurements in the Size group (see Figure 5-42). Click the Dialog Box Launcher to display the Size dialog box for more size options. To add alternative text for web pages, select the Alt Text tab in the Size dialog box.

Figure 5-42 *If the picture requires specific sizing, you can enter the dimensions in the Size group, without opening a dialog box.*

To crop two sides at the same time, select your picture and click the Crop button in the Size group. Then hold down Ctrl as you drag a center handle. To crop all four sides at the same time, click the Crop button and hold down Ctrl+Shift as you drag a corner handle.

Inserting Clip Art

When you click the Clip Art button in the Illustrations group, the Clip Art task pane appears, and you can search for Clip Art and media options just as you do in previous versions of Word. When the Clip Art object is selected, the Picture Tools Format tab is displayed, which provides the same options as described previously for pictures.

Inserting Shapes

When you click the Shapes button, a list of all the AutoShapes displays. The categories are the same as in earlier versions of Word, but you can view all of them at once in the drop-down menu. Notice, too, that the most recently used shapes are easy to find because they display at the top of the list.

When an AutoShape is selected, the Drawing Tools Format tab is displayed (see Figure 5-43). It is similar to the Picture Tools Format tab because it includes a group for styles, and it also displays the Arrange and Size groups. Instead of the Adjust group, the Insert Shapes group (see Figure 5-44) displays at the left. Click the More button in the Shapes list to display the entire list of AutoShapes.

Figure 5-43 *The Drawing Tools Format tab is very similar to the Picture Tools Format tab.*

Figure 5-44 *The most recently used AutoShapes display in the Insert Shapes group.*

To add text to a shape, select the object and then choose Add Text in the Insert Shapes group. (Or, right-click the shape and choose Add Text.) The Insert Shapes group is replaced with the Text Group to help you format the text (see Figure 5-45). You can position the text within the shape using the Text Direction button. By default, the text will wrap inside the shape. You can resize the shape so the text fits. Once the text has been added to the shape, you can format the text with bullets, numbering, and even Quick Styles. Select the text and use the Mini toolbar to change the formats. You can, of course, display the Home tab if you find it easier for formatting text. To show the Drawing Tools Format tab again, click the Text Box Tools Format tab on the Ribbon.

Figure 5-45 *When a text box is selected in the document, the Text group will display on the Ribbon.*

When freeform objects are selected, the Edit Shape button in the Insert Shapes group can be accessed. The Edit Points command enables you to adjust the freeform shape. Points are displayed in the border of the object (see Figure 5-46), and you can drag these points to adjust the shape.

Figure 5-46 *Drag the points to adjust a freeform shape.*

In the Lines category in the Shapes menu, you can choose connector lines to join shapes (see Figure 5-47). Although the connector line looks like a normal line, when locked to the shape, the connector line will always move with the shapes.

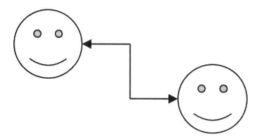

Figure 5-47 *Connector lines attach to other drawing objects.*

To attach and detach a connector line to a shape:

1. Display the shapes in the drawing canvas. (For more information on inserting and using the drawing canvas, see the next section, "Using the Drawing Canvas.")

2. Click the Shapes button and select a connector line in the Lines category.

3. Position the mouse pointer over the shape to which you want to attach the connector. Connector points (blue circles) will appear on the shape borders.

4. Click any one of these connector points to attach the line. The line can only be attached at one of these sites.

5. Point to the second shape to which you want the line to connect. The line will display as a dotted line, and as you move the mouse pointer, the dotted line will snap to the nearest connector point. When the line is attached where you want it, click once. The line will now display as a solid line, and the color of the connector point will turn from blue to red to indicate that the line is locked.

6. To unlock the connector line, click the line to select it. The line is selected when the connector points display.

7. Drag the line away from the shape. The connector points at both ends of the line will change from red to green to indicate that the connector line is unlocked.

When you reposition a shape with a locked connector line, the line will adjust to fit the change in space between the two shapes. Sometimes after moving the shape, there's a better way to connect the shapes. To reroute the connectors, click the Edit

Shape button and select Reroute Connectors. The connector line will be automatically adjusted for a more sensible connection between the two shapes.

Using the Drawing Canvas

You will also see the New Drawing Canvas command at the bottom of the Shape list. One of the advantages to using the drawing canvas is that you can move and resize multiple objects as a single unit. Another advantage to using the drawing canvas is that you can format a background behind the shapes and objects. To select the drawing canvas, click anywhere inside it. When the drawing canvas is selected, the Drawing Tools Format tab is automatically displayed. All the format options you need for inserting shapes and drawing objects are accessible on this tab. Before you begin adding objects, you can adjust the drawing canvas area by dragging the side or corner handles. If you know the exact dimensions for the drawing canvas, select the drawing canvas and enter the settings in the Height and Width boxes in the Size group. For more formatting options, click the Dialog Box Launcher in the Size group to display the Format AutoShape dialog box.

> **TIP** To align objects inside the drawing canvas, use the Align button in the Arrange group on the Drawing Tools Format tab.

To resize all the objects inside the drawing canvas as though they were a single object, right-click anywhere within the drawing canvas, but not on an object in the canvas. Choose Scale Drawing in the shortcut menu. The handles (small circles) on the drawing canvas border will change from black to blue. When you drag one of the blue handles, the drawing canvas and all the objects inside it will change size proportionally.

By default, the drawing canvas is positioned in the line of text. To reposition the drawing canvas on the page, you must change the wrapping style. With the drawing canvas selected, click Text Wrapping in the Arrange group, and select a different option. Because the borders of the drawing canvas are only visible when the drawing canvas is selected, it is easier to see the results if you reposition the canvas after you have entered one or more objects.

You can customize the settings so that the drawing canvas is automatically created when you insert an AutoShape. When the option is turned on, the drawing canvas will display as soon as you select an AutoShape and before you add it to the document.

To change the settings:

1. Click the Microsoft Office button.

2. Choose Word Options.

3. Select Advanced.

4. Under Editing options, turn on Automatically create drawing canvas when inserting AutoShapes and then click OK.

Formatting AutoShapes

Upon inserting most AutoShapes in your document, the tab will change to display the Drawing Tools Format tab. However, if you insert a callout shape, the Text Box Tools Format tab displays. Both of these tabs display groups for all the options you will need to format the objects. For example, you can apply shape styles, apply shadow and 3-D effects, arrange the objects, and resize them. And, to make it quicker and easier, you can use Live Preview to see the effects of most of these formats.

TIP To create a perfect square or circle, choose the shape and then hold Shift down as you drag the mouse to create the shape.

The Drawing Tools Format tab only displays when one or more objects or the drawing canvas are selected. For example, when you reposition the insertion point in the text of your document, the Home tab will display, and the drawing tools will temporarily disappear. Double-click the object to display the drawing tools or text box options again.

To save time formatting, select the object, click the More button in the Shape Styles group (see Figure 5-48), and use Live Preview to help you select a preset design. The designs include shape fills, gradients, and borders.

Figure 5-48 *The shape styles include formats for shape fills, gradients, and borders.*

Choose a shape style, and then if desired, edit the shape fill or outline colors. If you don't see the color combination you want in the Shape Styles group, first click the Shape Fill button in the Shape Styles group and select a color, and then click the Shape Fill button again and choose the gradient. To customize the style after you apply it, click the Dialog Box Launcher in the Shape Styles group to display the Format AutoShape dialog box.

TIP You can also apply shape styles, fills, borders, and outlines to the drawing canvas.

When you click the Shadow Effects or the 3-D Effects buttons (see Figure 5-49), menus of format options display. The Shadow options include theme colors and standard colors. The 3-D effects include options for color, depth, direction, lighting, and surface. You cannot apply shadow and 3-D effects to the same object. If you first apply a shadow effect and then apply a 3-D effect, the 3-D effect will remain, and the shadow effect will be removed.

Figure 5-49 *Live Preview is available for shadow and 3-D effects.*

To resize an object, you can drag a corner or side handle, or you can change the absolute height and width settings precisely by changing the measurements in the Size group. New in Word 2007 is the option to resize the AutoShape relative to the margins or the page. To do this, click the Dialog Box Launcher in the Size group to display the Format AutoShape dialog box. On the Size tab, under Height or Width, choose Relative, and then enter a percentage and select Margin or Page. To keep the AutoShape proportional when you resize it, select the Lock aspect ratio checkbox before accepting the changes and closing the dialog box.

NOTE To restrict the movement of an object as you reposition it, hold down Shift as you drag the object. When holding down Shift, the object will move only horizontally or vertically.

When you reposition the shape, the text will move with the shape. However, when you rotate or flip the shape, the text will not rotate and/or flip. Once you size and position the shape, you can add a picture to the shape (see Figure 5-50).

Figure 5-50 *You can add pictures to AutoShapes.*

To add a picture to an AutoShape:

1. Right-click the object.

2. Select Format AutoShape and display the Color and Lines tab.

3. Select Fill Effects.

4. Select the Picture tab, locate the picture, and click Insert.

The adjustment handle (a diamond shape) is available on some AutoShapes. This handle enables you to change the appearance of the shape. For example, you can insert the Smiley Face AutoShape, and then drag the adjustment handle to change the smile to a frown (see Figure 5-51).

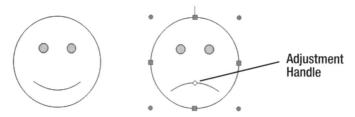

Figure 5-51 *Use the adjustment handle to modify the AutoShape.*

To keep the design of all AutoShapes consistent, you can set the default formatting for AutoShapes so that all the AutoShapes will look the same. Create an AutoShape and apply all the AutoShape formats, such as line colors, fill colors, and patterns. Then, right-click the AutoShape and choose Set AutoShape Defaults in the shortcut menu. All the new shapes you create will have the same formatting (see Figure 5-52).

Figure 5-52 *For a consistent look, set the AutoShape defaults so all AutoShapes have the same formatting.*

> **TIP** To copy the text formatting to text in a nearby AutoShape, select the formatted text and click Ctrl+Shift+C to turn on the Format Painter. Then select the text you want to format and drag the pointer across the text. If you want to copy the formats to other bodies of text, select the text and press Ctrl+Shift+V.

To align the objects you have created, select the objects (to select multiple objects, hold down Shift while clicking). Then click the Align button in the Arrange group and choose one of the alignment commands. When you choose either the Distribute Horizontally or Distribute Vertically command, the objects are arranged equal distances from each other. Here are some pointers for aligning objects:

- To align floating objects relative to a page, the objects cannot be positioned on a drawing canvas, and you must be working in Print Layout view.
- To align floating objects relative to a drawing canvas, the objects must be within the drawing canvas.
- To align objects down the center of a page, choose the Relative to Margin Guides and Align Center settings.

Inserting SmartArt

SmartArt is a new feature that greatly exceeds the Diagrams feature in earlier versions of Word. This new feature enables you to create a wide range of presentation graphics. And these are not ordinary graphics. The designs are based on contemporary layouts, combining text and graphics, and incorporating the colors and fonts from the selected document theme. The result is a professional-looking graphic that is sure to add impact to your document (see Figure 5-53).

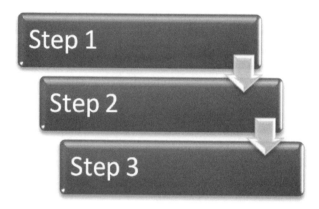

Figure 5-53 *SmartArt graphics help you visually communicate information.*

Creating a SmartArt Object

There are seven categories of SmartArt graphics. Each category arranges data in a different way. You choose a category that will most effectively present the concept of the data.

To insert a SmartArt object:

1. Position the insertion point where you want the object to display.
2. Click the SmartArt button in the Text group on the Insert tab.
3. Select a category.
4. Select a design from the gallery. Each design includes a brief description to help you choose the right design.

When the diagram is inserted in your document, the SmartArt Tools Design tab is displayed (see Figure 5-54).

Figure 5-54 *The SmartArt Tools Design tab automatically displays when you insert a SmartArt graphic.*

You can click the text boxes in the objects to add text, or you can enter the text in the separate text pane at the left. If you don't want to use this text pane, you can click the Close button to remove it. Some SmartArt shapes display the Picture button on one or more shapes in the object. Click the Picture button to add graphics to the shape.

Table 5-2 describes keystrokes you can use to edit in the SmartArt graphic.

Table 5-2. Keystrokes for Editing in a SmartArt Graphic

Press	To
Tab	Go to next element in the graphic.
Shift+Tab	Select the previous element in the graphic.
Arrow keys	Nudge the selected shape.
Ctrl+A	Select all shapes in the graphic.
Enter or F2	Edit text in the selected shape.
Shift+right arrow*	Enlarge the selected shape horizontally.
Shift+left arrow	Reduce the selected shape horizontally.
Shift+up arrow	Enlarge the selected shape vertically.
Shift+down arrow	Reduce the selected shape vertically.

* For the last four types of keystrokes, you can hold down the Ctrl key to make the adjustment more precise.

You can customize the diagram by adding and moving shapes and changing formats.

Modifying the SmartArt Object

After inserting a SmartArt graphic, you can modify the object by using the commands in the Create Graphic group (see Figure 5-55).

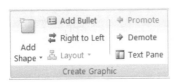

Figure 5-55 *You can modify a SmartArt graphic using the commands in the Create Graphic group.*

To add a new shape, click the Add Shape button in the Create Graphic group. You can add the shape before, after, or below the position of the insertion point. To rearrange the shapes by reversing the horizontal order, click the Right to Left button. Use the Add Bullet button to format a bulleted list within a text box. Use the Demote and Promote buttons to change the level of a bullet or shape (or group of shapes) within the hierarchy of the object.

Use the Task Pane button to toggle the display of the task pane on and off. To move a shape, simply drag it. Even after you've inserted the SmartArt graphic and added text to the object, you can change the layout of the shapes without losing text. The layout options are in the Layouts group (see Figure 5-56). Click the More button in the Layout group to see all the layout options. Click More Layouts to display the Choose a SmartArt Graphic dialog box (see Figure 5-57).

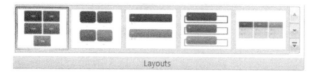

Figure 5-56 *You can change the SmartArt layout at any time.*

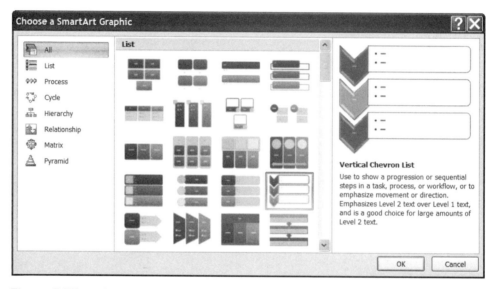

Figure 5-57 *Each layout option includes a description that will help you choose the appropriate design.*

Several preset formats are available in the SmartArt Styles group (see Figure 5-58). Click the More button to view all the options. The Best Match for Document styles do not include 3-D features. 3-D features include gradients, lines, fills, rotation, and depth. You can use Live Preview to see the results before you click.

Figure 5-58 *SmartArt styles provide predesigned formats that you can apply to SmartArt graphics.*

After you experiment with the options, you can also go back to the original design by clicking the Reset Graphic button in the Reset Group at the right side of the Ribbon. If you save a document that contains a SmartArt graphic, an image, a chart, or an equation in the Word 97–2003 format, the graphics and objects will be converted to a static image, which means you cannot edit the text or symbols inside the graphic or equation, nor can you change the general appearance. If you later convert the document back to an Office Word 2007 format, the graphics and objects will again be functional.

Inserting Charts

Word 2007 charts are integrated with OfficeArt, which enables you to create more powerful and flexible charts. PowerPoint 2007 and Excel 2007 charts are also integrated with OfficeArt. If Excel 2007 is installed on your computer, when you insert a chart in your Word document, you are actually using the Excel commands, and the Excel Ribbon will display. A few of the Excel editing and formatting commands are explained in the following text. If Excel is not installed on your computer, a Microsoft Graph Chart and a Word table with sample data will display. The Microsoft Graph Chart will also open if you are working with a document in compatibility mode. If you copy and paste a chart from applications other than Word 2007, PowerPoint 2007, and Excel 2007, the chart will be inserted as a picture, and you will not be able to edit the chart.

Creating a Chart

When you create a chart, you need to provide the data, but before you begin, you must choose a chart type (i.e., column, line, pie, or bar). Word will create the chart and format the data.

1. Click the Chart button in the Illustrations group. The Insert Chart dialog box is opened.

2. Select a chart style from the gallery and click OK. A chart is inserted and an Excel document with sample data is opened right next to the Word document.

3. Replace the spreadsheet data with your own data. The chart in the Word document will be updated to reflect the new data.

4. Close the Excel application. The data you entered is stored in Excel.

When the chart is selected, the Chart Tools Design tab displays (see Figure 5-59). This tab offers options for changing the chart type, editing the chart data, changing the chart layout, and applying chart styles. This tab is very similar to the tab that displays when you create a chart in Excel. A few of the features are discussed in the text that follows.

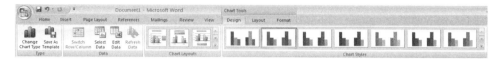

Figure 5-59 *The Chart Tools Design tab in Word is very similar to the Chart Tools Design tab in Excel.*

Editing Chart Data

If you need to change the data for a chart, you'll need to reopen the Excel spreadsheet. The Data group (see Figure 5-60) provides a shortcut. Click the Edit Data button, and the Excel spreadsheet will reopen on the right side of the screen. As you edit the data in the spreadsheet, the chart in the Word document will be updated to reflect the changes.

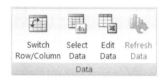

Figure 5-60 *The Edit Data button is a shortcut for reopening the Excel spreadsheet file.*

Changing Chart Layouts and Styles

If you change your mind and want to change the type of chart, you do not need to start over. Click the Change Chart Type button in the Type group (see Figure 5-61), and the Change Chart Type dialog box will display. Select the new chart type and click OK.

Figure 5-61 *Click the Change Chart Type button to change to a different type of chart.*

If you are satisfied with the chart type, but you want to change the layout, click the More button in the Chart Layouts group (see Figure 5-62) and select a predesigned layout.

After choosing the layout, you can quickly change the chart style. Click the More button in the Chart Styles group (see Figure 5-63) and select a built-in style to replace the current style.

Figure 5-62 *You can give the chart a new look by changing the layout and applying a new style.*

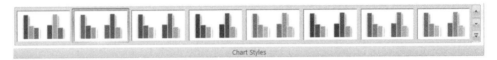

Figure 5-63 *Click the More button to display all the available chart styles.*

Customizing the Chart Layouts and Formats

You can also manually apply formats to customize the chart. The Chart Tools Layout tab displays tools for changing the layout of the elements within the chart, such as the chart title, the legend, and the data labels. For example, you can reposition the chart title, and you can insert an AutoShape to create a callout. The Chart Tools Format tab provides options for changing the formats of the elements within the chart. For example, you can convert the chart title to WordArt, and you can format the text for the callout.

Using Links

The three most common shortcuts for navigating documents and web pages (hyperlinks, bookmarks, and cross-references) are now displayed in the Links group (see Figure 5-64).

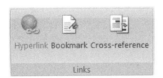

Figure 5-64 *Use these commands to create shortcuts for navigating documents.*

Creating Hyperlinks

The Hyperlinks command opens the Insert Hyperlink dialog box. You can still use the shortcut key combination Ctrl+K or select text and right-click and choose Insert Hyperlink in the shortcut menu.

It can be annoying to have every e-mail address or URL automatically converted to a hyperlink. To turn off this feature, click the Microsoft Office button, click Word Options, select Proofing, and click AutoCorrect Options. Then choose AutoFormat As You Type and turn off the option Internet and network paths with hyperlinks. If you leave the automatic hyperlink option turned on, you can remove an individual hyperlink as soon as it displays by pressing Ctrl+Z. Or, if you don't catch the AutoFormat immediately, you can right-click the formatted text and choose Remove Hyperlink.

Inserting Bookmarks

A bookmark serves as a shortcut for returning to a location in a document. You can use the Bookmark button in the Links group to add new bookmarks, delete existing bookmarks, or go to an existing bookmark.

By default, bookmarks do not display in the document. If you want to see where bookmarks are in the document, you must turn on an option in the Word Options menu. If you assign a bookmark to a selected group of text or an item, brackets display at the beginning and end of the selected text or item. If you assign a bookmark to a location, the bookmark displays as an I-beam (see Figure 5-65). The brackets do not print when the document is printed.

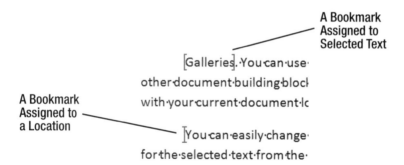

Figure 5-65 *To display bookmarks in the document, you must turn the option on in the Word Options menu.*

If the brackets do not display in the document:

1. Click the Microsoft Office button.

2. Choose Word Options and click Advanced.

3. Under Show document content, select Show bookmarks.

When you create a bookmark, you need to give it a name. The name must begin with a letter, and it can contain numbers, but it cannot contain blank spaces. You can cut, copy, and paste bookmarked items. The following summarizes the status of the bookmark when it is edited:

- If you copy all or part of a marked item to another location in the same document, the copied material is not marked. The original bookmark remains intact.

- If you copy all of a marked item to a new document, both documents contain identical bookmarks.

- If you delete part of a marked item, the bookmark remains intact. If you cut and paste all of a marked item, the item and the bookmark are moved to the new location.

- If you add text between the two brackets identifying a bookmark, the addition is included in the bookmark.

Inserting Cross-References

Cross-references are very similar to bookmarks. Both enable you to jump to other locations within the same document. The difference is a cross-reference also adds information in the document to refer the reader to other locations in the document. Cross-references are useful when content is moved within a document, because the cross-reference information is automatically updated. For example, you create a cross-reference to the page number for a heading in the same document. As you work with the document, the heading and its subtext get moved to a new location. When you update the fields in the document, the page number in the cross-reference information is updated.

You can create cross-references to numbered items, headings, bookmarks, footnotes and endnotes, and captions for figures or tables. To cross-reference a heading, heading styles must be applied. To cross-reference a table or a figure, a caption must be included.

To create a cross-reference:

1. Position the insertion point in the document where you want the cross-reference to display.

2. Enter the introductory text you want to display for the reference in the document (for example, **Learn more about the research**). You can change this introductory text at any time.

3. Select the reference text and then click the Cross-reference button in the Links group. The Cross-reference dialog box will display.

4. In the Reference Type list, select the item you want to reference. For example, choose Heading.

5. Under For which, select the text or object that that identifies the reference (for example, Recent Findings).

6. Under Insert reference to, select what you want to refer the reader to (for example, the page number).

7. To add the words "above" or "below" to the reference information, turn on the Include above/below option.

8. Click Insert, and then click Close. A cross-reference field is inserted in the document, and the results of the field will display in the document (see Figure 5-66).

See·the·table·on·page·4.

Figure 5-66 *The cross-reference will display as normal text until you click it. Then, it will display as a field.*

9. To update the field, click the field and then press F9. To update all fields in the document, select the entire document and then click F9.

Chapter 7 provides more information on working with fields.

Formatting Headers, Footers, and Page Numbers

A header contains information you want to repeat on multiple pages in your document. It appears at the top of the page. A footer serves the same purpose and appears at the bottom of the page. You can use a header or footer to provide useful information in a creative format. Consider including page numbers, time and date, document titles, file names, author names, and/or a company logo.

Headers, footers, and page numbers have their own group on the Insert tab (see Figure 5-67).

Figure 5-67 *Clicking any of these buttons will display several building block options.*

Several header/footer designs are provided in header and footer building blocks. Click the Header or Footer button and then choose the design you like, and the header/footer is automatically added to the document. If you prefer to create your own header, simply choose Edit Header under the designs that appear when you click the Header button. Once inserted, the document displays the header/footer area so you can edit the content. Also, once the header or footer is inserted in a document, and the header/footer is selected, the Header Footer Tools Design tab displays (see Figure 5-68). The Header & Footer group displays again on the Header & Footer Tools Design Tab.

Figure 5-68 *When a header or footer is selected, the Header & Footer Tools Design tab will display.*

Headers, footers, and page numbers will only display in Print Layout view or Print Preview. To display the header/footer panes, double-click at the top or bottom of the page. To return to the document, double-click in the document or click the Close Header/Footer button on the right side of the Header & Footer Tools Design tab. To remove a header or footer, click Header or Footer in the Header & Footer group on the Insert tab and choose Remove Header or Remove Footer at the bottom of the menu.

Adding Building Blocks

Headers and footers commonly include the date and time. When you insert a date or time field, you can select the option to automatically update the field. When you click the Date & Time button in the Insert group (see Figure 5-69), you can choose from several formats.

Figure 5-69 *Use the buttons in the Insert group to add date and time fields and graphics to a header or footer.*

Pictures and art, such as company logos, are also commonly displayed in headers and footers. You can use the Picture and Clip Art buttons to locate the graphics, or you can use the Quick Parts button if you have saved the graphics in the Building Blocks Organizer.

Creating Different Headers and Footers in Each Section

If your document has several multipage sections, you may want to create a different header or footer for each section. By default, when you insert a header or footer, Word will insert the header or footer in all sections in the document, but you can change those settings using the options in the Navigation group on the Header & Footer Tools Design tab (see Figure 5-70). You can change the settings either before or after the header or footer is created. Chapter 6 provides more information about formatting sections.

Figure 5-70 *Use the buttons in the Navigation group to move between headers and footers and to change the section formats.*

To create different headers and footers in each section, follow these steps:

1. Position the insertion point in the header or footer pane, within the section where you want to create a different header or footer.

2. Click Link to Previous in the Navigation group. This will break the connection between the header or footer in the new section and the previous section.

If there are multiple sections in the document, and there are multiple headers or footers, you can edit the document so it displays the same header or footer in all sections. Follow these steps:

1. Position the insertion point in the section where you want to create a different header or footer.

2. Click Link to Previous in the Navigation group on the Headers & Footers tab. This will create a connection between the header or footer in the new section and the previous section.

3. When prompted to delete the header and footer and connect to the header and footer in the previous section, click Yes.

Creating Different Headers and Footers for the First Page and Odd and Even Pages

The commands in the Options group (see Figure 5-71) enable you to format a different header/footer for the first page and for odd and even pages. By default, the Show Document Text option is turned on. You can turn off this option so that only the header/footer text displays.

The options in the Position group shown in Figure 5-72 control the placement of the text in the header/footer panes.

Figure 5-71 *These options enable you to format different headers and footers.*

Figure 5-72 *The Insert Alignment Tab command includes options for adding leaders to the tab setting.*

If the document has multiple sections, you can insert a different header or footer for each section, or you can use the same header or footer for all sections. If your document does not have multiple sections and you want to create a different header or footer for part of a document, you must first create a new section in the document. To create a new section, display the Page Layout tab, and click the Breaks button in the Page Setup group.

Using Graphics to Enhance Text

Newsletters and magazine articles often include special sections to draw attention and focus on the contents of the articles. For example, sidebars are used to provide a summary of the document content, or a quote from the article is displayed in a box centered right in the middle of the article. You can easily create these special sections using text boxes. Text boxes enable you to position text exactly where you want it on the page. To add a text box, use the Text Box command in the Text group on the Insert tab (see Figure 5-73).

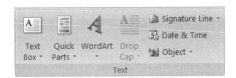

Figure 5-73 *You can use graphics to enhance text.*

But before you start creating text boxes to create a sidebar or a pull quote, scroll through the several building blocks Word 2007 provides. When you select one of these designs, a text box with sample text is entered at the location of your insertion point in the document. You can replace the sample text and reposition the text box as needed. You can also change the colors and borders by selecting the text box and choosing from the options in the Text Box Tools Format tab. If you are looking for something plain and simple, or if you want to design your own text box, click the Draw Text Box command at the bottom of the menu. After you enter the text in the text box, drag and drop the text box where you want it to display. Apply a text wrapping option and position the text box where you want it to display in the document.

The WordArt button displays the design options, which are all consistent with earlier versions of Word. You can add shadows and 3-D effects. Like pictures, you cannot add shadows and 3-D effects at the same time. If you apply a 3-D effect and then add a shadow, the shadow will override the 3-D effect. You resize and reposition the WordArt object the same as other drawing objects.

The Drop Cap button is also in the Text group. The drop cap feature automatically creates a large dropped initial capital letter. Drop caps can be used to add style to a document and draw attention to something in the document, such as the beginning of an article. Figure 5-74 shows examples of the two styles—Dropped and In margin. To format a drop cap letter, position the insertion point in a paragraph, click the Drop Cap button, and select one of the styles. To apply the format to the entire first word, select the first word before you click the Drop Cap button. Of course, formatting the entire word is most effective for short words, such as "It," "An," or "On." You can adjust the size of the drop cap format by clicking the Drop Cap button and selection Drop Cap Options at the bottom of the menu.

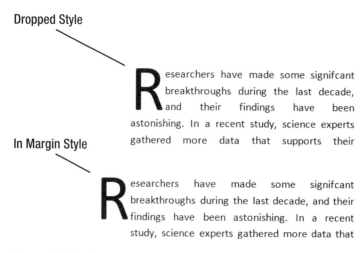

Dropped Style

Researchers have made some signifcant breakthroughs during the last decade, and their findings have been astonishing. In a recent study, science experts gathered more data that supports their

In Margin Style

Researchers have made some signifcant breakthroughs during the last decade, and their findings have been astonishing. In a recent study, science experts gathered more data that

Figure 5-74 *There are two drop cap styles.*

Adding a Signature Line

When you need to add a visible signature to a document, you can add a signature line (see Figure 5-75). In earlier versions of Word, the Signature setup options are in the Tools Options dialog box. In Word 2007, the options are in the Text group on the Insert tab. When you click the Signature Line button, the Signature Setup dialog box is displayed. Stamp signature lines can only be inserted into Word and Excel documents. You must have a digital signature certificate. If you don't have a certificate from a third party, you can create a self-signed certificate (see Chapter 10).

2/5/2007

X _Chris A. Maxwell_

Chris A. Maxwell
President   ¶

Figure 5-75 *You can add signature lines to a document.*

To create a signature line:

1. Position the insertion point in the location in your document where you want to add a signature line.

2. On the Insert tab, in the Text group, click Signature Line.

3. In the Signature Setup dialog box, type the information about the person who is signing this document. This information is displayed in the stamp signature line. Do any of the following:

    - Type the signer's name in the Suggested signer box.
    - Type the signer's organizational title (if any) in the Suggested signer's title box.
    - Type the signer's e-mail address (if any) in the Suggested signer's e-mail address box.

4. If you want to provide the signer with any instructions, type these instructions in the Instructions to signer box. These instructions are displayed in the Signature dialog box that the signer uses to sign the document.

5. If you want the signer to be able to add comments along with the signature, select the Allow the signer to add comments in the Sign dialog checkbox.

6. If you want to show the date when the signature is added in the signature line, select the Show sign date in signature line checkbox.

7. Click OK. The signature line is inserted in the document.

8. To add an additional signature line, repeat steps 1 through 7.

Now that the signature setup is complete and a signature line is inserted in the document, you can sign on the line. You can print the document, and sign on the paper. But if you want to e-mail the document, you need to sign the document on your computer. If you have a Tablet PC, you can use the inking feature to sign on the line. You can write your signature on a plain piece of paper, scan the image into your computer, and then insert the image of the signature on the signature line.

To add the signature image to the signature line:

1. Double-click the signature line in the document. The Sign dialog box will display.

2. Click the link for Select Image and locate the image of the signature. The image will display on the line in the dialog box.

3. Click Sign, and then click OK to close the message box. The signature line in the document is updated with the signature, and the document is locked.

> **NOTE** If the alert "Invalid signature" displays above the signature line, double-click the signature line to display the Signature Details box. Click the link at the top of the dialog box to confirm that you trust the user's identity, and then click Close.

Once the signature line is complete, the document is locked and cannot be edited. To unlock the document for editing, you need to remove the signature line from the document.

To remove the signature line:

1. Click the Microsoft Office button, choose Prepare, and select View Signatures. The Signatures task pane will display.

2. Select the signature to be removed.

3. Click the down arrow next to the signature name, and choose Remove Signature.

4. Click Yes to confirm the deletion.

Creating Equations

Because equations contain various symbols, it's convenient to have the Equation and Symbol options in the same group on the tab (see Figure 5-76).

Figure 5-76 *The Equation tools enable you to create complex equations.*

To create an equation, you can start by choosing a preformatted equation from a gallery of commonly used equations, or you can create your own equation from scratch. To choose from the built-in gallery, position the insertion point where you want the equation to appear, click the down arrow next to the Equation button in the Symbols group, and select an equation from the menu (see Figure 5-77). The built-in equation is inserted in the document at the location of the insertion point.

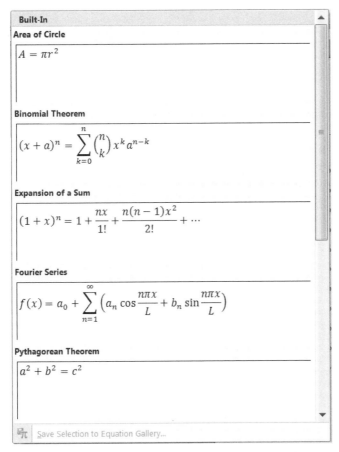

Figure 5-77 *You can insert a built-in equation and then edit it.*

When the equation is selected, the Equation Tools Design tab shown in Figure 5-78 will display as well. The tab includes numerous symbols and math structures.

Figure 5-78 *When you insert a built-in equation, the Equation Tools Design tab displays.*

To create an equation from scratch, position the insertion point where you want the equation to appear. Click the top portion of the Equation button in the Symbols group. An equation text box will be inserted at the location of the insertion point, and you can begin entering the equation using the options in the Symbols and Structures groups on the Equation Design Tools tab.

The Tools group (see Figure 5-79) includes the Equation command and options for formatting the equation layout.

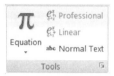

Figure 5-79 *You can easily swtich between Professional and Linear formats.*

By default, Word automatically enters an equation in a professional format, which is a two-dimensional format (see Figure 5-80). For example, exponents are shown as superscripts, and fractions are displayed with the numerator above the denominator. Click the Professional button to convert an equation to the two-dimensional format.

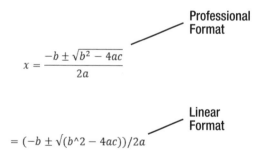

Professional
Format

$$x = \frac{-b \pm \sqrt{b^2 - 4ac}}{2a}$$

Linear
Format

$$= (-b \pm \sqrt{(b^2 - 4ac))/2a}$$

Figure 5-80 *It is easier to edit equations in the linear format.*

To display the equation in a one-dimensional format on one line (see Figure 5-80), with exponents indicated by a caret ($^\wedge$) and fractions shown as x/y, click the down arrow on the right side of the equation box and select Linear. Linear equations are easier to edit. To change to Normal text in a math area, click the Normal Text button. You can also access these format options by clicking the down arrow on the Equation Editor.

To remove an equation from a document, select the entire equation by clicking the small tab on the left side of the Equation Editor. The equation is selected when it is shaded blue. Press the Delete key.

Word offers more than 500 symbols for creating math equations. To view the symbols, click the More button in the Symbols group (see Figure 5-81). There are eight categories from which to choose. Click the down arrow next to Basic Math to view all the categories.

Figure 5-81 *Click the down arrow next to Basic Math to view the eight categories of symbols.*

The Structures group includes 11 options for fractions, operators, functions, and so forth (see Figure 5-82). Each option in the group includes further options for the math structure.

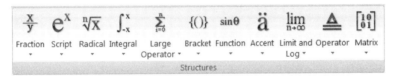

Figure 5-82 *Structures are symbols and placeholders that help you create math expressions.*

When you add placeholders to an equation, the placeholders display as small, dotted boxes. The placeholders are not visible when the document is displayed in Full Screen Reading view or in Print Preview. Also, the placeholders do not appear in printed documents.

To use Math AutoCorrect rules outside of an equation, you need to change the default settings.

1. Click the Microsoft Office button.

2. Choose Word Options.

3. Click Proofing.

4. Click AutoCorrect Options.

5. Select the Math AutoCorrect tab and turn on the option Use Math AutoCorrect rules outside of math regions.

Saving Documents with Equations

If you convert a document with equations to the Word 2007 file format, you will not be able to change the equations. Earlier versions of Word use Microsoft Equation 3.0 or Math Type add-ins. To edit the equations, you need the add-in that was used to write the equation.

If you create an equation in Word 2007 and then save the document in Word 97–2003 format, the equations in the document will be converted to images, and you will not be able to edit those equations. However, if you later convert the document to the Word 2007 file format, the equations will become text again, and you will be able to edit them.

Using Symbols

As you have already seen, many of the symbols available in Word 2007 can be used in math equations. However, there are many more symbols that can be used in general documents. You can access these symbols by clicking the Symbol button. The most recently used symbols will display. To choose from the entire gallery and to select font styles, click More Symbols to open the Symbol dialog box.

CHAPTER 6

Designing Page Layouts

It's easy to take page layout for granted because when you create a new document, it is already formatted with default settings for margins, page orientation, tabs, and paragraph spacing. You've always had the ability to change those default settings, but you probably never gave it much thought. Now with the Page Layout tab (see Figure 6-1), all the options for changing the layout are in one place and are more visible.

Figure 6-1 *The Page Layout tab provides many tools to help you create professional-looking documents.*

Using Themes

A *theme* is a set of integrated formats including color, fonts, and effects. Themes enable you to format font, text color, and text effects, all with a single click. The tools for applying themes are available in the Themes group (see Figure 6-2). The default theme in the Normal template uses Calibri (no longer Times New Roman) as the font for body text and Cambria as the font for headings.

You will find dozens of predefined themes in the Themes gallery (see Figure 6-3). You can apply one of the designs, modify the formats if desired, and then save your customized theme. The same themes are available in Word, Excel, and PowerPoint, so you can maintain a consistent look among all your documents.

Figure 6-2 *Themes integrate formats for fonts, colors, and effects.*

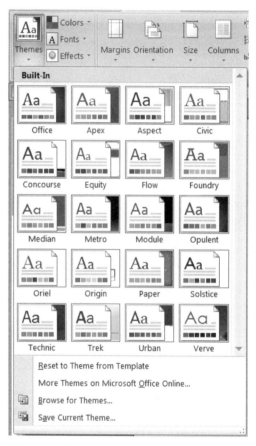

Figure 6-3 *The Themes gallery offers several built-in themes.*

Applying a Theme

When you apply a theme to a document, the formats defined in the theme affect the styles that already exist in the document. Therefore, you see more effects of the theme if you have various styles such as headings, bulleted and numbered lists, and headers and footers in your document. Even if you have just a few paragraphs of text in the default Normal style, you see changes to the font style when you apply a theme. However, if there are no headings, you may not see a change in the font color.

To apply a theme:

1. Display the Page Layout tab.

2. In the Themes group, click the Themes button.

3. Position the mouse pointer over a theme option in the gallery and use the Live Preview feature to see how the theme will look applied to your active document.

4. Select one of the themes.

Modifying a Theme

To modify a theme, you first apply the theme and then you click the Colors, Fonts, and Effects buttons in the Themes group and select different formats.

Changing Theme Colors

The Colors options affect the font colors for headings and some body text. When you click the Colors button in the Themes group, each option displays a bar of eight colors (see Figure 6-4). These color combinations affect text, backgrounds, accents, and hyperlinks. You can use Live Preview to see the effect of the change in color. If the built-in color schemes do not meet your needs, you can create your own theme colors.

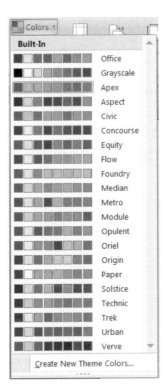

Figure 6-4 *The built-in Colors options affect the font colors for headings, text, backgrounds, and more.*

To customize the Colors options:

1. Display the Page Layout tab.

2. Click the Colors button in the Themes group.

3. At the bottom of the menu, click Create New Theme Colors. A dialog box will display.

4. Select the desired colors. As you make new selections, the changes will show in the preview sample provided in the dialog box.

> **NOTE** If you are not satisfied with your new changes, you can click the Reset button in the bottom-left corner of the dialog box, and then start again.

5. Enter a name for the new colors theme in the Name box and then click Save.

Changing Theme Fonts

The Fonts options affect the font style for headings and body text. When you click the Fonts button in the Themes group, a list of the available font combinations for each theme are displayed (see Figure 6-5). As you scroll through the Fonts options, you can use Live Preview to see the effect of the font changes. If you don't see a font combination that's right for your document, you can create your own font theme.

To customize the font style used for headings and body text:

1. Display the Page Layout tab.

2. Click the Fonts button in the Themes group.

3. At the bottom of the menu, click Create New Theme Fonts. A dialog box will display.

4. Select the desired font in the Heading font and Body font boxes. The new settings for the heading and/or body text fonts will display in the preview sample box.

5. Enter a name for the new font theme in the Name box and then click Save.

Figure 6-5 *The Fonts button in the Themes group displays the font combinations for each of the built-in themes.*

Changing Theme Effects

The Effects options affect the lines and fill effects in the graphics in the document, such as SmartArt. When you click the Effects button in the Themes group, you can quickly see how lines, fills, and special effects can change the appearance of a graphic (see Figure 6-6). You can use Live Preview to see the results of applying these various theme effects. Sometimes, though, the changes are very subtle, so as you use Live Preview, you must take your time previewing each option and focus very carefully on the results from applying the different effects. Notice, however, that there is no option for customizing the available theme effects. It is not possible to create your own set of theme effects.

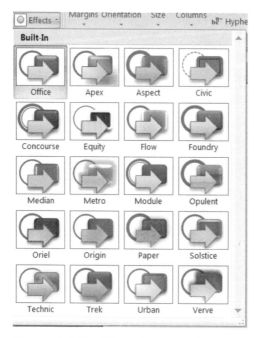

Figure 6-6 *The Effects button in the Themes group displays the effect options for each of the built-in themes.*

Saving Customized Themes

When you customize the theme settings, the new theme formats apply only to the active document. If you want to use the custom theme settings again for other documents, you need to save the modified theme.

To save a customized theme:

1. Click the Themes button in the Themes group.

2. At the bottom of the menu, select Save Current Theme. A dialog box will display.

3. Enter a name in the File name box and click Save.

By default, the customized theme is saved in the Document Themes folder. Once you save a customized theme, the options in the Themes menu are organized in two categories: Custom and Built-In. The customized themes will display at the top of the list. If you do not see a customized theme that you want to use, open the Themes menu and select Browse for Themes to search for the theme on your computer or network.

> **TIP** To search for other document themes on Office Online, click the Themes button and select More Themes on Microsoft Office Online.

To delete a customized theme, click the Themes button in the Themes group to display the list of themes. Then, right-click the theme you want to remove and select Delete in the shortcut menu.

> **NOTE** When you open a Word 2007 document in a previous version of Word, the themes (including colors, effects, and fonts) are permanently converted to styles. You can edit those styles and even apply new themes in the older version of Word. However, if you reopen the file in Word 2007, you cannot automatically change the style back to the theme settings. The buttons in the Themes group will not be available, and you will need to make all the theme changes manually.

Generating Filler Text

To experiment with some of the features introduced in the remaining topics in this chapter, you will need documents with multiple pages. Did you know that you can create a document of any size quickly by generating random text?

To insert random text:

1. Open a new document.
2. Type **=rand(12,10)**.
3. Press Enter.

The document will fill with 12 paragraphs, each paragraph containing 10 sentences. You can determine the size of the document by changing the number of paragraphs and the number of sentences within each paragraph. You can also insert random text within an existing document. If you want the random text to include paragraph formats such as line spacing and paragraph indents, apply the desired formats before you press Enter.

Changing Page Orientation and Paper Size

There are many adjustments you can make to the page layouts to present document information effectively. The Page Setup group shown in Figure 6-7 offers many ways to make such adjustments.

The page orientation setting determines whether the document displays on the page vertically or horizontally. The default setting is portrait, which is vertical. The landscape option displays the document horizontally. When you change the page orientation, the galleries for cover page options also change. You can quickly change the orientation by clicking the Orientation button in the Page Setup group.

Figure 6-7 *Use the commands in the Page Setup group to make adjustments to page layouts.*

To use portrait and landscape orientation in the same document:

1. Select the text that you want to change.
2. Click the Dialog Box Launcher in the Page Setup group to display the Page Setup dialog box.
3. Under Orientation on the Margins tab, select Portrait or Landscape.
4. In the Apply to list, choose Selected text and click OK. Word will automatically insert a section break above the selected text and position the selected text on a new page.

If you're going to print the document, the page layout must, of course, also fit the paper. The default setting for the paper size is Letter 8.5x11 in. If you will be printing on a different size paper, the Paper Size button in the Page Setup group makes it convenient to change the settings. This feature is especially useful when you are printing documents such as invitations or announcements on custom-size paper stock.

Setting Page Margins

If your document has multiple pages, your margin settings will depend upon how you want to publish the pages. For example, will you bind the pages? Punch holes in the margin and put the pages in a binder? Fold the pages into a booklet? Word offers several options to help you choose the appropriate margin settings for all of these options.

Margins display only in Print Layout view and Full Screen Reading view. You can also use Print Preview to see the effect of your margin settings. Sometimes projects require specific margin settings, so you will need to adjust the margins. You may also want to adjust margins so you can fit more on a page.

> **NOTE** If the margins do not display in Print Layout view or Full Screen Reading view, click the Microsoft Office button and choose Word Options. Click Display, and under Page display options, turn on Show white spaces between pages in Print Layout view, and click OK.

Most printers cannot print all the way to the edge of the page, so depending on your printer, there may be a required minimum width for margin settings. Check your printer manual for information about the minimum margin settings for your printer.

Changing Margins for the Entire Document

The default setting applies changes to margin settings to the whole document. So, if you want to change the margins for the entire document, you can click anywhere in the document and then edit the margin settings. To change the current margin settings, you can use the Margins command in the Page Layout group. You can choose from a list of preset options (see Figure 6-8), or you can customize your own. If you create a custom setting, the last custom setting will be included at the top of the list.

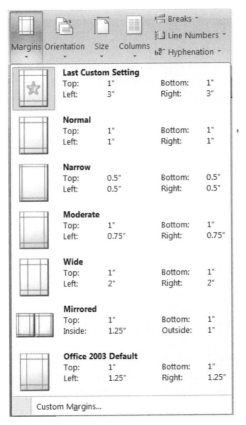

Figure 6-8 *You can choose from a list of predefined margin settings.*

To change margin settings:

1. Display the Page Layout tab.
2. Click the Margins button in the Page Setup group.
3. Select the desired preformatted margin settings, or click Custom Margins. The Page Setup dialog box will open, and you can enter your own settings.

> **TIP** To open the Page Setup dialog box, double-click in the margin areas on the Ruler.

Changing Default Margin Settings

One change in Microsoft Word 2007 you may not have noticed is that the default settings for a document have changed. Previous versions of Word have default settings of 1.25" for the left and right margins. The new default settings include formats for 1" margins on all four sides of the document. If these new margin settings aren't what you need for most documents, you can modify the default settings. Default margin settings are saved in the template on which the document is based, so if the document was created using the Normal template, the changes will be made to the Normal template.

To change the default margin settings:

1. Click the Margins button in the Page Setup group.
2. Select Custom Margins at the bottom of the menu. The Page Setup dialog box will display.
3. Select the desired settings.
4. Click the Default button in the lower-left corner of the dialog box.
5. Click Yes to confirm the change.

When you change the default settings to custom margins, the new default settings will not display in the Margins menu.

Setting Margins for a Section in the Document

If your document has multiple sections, you may want to change the margins for only selected sections throughout the document. When you position the insertion point within the section, Word applies the changes to margin settings for only the current section.

To change the margin settings for a section in a document:

1. Click anywhere within the section you want to change.
2. Click the Margins button in the Page Setup group.
3. Choose one of the margin setting options in the menu.
4. If you do not see the margin settings you need, click Custom Margins at the bottom of the menu. The Page Setup dialog box will display, and you can enter your desired settings.

Setting Margins for a Portion of the Document

If your document does not have section formats, you can still change the margin settings for a portion of the document.

To change the margin settings for only a portion of a document:

1. Select the text you want to format.
2. Click the Margins button in the Page Setup group.
3. Click Custom Margins at the bottom of the menu. The Margins tab in the Page Setup dialog box will display.
4. Under Margins, enter your desired settings.
5. Under Preview, in the Apply to box, click the down arrow and choose Selected text.
6. Click OK. Section breaks will automatically be inserted above and below the selected text. If the selected portion of the document displays on a separate page, you can edit the section breaks as described in the section "Editing a Section Break" later in this chapter.

Adding a Gutter Setting

If you plan to bind the pages of your document, you will want to add extra space to the side or the top margin of the document (see Figure 6-9). This extra space is called a *gutter*.

To add a gutter setting to document margins:

1. Click the Margins button in the Page Setup group.
2. Select Custom Margins in the Margins menu to display the Page Setup dialog box.
3. Under Margins, select a setting in the Gutter box and select Left or Top in the Gutter position box. As you change the settings, the sample in the dialog box under Preview will change to show the effect of the new settings.

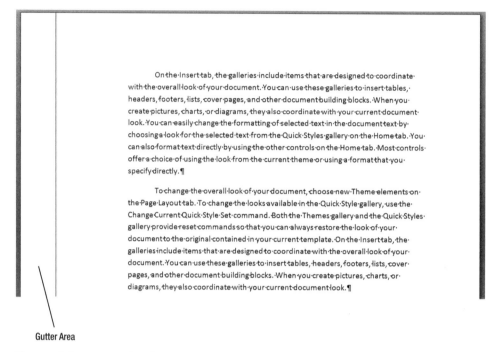

Gutter Area

Figure 6-9 *A gutter has been added to the left side of the document to allow extra space for binding.*

Formatting Mirror Margins

If the pages are to be displayed side-by-side and double-sided (duplex), such as in books or magazines, then you want to create *mirror margins*. This is sometimes referred to as *facing pages*. With mirror margins, the margins on the left page mirror the margins on the right page. In other words, the outside margin on the left page is identical to the outside margin on the right page. When you format mirror margins, the inside and outside margins are often different. For example, if you plan to bind the pages in a book format, the inside margin may need to be wider. But you can't solve the problem with a gutter setting, because the extra space needs to be alternated between the left and the right pages. That's where mirror margins become useful. Word will automatically alternate the extra space on the right and left pages as shown in Figure 6-10. The right margin on an even-numbered page is the inside margin. The right margin on an odd-numbered page is the outside margin.

Extra Space
Added for Binding

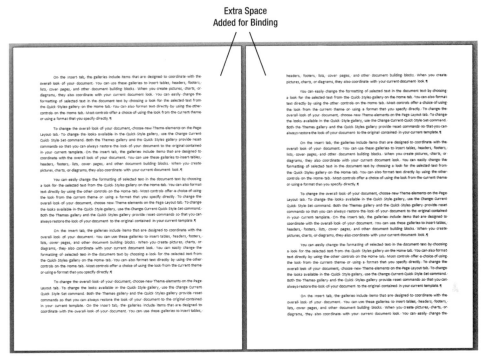

Figure 6-10 *The margins on the left page mirror the margins on the right page.*

To create mirror margins:

1. Click the Margins button in the Page Setup group.

2. Do one of the following:

   • Choose Mirrored from the preset options.

   • Select Custom Margins in the Margins menu to display the Page Setup dialog box. Under Pages in the Multiple pages box, select Mirror margins. The settings will automatically display the default settings of 1" for all margins. You can, of course, change these settings.

3. To view how the pages will look side by side, display two pages in Print Layout view.

You can add gutter margins to mirror margins and booklets, but you cannot adjust the gutter position. The gutter position is automatically determined based on the type of margin selected. For example, if you have chosen the mirror margin or the book fold formats, the extra space for the gutter setting is added to the inside margins. If you have chosen 2 pages per sheet, the extra space is added to the outside margins.

Formatting Margins for Printing Two Pages on One Sheet

You also have the option of printing two half-sized pages on one sheet of paper, and you can print the half-size pages on both sides of the paper as well. Word will automatically set the margins when you choose this option. The pages will print in the order they occur in the document. You can choose either portrait or landscape orientation. Figure 6-11 shows examples of two pages on one sheet in both portrait and landscape orientations. However, because the pages print in order, you cannot fold these pages to create a booklet.

Figure 6-11 *You can print two pages per sheet in portrait or landscape orientation.*

Formatting Margins for a Booklet

You might want to fold printed pages to create a booklet, such as a menu or a program. If you plan to fold the printed pages to create a booklet, the document must be formatted in landscape orientation. You will fold the page from left to right. Also, you must print in duplex (print on both sides of the page) so the pages remain in order when you fold them. Word will automatically adjust the margin settings when you use the book fold, and the margin settings must be applied to the entire document. The preview of the document will display exactly the same as two pages per sheet in landscape orientation. The difference, though, is that the document pages will print in the order needed when the pages are folded.

To create a booklet:

1. Make sure Landscape orientation is selected.

2. Click the Margins button in the Page Setup group.

3. Select Custom Margins in the Margins menu to display the Page Setup dialog box.

4. Under Pages in the Multiple pages box, select Mirror margins.

5. Make any necessary adjustments to the margin settings and then click OK.

The preview in the dialog box will change to reflect the format you have chosen. If you work with the document in Print Layout view, the arrangement of pages on the screen will reflect the settings you have chosen. You can continue to work with the document as you normally would. Printing a book fold document is also addressed in Chapter 12.

If you chose margin settings for mirror margins, 2 pages per sheet, or book fold, you should consider creating headers or footers that will also be mirrored. To do so, click inside the header section to display the Header & Footer Tools Design tab. Turn on the option Different Odd & Even Pages. Then, edit the even-page header or footer so that the format mirrors the format of the odd-page header or footer. For example, align the document title and date at the left on the odd-numbered pages and align that same information at the right on the even-numbered pages.

Formatting Text in Columns

There's nothing new about formatting columns except that now there's a button on the Page Layout tab to get you to the columns feature faster. Clicking the Columns button in the Page Setup group will display the Columns menu. Selecting More Columns will display the Columns dialog box, including more formatting options for column layouts. You can apply the column formats before or after you enter text. When you select text and then apply a column format, Word creates a Continuous section break above and below the selected text. You must display the document in Print Layout view to see how the text will appear in multicolumn formats. The multiple columns are not visible in any of the other views.

Automatically Hyphenating Text

When you format text in columns, you can create more uniform spacing within each line of text by hyphenating the text when text wraps to the next line. Of course, you can manually hyphenate text, but if you edit the document and the line wraps change, the hyphenation may be unnecessary or improperly placed. The advantage of using the automatic hyphenate feature is that Word will automatically hyphenate every time line wraps change.

To turn the automatic hyphenation feature on and off:

1. Click the Hyphenation button in the Page Setup group.

2. Click Automatic. The Automatic option is turned on.

3. To turn the Automatic option off, click the Hyphenation button and select None. All automatic hyphenation will be removed.

When you use the Automatic Hyphenation feature, Word hyphenates the entire document. If there are parts of the document that you don't want hyphenated, you can mark those paragraphs to be excluded. You can mark paragraphs for exclusion both before and after you automatically hyphenate.

To exclude paragraphs for automatic hyphenation:

1. Select the paragraph(s).
2. Click the Dialog Box Launcher in the Paragraph group on the Page Layout tab. If necessary, display the Line and Page Breaks tab.
3. Under Formatting exceptions, turn on Don't hyphenate and click OK.

Because the Automatic Hyphenation feature is applied to the entire document, Word will automatically hyphenate the excluded paragraphs if you turn this option off.

Working with Document Sections

Section formats include margins; page orientation; page borders; vertical alignment; headers, footers, and page numbers; footnotes and endnotes; columns; and line numbers. Settings for paper size and paper source for a printer are also included in section formats. Each section can have its own formats. Many sections are automatically created, but you can also create new sections manually.

Creating a New Section

When you create a new section, you choose whether the document content will start on a new page or continue on the existing page. For long documents containing several chapters, you can create a section break that will begin on a new odd or even page. Until you change the formats, the new section contains the same formats as the section where it was created.

To create a new section:

1. Position the insertion point where you want the new section to begin.
2. Click the Breaks button in the Page Setup group.
3. Under Section Breaks, select an option. A section mark displays in Draft or Outline view, or when Show/Hide ¶ is turned on in Print Layout view (see Figure 6-12).

⸺Section Break (Continuous)⸺

Figure 6-12 *The section mark displays at the end of a section.*

Editing a Section Break

The section formats are saved in the section mark at the end of each section. Therefore, the section mark controls all the text that precedes it.

To edit a section break:

1. Double-click the section break line. The Page Setup dialog box will display. If necessary, display the Layout tab.
2. Under Section, select from the list in the Section start drop-down list.
3. Click OK.

Generally, section marks do not display at the end of the last section in a document. You can, of course, still change the section formats. Click in the last paragraph of the document before you begin to change the settings.

Deleting a Section

When a section mark is deleted, all the section formats are removed. The text above the deleted section mark becomes part of the section below, and the formats in the section below are applied to the text above.

To delete a section:

1. If necessary, display the document in Print Layout, Draft, or Outline view so the section break marks display.
2. Click the section break mark. Make sure the insertion point displays immediately to the left of the section break mark.
3. Press Delete.

Changing Vertical Text Alignment

When you want to position the text on the page relative to the top and bottom margins, you need to align the text vertically. You can align the text at the top of the page, in the center of the page, or at the bottom of the page. You can also vertically justify the text, which means the paragraphs are spread out evenly between the top and bottom margins. You can align an entire section of text, or you can select a portion of the text and align only the selection.

To align text vertically:

1. Click the Dialog Box Launcher on the Page Setup group to display the Page Setup dialog box.
2. Display the Layout tab.
3. In the Vertical alignment box, select the desired option.
4. In the Apply to box, select the desired option.
5. Click OK.

Using Watermarks

A *watermark* is text or a graphic that displays behind document text. Watermarks can be used to draw attention to a document, or they can be used to identify the status or source of a document. For example, you can add a watermark to a document to label the document as "Confidential" or "For Office Use Only." Usually, the graphic or text is lightened or "washed out" so the document text is still easy to read. Formatting watermarks in Word 2007 is much easier with the new Watermark command in the Page Background group (see Figure 6-13).

Figure 6-13 *The new Watermark button makes it much easier to add watermarks to document pages.*

Adding a Predesigned Watermark

When you create a watermark, the contents and formatting are stored in the header pane of the document. By adding the watermark to the header, the watermark will be repeated on all pages in the document. The watermark will display behind the text in the document, and it will not display in the header.

> **NOTE** Watermarks are visible only when the document is displayed in Print Layout view.

To add a predesigned watermark:

1. If necessary, switch to Print Layout view.
2. Double-click at the top of the document to open the header pane. Make sure the insertion point is positioned in the header pane.
3. Click the Watermark button in the Page Background group and select a watermark design.

> **NOTE** When you insert a cover page in a document, it is created in a separate section of the document and it has its own separate header. Therefore, if you create a watermark for the other pages in the document, the watermark will only apply to the current section and will not appear on the cover page.

Creating a Custom Watermark

If you want to choose the text and/or graphics for your watermark, you will need to create a custom watermark. Word 2007 makes it very easy.

To create a custom watermark:

1. If necessary, switch to Print Layout view.
2. Double-click at the top of the document to open the header pane. Make sure the insertion point is positioned in the header pane.
3. Click the Watermark button in the Page Background group.
4. Select Custom Watermark at the bottom of the menu. The Printed Watermark dialog box will display.
5. Choose either Picture watermark or Text watermark.
6. Do one of the following:
   a. If you chose to create a picture watermark, click Select Picture and locate the picture.
   b. If you chose to create a text watermark, enter the text, and if desired, change the font, font size, and font color. You can also change the layout of the text.
7. Click OK.

> **NOTE** To edit a watermark object, you must first select it. To select the watermark, display the header pane and position the insertion point in the header pane. Then, you should be able to select the watermark object.

Creating a Watermark with a Clipart Image

You can also create a watermark by inserting a clipart image in the header/footer pane. After inserting the clipart image in the header pane, you format the image to display behind the text in the document.

To create a watermark with a clipart image:

1. If necessary, switch to Print Layout view.
2. Double-click at the top of the document to open the header pane. Make sure the insertion point is positioned in the header pane.
3. Locate and insert the clipart image.
4. Select the image and display the Picture Tools Format tab.
5. In the Arrange group, select Text Wrapping, and then choose Behind Text.
6. Resize and reposition the image anywhere on the document page.
7. Select the image and select Recolor in the Adjust group on the Picture Tools Format tab. Under Color Modes, select Washout.

Assigning a Watermark to Specific Pages

You can change the header format so the watermark appears only on specific pages within the document. Because the watermark is stored in the header, your document must be divided into sections, which will enable you to format a different header for each section.

If your document is already divided into sections, when you add a watermark, the watermark is applied to all sections. If you format the sections after you add the watermark, the watermark will apply to all new sections. This is because the headers for all sections are linked together. When you remove that link, you can format a different header for each section.

To format a different header for each section:

1. Go to the second section in the document.
2. Double-click in the header pane at the top of the document and display the Header & Footer Tools Design tab.
3. In the Navigation group, click Link to Previous to turn off the link.
4. Remove the links for all other succeeding sections in the document.
5. Position the insertion point in the section where you want to change the watermark, and create (or remove) the watermark.

Removing a Watermark

If you used the Watermark button to create the watermark, you can use the button again to remove the watermark.

To remove a watermark created with the Watermark button:

1. Position the insertion point in the section of the document where you want to remove the watermark.
2. Click the Watermark button in the Page Background group.
3. Select Remove Watermark at the bottom of the menu.

To remove a watermark created with clipart:

1. Position the insertion point in the section of the document where you want to remove the watermark.
2. Click inside the header box, select the clipart image, and press Delete.

Adding Background Color to Pages

In earlier versions of Word, background colors and images were visible only when you viewed a document online. Word XP first introduced the capability of printing background colors and images. Background formats and page colors are primarily used in a web browser to create a more interesting background for online viewing. You can also display backgrounds in all views, except Draft view and Outline view.

You can use gradients, patterns, pictures, solid colors, or textures for backgrounds. The background is created by tiling or repeating the gradients, patterns, pictures, and textures to fill the page. When a document with backgrounds is saved as a web page, the patterns used to create the background are saved as GIF files, and textures and gradients used to create the background are saved as JPEG files.

NOTE If no background is specified for a web page, the page displays with the default background color that has been set for the web browser.

To add a color to a page:

1. On the Page Layout tab, in the Page Background group, click Page Color.
2. Select the color that you want under Theme Colors or Standard Colors.

TIP Select the color that you want before you apply a gradient or pattern.

3. Click Fill Effects to change or add special effects, such as gradients, textures, or patterns.

Adding Borders to Pages

The features for formatting page borders are similar to earlier versions of Word, but there is no longer a Borders toolbar. All the options you need are easily accessed by clicking the Page Borders button in the Page Background group. The Borders and Shading dialog box will display, and you can choose your border settings.

Indenting Paragraphs

An *indent* is the distance set between the document text and either the left or the right margin. You can increase or decrease the width of indentations for a single paragraph or for a group of paragraphs.

Formatting a First Line Indent

The first line indent is the most commonly applied indent, and the standard space of the indent is either .25" or .5". The quickest and easiest way to create a first line indent is to press the Tab key at the beginning of a sentence. This will indent the first line according to your default settings for tab stops.

If you cannot automatically create an indent by pressing the Tab key:

1. Click the Microsoft Office button.

2. Choose Word Options.

3. Select Proofing.

4. Under AutoCorrection options, select AutoCorrect Options.

5. Display the AutoFormat as You Type tab.

6. Select Set left- and first-indent with tabs and backspaces.

7. Click OK.

Formatting a Full-Paragraph Indent

Another commonly applied indent is to move all the lines in a paragraph to the right. There are several options to achieve this format. The quickest and easiest option is at the top of the list.

- Click in front of any line but the first line in the paragraph, and then press the Tab key. If you change your mind, immediately press the Backspace key to remove the indent (or click the Undo button).

- Click anywhere within the paragraph and then drag the indent markers on the Ruler.

- Enter the indent settings in the Indent Left and Indent Right boxes in the Paragraph group on the Page Layout tab (see Figure 6-14).

- Click the Dialog Box Launcher on the paragraph group to display the Indents and Spacing tab of the Paragraph dialog box. Under Indentation, enter the indent settings in the Paragraph dialog box.

- Use the Increase Indent and Decrease Indent buttons in the Paragraph group on the Home tab.

Figure 6-14 *Use these options to enter specific settings for full paragraph indents and paragraph spacing.*

Formatting a Hanging Indent

A *hanging indent* is a format that leaves the first line of a paragraph aligned with the left margin, and all the subsequent lines in the paragraph are indented to the right. Again, there are several options for creating the indent.

The fastest way, of course, is to use a shortcut key combination. Position the insertion point anywhere within the paragraph and then press Ctrl+T. This will format a .5" hanging indent.

To create a hanging indent using the Ruler:

1. Select or position the insertion point in the paragraph in which you want to indent all but the first line of the paragraph, also referred to as a hanging indent.

2. If you don't see the horizontal Ruler that runs along the top of the document, click the View Ruler button ⬚ at the top of the vertical scroll bar at the right side of the window. The Ruler displays two indent markers (see Figure 6-15).

First Line Indent Marker

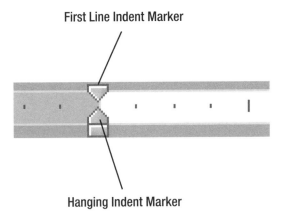

Hanging Indent Marker

Figure 6-15 *The indent markers display at the left side of the Ruler.*

3. On the horizontal Ruler, drag the Hanging Indent marker to the position at which you want the indent to start (see Figure 6-16).

Figure 6-16 *Drag the indent markers on the Ruler to set paragraph indents.*

Instead of sliding the indent markers along the Ruler, you can toggle through the options on the Tab button on the Ruler (see "Setting Tabs Using the Ruler" later in this chapter). Select either the First Line Indent button ⬚ or the Hanging Indent button ⬚ and then click the Ruler to position the indent tab.

When you use the Ruler to set indents, the settings are approximate. If you want to format precise settings, use the options available in the Paragraph dialog box.

To create a hanging indent using the Paragraph dialog box:

1. Click in the paragraph in which you want to indent all but the first line of the paragraph, also referred to as a hanging indent. (To format multiple paragraphs, select all of the paragraphs.)

2. Click the Dialog Box Launcher on the Paragraph group and display the Indents and Spacing tab. Under Indentation, click the down arrow in the Special box, and select Hanging.

Formatting a Negative Indent

You can also create a *negative indent*, which is sometimes referred to as an *outdent*. A negative indent extends the paragraph out into the left margin.

To create a negative indent:

1. Select or position the insertion point in the paragraph that you want to extend into the left margin.

2. In the Paragraph group on the Page Layout tab, click the down arrow in the Indent Left box.

3. Continue to click the down arrow until the selected text is positioned where you want it in the left margin.

Setting Tabs

Not only are tabs useful for indenting paragraphs, but they can also be used to align text on the page. When using the normal template to create documents, the default setting for tabs is every 0.5". These default tab settings do not display on the Ruler. When you create your own tab stops, the manual settings override all default settings to the left of the new manual settings.

Setting Tabs Using the Ruler

You can quickly set tabs and edit tabs using the Ruler. When you open a new blank document, no tab settings will display on the Ruler. The Tab button displays at the left side of the Ruler (see Figure 6-17).

Tab Button

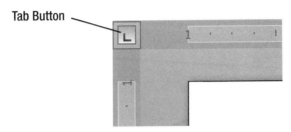

Figure 6-17 *The Tab button is at the far left side of the horizontal Ruler and the top of the vertical Ruler.*

As you click the Tab button, it will toggle through seven tab and indent setting options:

- *Left*: Text will run to the right of the tab setting.
- *Center*: Text will be centered at the position of the tab setting.
- *Right*: Text will run to the left of the tab setting.
- *Decimal*: Numbers are aligned around the decimal point, which is always positioned at the tab setting.
- *Bar*: A vertical bar is inserted at the tab setting.
- *First Line Indent*: This controls the indent for the first line of the paragraph.
- *Hanging Indent*: This controls the indent for all lines except the first line of the paragraph.

Tab settings are stored with the paragraph. You can set tab stops before or after you enter text. If you want to apply the same tab settings to multiple paragraphs, select all the paragraphs before you apply the tab settings. Obviously, tab settings will vary throughout the paragraphs in a document. If multiple paragraphs are selected, only the tab settings for the first paragraph will display on the Ruler.

To change the position of existing tab stops, drag the tab markers left or right along the Ruler. To remove a tab stop, drag the tab marker (up or down) off the Ruler. When you release the mouse button, the tab stop disappears.

Setting Tab Stops Precisely

It can be difficult to position tabs precisely using the Ruler. If you want your tab stops set at precise positions, or if you want to insert a specific character (leader) before the tab, use the Tabs dialog box.

To create precise tab stop settings:

1. On the Page Layout tab, in the Paragraph group, click the Dialog Box Launcher.

> **TIP** Double-click a tab stop marker to open the Tabs dialog box.

2. At the bottom-left corner of the Paragraph dialog box, click Tabs.
3. In the Default tab stops box, enter the tab stop positions or the amount of spacing that you want between the default tab stops.

Adjusting Paragraph and Line Spacing

You may have noticed that there are two Paragraph groups—one on the Home tab and one on the Page Layout tab. Both groups make it very convenient to change paragraph formats. The Home tab Paragraph group (see Figure 6-18) includes a button for selecting line spacing, and you can also access options to add or remove spacing before and after paragraphs. The Paragraph group on the Page Layout tab offers buttons for setting specific spacing before and after paragraphs.

Figure 6-18 *The Paragraph group on the Home tab includes options to change line spacing and remove space before and after paragraphs.*

Line spacing refers to the amount of space between lines of text. For example, the default setting is single line spacing. When you change to double line spacing, there is more white space between the lines of text.

To change the line spacing in a paragraph:

1. Select or position the insertion point in the paragraph for which you want to change the line spacing.
2. On the Home tab, in the Paragraph group, click Line Spacing.

3. Do one of the following:

   a. To apply a new setting, click the number of line spaces that you want. For example, if you click 1.0, the selected text is single-spaced.

> **TIP** The shortcut key combination for single spacing is Ctrl+1. For 1.5 spacing, press Ctrl+5, and for double spacing, press Ctrl+2.

   b. To set more precise spacing measurements, click Line Spacing Options, and then select the options that you want under Line spacing.

> **NOTE** If a line contains a large text character, graphic, or formula, Word increases the spacing for that line.

- *At least*: Sets the minimum line spacing needed to fit the largest font or graphic on the line.
- *Exactly*: Sets a fixed line spacing.
- *Multiple*: Sets line spacing relative to single line spacing. For example, 1.4 increases the space by 40 percent and .9 decreases the single line spacing by 10 percent.

> **NOTE** Line spacing is not the same as allowing extra space formatted above or below paragraphs. By default in Word 2007, extra spacing is now automatically added after a paragraph. To remove the extra spacing, show the Home tab, click the Line Spacing button in the Paragraph group, and select Remove Space After Paragraph.

To change the spacing before or after paragraphs:

1. Select or position the insertion point in the paragraph for which you want to change the before or after spacing

2. Display the Page Layout tab.

3. In the Spacing section of the Paragraph group, click an arrow next to Before or After and select the amount of space that you want.

> **TIP** Double-click an indent marker to open the Paragraph dialog box.s

CHAPTER 7

Using Reference Features

Creating tables of contents, footnotes, citations, and bibliographies can be tedious work, but Word 2007 has streamlined its reference features to make these tasks much easier. First, all the features are grouped together on the References tab (see Figure 7-1), so they're all easy to find. Second, the process of applying the formats has been simplified. For example, you can specify a document style such as MLA or APA and apply the document formats with a single click.

Figure 7-1 *The References tab streamlines options for formatting footnotes, citations, bibliographies, and more.*

Creating a Table of Contents

Word automatically creates a table of contents (TOC) by searching the document for text entries marked for use in the TOC. The templates for the TOC formats are the same as those in earlier versions of Word, but the Table of Contents group (see Figure 7-2) offers some new options.

Figure 7-2 *The features for creating a TOC are easy to access in the Table of Contents group.*

To create a TOC, you must first identify the text entries to be included. There are three ways to identify text entries:

- Use any of the nine built-in heading styles provided in the Word Normal template.
- Use custom styles that you have created and applied to text entries in the document.
- Create TOC entries manually.

Creating a TOC Using Built-In Heading Styles

The Table of Contents button displays a menu with built-in styles, but you can also access TOC styles and options by choosing the Insert Table of Contents option at the bottom of the menu (see Figure 7-3).

If you have applied heading styles to text in your document, you can use the heading styles to help you identify the TOC entries. You can choose to include some or all of the heading styles. For example, you can specify only heading levels 1 through 3, or you can specify all headings in the document. When you use styles to identify TOC entries, Word includes the entire paragraph in the TOC entry.

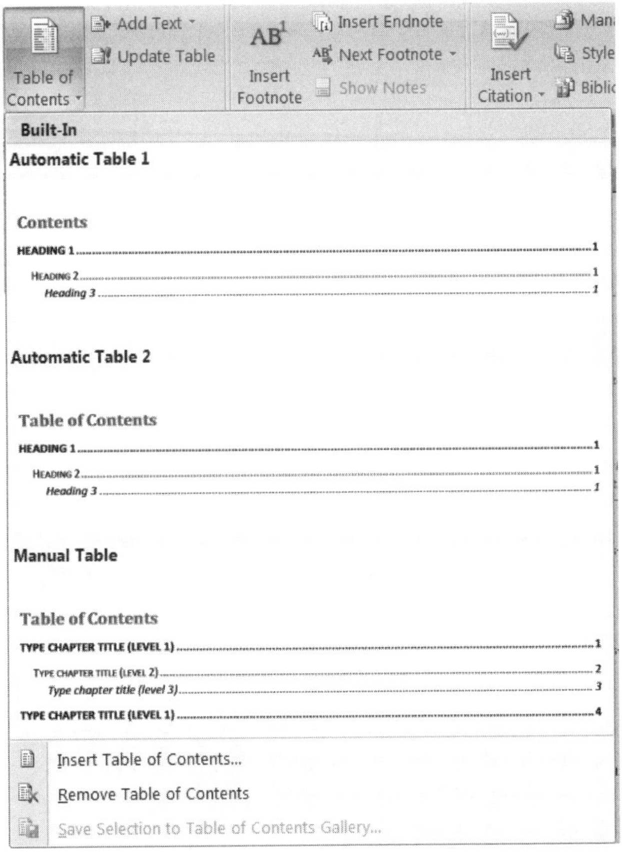

Figure 7-3 *The Table of Contents menu includes built-in TOC styles.*

To create a TOC using built-in styles:

1. Position the insertion point where you want the TOC to appear.

2. Click the Table of Contents button in the Table of Contents group on the References tab.

3. Do one of the following:

    a. Select one of the two automatic table styles in the drop-down menu. A TOC will be created and formatted based on the Level 1 through 3 heading styles already formatted in the document. (The Manual Table option provides a template for the TOC structure, but you must manually enter all the TOC entries.)

    b. Select Insert Table of Contents at the bottom of the menu. The Table of Contents dialog box will display (see Figure 7-4). Under General, you can choose from several formats, and you can select which heading levels you want to display in the TOC.

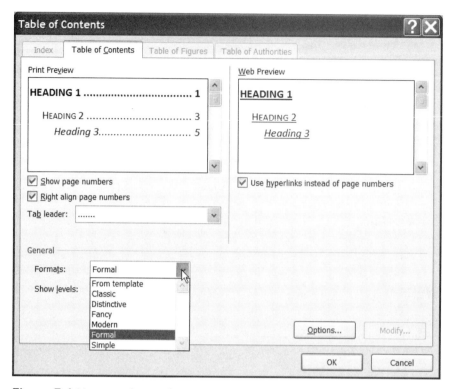

Figure 7-4 *You can choose from more TOC template styles in the Table of Contents dialog box.*

> **NOTE** If you plan for readers to view the document online, click the Table of Contents button in the Table of Contents group, and select Insert Table of Contents. In the Table of Contents dialog box, under Web Preview, turn on the option Use hyperlinks instead of page numbers.

If you used the built-in styles to generate the TOC, click anywhere within the TOC and then move the mouse pointer to the upper-left corner to display the buttons to update the table or display the Table of Contents menu (see Figure 7-5). The document must be displayed in Print Layout view.

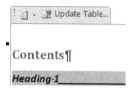

Figure 7-5 *When you use a built-in TOC style, a menu can be displayed at the top-left corner of the TOC.*

Adding More Entries to the TOC

You can quickly add additional entries to the TOC using the Add Text button in the Table of Contents group. When you choose additional text, make sure the text is from a short and concise paragraph, because Word will include the entire paragraph in the TOC entry.

To add an entry to the TOC:

1. Select the text you want to add. Note that even if you select only a few words within a paragraph, the entire paragraph will be included in the TOC entry.

2. Click the Add Text button. A drop-down list will display. The default setting is Do Not Show in Table of Contents.

3. Select a level for the TOC entry. If the selected text already has a paragraph style applied, the text will remain unchanged, and the entry will be formatted at the designated level in the TOC. However, if the current paragraph is formatted with the Normal style, Word will automatically format the entire paragraph with the heading paragraph style for the level you select (for example, Heading 1).

4. To reflect the changes in an existing TOC, click the Update button in the Table of Contents group (or click anywhere within the TOC and press F9).

Creating a TOC Using Custom Styles

By default, Word automatically marks the first three heading style levels for the TOC entries. If you have created and applied custom styles to portions of text in the document, you can open the Table of Contents Options dialog box (see Figure 7-6) and specify that the custom styles also be included for marking TOC entries. For example, you apply a custom style for the title of a poem in your document. Even though the poem title is not formatted with a heading style, you want that title to be included in the TOC. Remember, though, that even if only selected words within a paragraph are formatted with the custom style, the entire paragraph of text will display in the TOC.

To use the Table of Contents dialog box to identify custom styles for TOC entries:

1. Position the insertion point where you want the TOC to appear.

2. Click the Table of Contents button in the Table of Contents group on the References tab.

3. Select Insert Table of Contents. The Table of Contents dialog box displays.

4. Click Options.

5. Locate the desired style under Available styles, and in the TOC level box to the right of the style name, enter a number to assign a level number for the style.

6. If you do not want one or more of the three built-in heading styles to appear in the TOC, delete the level numbers in the related TOC level boxes.

7. Click OK twice to save the settings and insert the TOC.

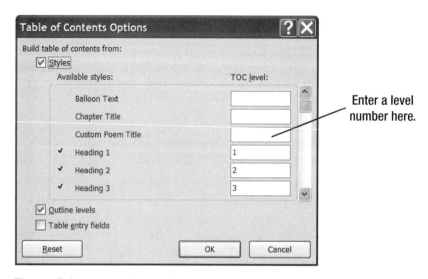

Figure 7-6 *You can change the options so that text formatted with customized styles is also marked for TOC entries.*

Marking TOC Entries Manually

If your document text is not formatted with heading and paragraph styles, you can still create a TOC. To mark the TOC entry, you create a TC field that identifies the text and page number to be displayed in the TOC entry. There are two advantages to marking TOC entries manually. You can avoid displaying whole paragraphs of text in the TOC, and the format for the text you mark will not change.

To create a TC field manually:

1. Select the text you want to include in the TOC.

2. Display the Insert tab and click Quick Parts in the Text group.

3. Choose Field in the drop-down menu to display the Field dialog box.

4. Under Field names, scroll down and select TC (see Figure 7-7).

5. In the Text entry box, enter the text you want to display in the TOC.

6. Click OK. If you have nonprinting characters displayed, the TC field will display to the right of the selected text. The TC field will not print. To hide the TC field, click the Show/Hide ¶ button in the Paragraph group on the Home tab.

> **TIP** You can also use shortcut keys to mark entries for the TOC. Select the text and then press Alt+Shift+O. The Mark Table of Contents Entry dialog box will display. Select a level, click Mark, and then click Close.

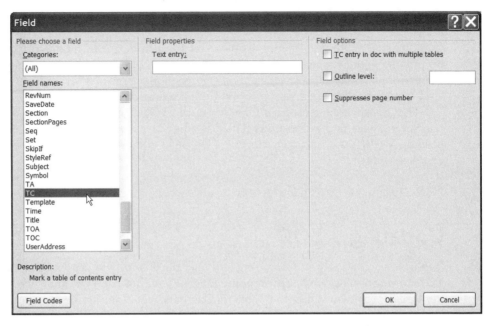

Figure 7-7 *You can mark TOC entries manually by inserting TC fields.*

When you generate the TOC, you must turn off the Styles option and select Table entry fields in the Table of Contents Options dialog box (see Figure 7-6 earlier).

Displaying TOC Field Codes

When you create a TOC, Word inserts a TOC field. The TOC field builds the TOC based on the specified entries. By pressing Alt+F9, you can toggle between viewing the TOC (field results) and TOC field code.

Following is an example of a TOC field code, with a description of each of the code elements:

{ *TOC \o "1-3"\p " " " " \h \z* }

- TOC identifies the type of field.
- The backslash (\) is called a *switch*. The switch provides additional instructions.
- \o indicates that the TOC is created from paragraphs formatted with built-in heading styles.
- "1-3" indicates that only headings 1 through 3 are included in the TOC.
- \p indicates the separators between the entry and its page number. In this example, the separators are the leaders shown after each of the three quotation marks.
- \h specifies that the TOC entries are formatted as hyperlinks.
- \z specifies that the tab leader and page numbers are hidden when the TOC is displayed in Web Layout view.

Editing Field Codes

Comprehending the field codes enables you to customize the format of the TOC beyond the options available in the Table of Contents dialog box. For example, if you want to display all heading levels, but you want to display page numbers only for heading level 1, you can remove the page numbers from heading levels 2 and beyond.

The \n switch controls page numbers in the TOC. You can use the \n switch to remove the page numbers from specified heading levels by including a range for the heading levels. Using this scenario, the TOC field code shown previously would be edited as follows:

{ *TOC* \o "*1-3*"\p " " " " \h \z \n "*2-3*"}

Updating a TOC

If you move content or add headings to your document, you can easily update the TOC by positioning the insertion point anywhere within the TOC and then clicking the Update Table button in the Table of Contents group on the References tab. The Update Table of Contents dialog box will display, and you can choose to update the page numbers only or update the entire table. You can also quickly display the Update Table of Contents dialog box by clicking anywhere within the TOC and then pressing F9. If you used the built-in styles to create the TOC, you can click Update Table on the tab at the top-left corner of the table.

Removing a TOC

To delete a TOC, simply click the Table of Contents button and choose Remove Table of Contents. Or, select all the paragraphs in the TOC, and then press the Delete key. If you used the built-in styles to create the TOC, you can click the Table of Contents button on the tab at the top-left corner of the table, and then choose Remove Table of Contents.

Creating Multiple TOCs in the Same Document

There may be times when you need to create more than one TOC for a single document. For example, if you create TOCs for a travel catalog with information about numerous destinations, it would be helpful to create a main TOC for all the destinations and then create a separate TOC for each destination to reference hotels/resorts, transportation, events, and so forth.

Using TC Fields to Create Multiple TOCs

You can create multiple TOCs by marking text with TC field codes that reference different TOCs.

To create multiple TOCs using TC fields:

1. Insert the first TOC:

    a. Position the insertion point where you want the first TOC to appear.

    b. Insert the first TOC, using the desired settings.

2. Mark TC fields for the second TOC.

    a. Select the first occurrence of desired text to appear in the TOC.

    b. Press Alt+Shift+O. The Mark Table of Contents Entry dialog box will display.

    c. Select a table identifier. The default setting is C. You can keep this setting, but subsequent tables will need a different table identifier (such as D or E).

    d. Select a level number and click Mark. Leave the dialog box open.

    e. Click in the document and select the next text entry for the TOC.

    f. Select the level number in the Mark Table of Contents Entry dialog box, and then click Mark.

    g. Mark all additional text entries.

    h. Close the Mark Table of Contents Entry dialog box.

3. Create a second TOC.

    a. If necessary, press Alt+F9 to display all field codes.

    b. Position the insertion point where you want the second TOC to appear.

    CAUTION There must be a blank paragraph between the two TOCs.

    c. Press Ctrl+F9 to insert a blank field.

    d. Inside the brackets, enter **TOC \f C**. This instructs Word to include all the TC fields with the table identifier C.

    e. With the new TOC field selected, press F9 to update the new TOC.

    f. Press Alt+F9 to display the results.

4. Repeat Steps 2 and 3 to create subsequent TOCs. Remember to change the table identifier for each subsequent TOC.

Using Bookmarks to Create Multiple TOCs

If you want to create a subsequent TOC for a large section of text, you can create a bookmark and then create the table based on the heading styles within the contents of the bookmark.

To create a subsequent TOC using a bookmark:

1. Select the entire section of text that you want to appear in the TOC. (The section must contain text formatted with heading or paragraph styles.)

2. Click the Bookmark button in the Links group on the Insert tab, enter a name for the bookmark (for example, BM1), and click Add.

3. Position the insertion point where you want the new TOC to appear.

4. If necessary, press Alt+F9 to display all field codes.

5. Press Ctrl+F9 to insert a blank field.

6. In the new field, enter **TOC \b BM1** (or the name of the bookmark you created).

7. With the new TOC field selected, press F9 to update the fields.

8. Press Alt+F9 to display the results.

Creating Footnotes and Endnotes

Although the features for footnotes and endnotes are similar to those in earlier versions of Word, the Footnotes group on the References tab (see Figure 7-8) provides some shortcuts for inserting footnotes and endnotes.

Figure 7-8 *The new buttons in the Footnotes group make it much faster to insert and navigate footnotes and endnotes.*

Inserting and Deleting a Footnote or an Endnote

Instead of opening the Reference dialog box, you can quickly insert a footnote or an endnote by simply clicking Insert Footnote or Insert Endnote in the Footnotes group on the References tab. The shortcut key combination for inserting a footnote is Ctrl+Alt+F. To insert an endnote, press Ctrl+Alt+D.

When you delete the content of the note in the note pane, the reference mark remains in the body of the document where the footnote/endnote was inserted. Therefore, if you want to remove a footnote or an endnote, you must delete the reference mark in the body of the document. When the mark is deleted, the content of the note is also removed.

Changing the Reference Mark Format

The default footnote/endnote mark is in the 1, 2, 3 number style. You can change the mark to a different number style, such as A, B, C, or you can use a symbol for the footnote mark. If desired, you can apply different numbering schemes for each section of the document.

1. Position the insertion point anywhere in the section where you want to change the reference mark format.

2. Click the Dialog Box Launcher in the Footnotes group. The Footnote and Endnote dialog box will display.

3. Select Footnotes or Endnotes.

4. Do one of the following:

   a. Under Format, choose a number format. If the document has multiple sections, under Apply changes, select This section or Whole document, and then click Apply. All the existing numbers in the document will automatically convert to the new number format.

   b. Click Symbol, choose a symbol to be used as a reference mark, click OK, and then click Insert. The symbol will apply only to the new footnote/endnote you are creating. All existing number formats will remain intact.

Restarting Reference Mark Numbering

There may be occasions when you want to start the footnote reference mark numbering over again. For example, you may have multiple sections within a document, and you want the first reference mark in each section to begin with 1.

1. Click the Dialog Box Launcher in the Footnotes Group on the References tab.

2. Select 1 in the Start at box.

3. In the Numbering box, click the down arrow and select Restart each section.

4. Click Apply.

Navigating Among Footnotes and Endnotes

In earlier versions of Word, you can use the Go To command in the Edit menu to move from one footnote/endnote to another. Now you can access these options much quicker on the References tab. Click the Next Footnote button in the Footnotes group. Or, to navigate to previous footnotes and/or endnotes, click the down arrow on the Next Footnote button and then select Previous Footnote or Previous Endnote.

To view the footnote/endnote area, click the Show Notes button in the Footnotes group. The footnotes for the current page will display, or the endnotes at the end of the document will display. An alternative to using this button is to double-click the reference mark in the document.

Creating a Footnote or Endnote Continuation Notice

If the text content for the footnote or the endnote does not fit on the page, you can add a notice that the content is continued on the next page. To utilize this feature, the document must be displayed in Draft view.

1. If necessary, change to Draft view.
2. Click Show Notes in the Footnotes group on the References tab. If your document contains both footnotes and endnotes, a prompt will display asking you to choose to view either the footnote or the endnote area.
3. When the note pane displays, click the down arrow in the Footnotes or Endnotes box and do one of the following:
    a. Select a Footnote Continuation Separator or Endnote Continuation Separator. A long, horizontal line will be inserted.
    b. Click the down arrow in the Footnotes or Endnotes box again, and then select Footnote Continuation Notice. Then enter text indicating that the content will be continued on the next page.

Converting Selected Notes to Footnotes or Endnotes

At any time, you can change a footnote to an endnote and an endnote to a footnote. The quickest way to change selected notes within the document is to show the notes on the screen. To do so, the document must be displayed in Draft view or Print Layout view.

1. Click Show Notes in the Footnotes group on the References tab. If your document contains both footnotes and endnotes, a prompt will display asking you to choose to view either the footnote or the endnote area.
2. When the note pane displays, select the note(s) you wish to convert.
3. Right-click and choose Convert to Footnote or Convert to Endnote.

Converting All Notes to Footnotes or Endnotes

You can also convert all notes to footnotes, or all endnotes to footnotes.
    To convert all notes:

1. Click the Dialog Box Launcher in the Footnotes group on the References tab.
2. Click Convert.
3. Choose the desired option and click OK.

Creating Citations and Bibliographies

For many of us, citing sources can be the most frustrating task when completing a report. Not only is a lot of detail required, but a specified format for each citation is also required. The new features in the Citations & Bibliography group on the References tab (see Figure 7-9) certainly make the process of documenting source information more efficient.

Figure 7-9 *The Citations & Bibliography group helps you document source information more efficiently.*

Choosing a Documentation Style

Citations and bibliography formats are driven by the documentation style used for a document. There are many styles to choose from. The more commonly used (or requested) styles are APA, Chicago, MLA, and Turabian.

To choose a documentation style:

1. Click the down arrow next to the Style button in the Citations & Bibliography group on the References tab.

2. Choose the desired style. You can change the style at any time, and Word will automatically make the necessary adjustments to all existing citations and bibliographies.

> **CAUTION** Verify that the documentation styles for both the citations and the bibliography are consistent with your requirements.

Inserting a Citation

The citation feature will save you time and help you work more efficiently in your current document and in future documents. When you add a citation to a document, Word automatically saves the information in a source database, so you won't have to reenter the information when you create the bibliography or when you create future documents.

To insert a citation by adding a new source:

1. Position the insertion point where you want the citation to appear.

2. Click the Insert Citation button in the Citations & Bibliography group on the References tab.

3. Select Add New Source. The Create Source dialog box displays (see Figure 7-10).

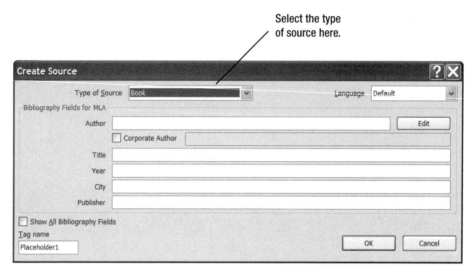

Select the type
of source here.

Figure 7-10 *The fields vary when you choose the type of source because the information required for each type of source is different.*

4. Select the type of source. The dialog box fields will vary depending on the source selected.

5. Enter the source information in the fields. To display all fields for bibliography information, turn on the option Show All Bibliography Fields. Complete as many fields as possible to ensure that you have adequate information for both the citation(s) and the bibliography.

6. When all information is entered, click OK. A source reference enclosed in parentheses is inserted at the location of the insertion point.

It is good practice to insert citations as you write and develop your document. If the source information is not readily available, you can create a placeholder and insert the source information at a later time. To insert a placeholder for a citation, click the Insert Citation button and select Add New Placeholder. Word automatically provides the name Placeholder1, but you can change the name if desired.

You can also use the Insert Citation button to search libraries including dictionaries, encyclopedias, and other references. The advantage to accessing these resources is that the required information for the bibliography is often available at the end of the article or web page. For example, you may see a link "How to cite this article."

Managing Sources

To view a list of your sources, click the Manage Sources button in the Citations & Bibliography group on the References tab. The Source Manager dialog box will display (see Figure 7-11).

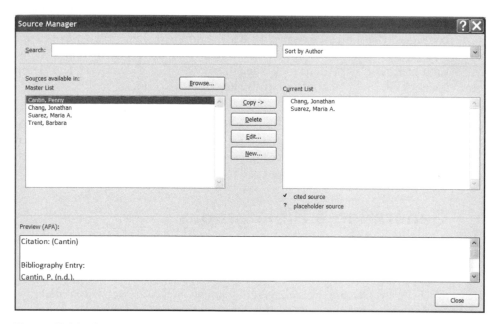

Figure 7-11 *The Source Manager displays a Master List of all sources ever used and a Current List of sources used for the current document.*

On the left side, the Master List displays all sources you have ever used, including the current document. On the right side, the Current List displays only sources for the current document. All sources are listed in alphabetical order. To locate a specific source, you can use the Search boxes to sort by author, title, year, or citation tag.

You can quickly select sources from your Master List and copy them to the Current List so you have access to them for the current document. At any time, you can update information for your sources. You can make the edits in the Source Manager, or you can select a citation or placeholder in the document and make the edits there. Any changes you make in the citation are immediately reflected in the Source Manager, and vice versa. To complete the edits in the Source Manager, select the source in either the Master List or the Current List, and click the Edit button. To complete the edits directly in the citation or placeholder, select the citation in the document. Then, click the down arrow to the right of the selected citation and choose Edit Source from the shortcut menu.

Citation tags are automatically assigned, but you can edit them if desired. If you inserted a placeholder in the current document, Word will display the placeholder in the Current List with a question mark to remind you that you need to provide information for that source.

The Master List is a database of information about sources, and you can easily share that information with others. If you have access to a network, you can use the Browse button to locate and access a different Master List. Then, you can copy sources from that list to your Current List. You can share your Master List by e-mailing it to a colleague. The sources are saved as XML, and the documentation styles are saved as XSLTs. To locate the Master List on your computer, search for the Bibliography subfolder. The path may look something like this: Documents and Settings\User Name\Application Data\Microsoft\Bibliography.

> **NOTE** If you choose the GOST or ISO 690 style and you have multiple sources with the same year, you can add an alphabet character after the year to create a unique citation. If you are using the ISO 690 style, you must select the style again after adding citations so the citations are correctly ordered.

Generating a Bibliography

If your sources are accurate, and you've entered citations in your document, creating a bibliography is a cinch. You simply indicate the style you want and you click a button to create the bibliography.

Before you create the bibliography, though, make sure you have replaced all placeholders with a proper citation. If you inserted a placeholder for a citation, the source will not appear in the bibliography. However, if you later replace the placeholder with source information, the bibliography will be automatically updated, and the new source will be added to the bibliography.

To create a bibliography:

1. Position the insertion point where you want to insert the bibliography.

2. Do one of the following:

   a. Click the Bibliography button in the Citations & Bibliography group on the References tab and then choose one of the built-in styles in the drop-down menu.

   b. Click the Bibliography button in the Citations & Bibliography group on the References tab. Select Insert Bibliography at the bottom of the menu. You will need to add a heading, and you cannot automatically update the bibliography.

Word creates the Bibliography page and the Works Cited page based on the sources that appear in the Current List of the Source Manager. All of the sources in the Current List of resources are included, even if all the sources were not cited in the document. Therefore, it is important that you verify the Current List of resources before you create the bibliography.

Displaying Bibliography Field Codes

When you create a bibliography, Word inserts a Bibliography field. By pressing Alt+F9, you can toggle between viewing the bibliography (field results) and the Bibliography field code.

Following is an example of a Bibliography field code:

{ BIBLIOGRAPHY \l-1033 }

> **TIP** To toggle between displaying a single field code and its results, click the field (or the results) to select it and then press Shift+F9. To toggle between displaying all the field results and the field codes, press Alt+F9.

Formatting Captions

The caption features parallel those in earlier versions of Word. The Insert Caption button in the Captions group on the References tab (see Figure 7-12) will display the Caption dialog box.

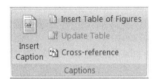

Figure 7-12. *Click the Insert Caption button to add a caption to a picture, table, equation, or figure.*

To insert a caption:

1. Position the insertion point where you want the caption to appear.
2. Click the Insert Caption button in the Captions group on the References tab. The Caption dialog box is displayed (see Figure 7-13).

When you insert a caption, you can choose the label Figure, Equation, or Table followed by an autonumber. However, you can also create your own labels. When you click the AutoCaption button, you can change the settings so that Word will automatically create captions when you insert objects in your document. For example, you can set options to automatically create captions with labels and numbers for each Word table you insert in a document. When you insert a caption, a SEQ field is created. A field code for a caption looks similar to one shown here:

{ SEQ Table * ARABIC }

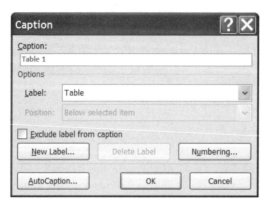

Figure 7-13 *You can customize the labels for the caption and set options to automatically create captions.*

CAUTION If you add a table, Word will update the following table caption numbers. However, when you delete a table and its caption, the following table captions will not be automatically updated, and you must make the adjustments manually.

Creating a Table of Figures

If your document includes several tables, figures, or equations, you can create a table of figures to show their locations in the document. A table of figures serves the same purpose as a TOC, helping the reader find information. Creating a table of figures is similar to creating a TOC. Instead of using marked text, you specify whether you want to use captions for tables, figures, or equations. Word then identifies the captions in the document and compiles the list of figures. If you rearrange the sequence, or if you add or delete tables or figures, or if you edit the captions, you can easily update the table of figures.

To create a table of figures using caption styles:

1. Position the insertion point where you want the table of figures to appear.

2. Click the Insert Table of Figures button in the Captions group on the References tab.

3. Under General, click the down arrow in the Formats box, and choose a table of figures style (see Figure 7-14).

4. Click the down arrow in the Caption label box, select a caption type, and then click OK.

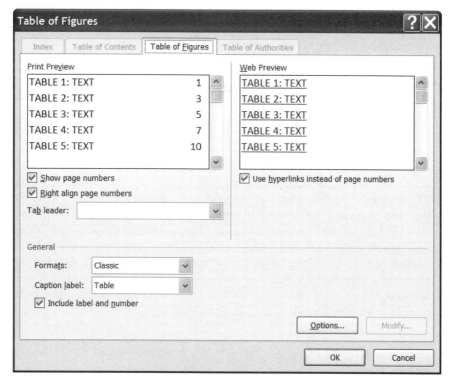

Figure 7-14 *Word creates a table of figures by identifying all the captions in a document.*

When you create a table of figures, Word inserts a TOC field, but instead of referencing heading levels or TC entries, the TOC code includes references to the captions used to create the table. Following is an example of a TOC field code for a table of figures:

{ *TOC \h \z \c "Figure"* }

If you edit the document after the table of figures is inserted, click the Update Table button in the Captions group to make sure all references and page numbers are correct.

Formatting Cross-References

Another way to help a reader navigate in a document is to provide *cross-references*. For example, you can create a reference on page 1 that tells the reader "For more information, see Figure 2 on page 3." Cross-references can link to headings, footnotes, bookmarks, captions, and numbered paragraphs.

> **TIP** Cross-references must refer to locations in the same document. Therefore, if you want to cross-reference something between two separate documents, combine the two subdocuments in a master document.

Creating a Cross-Reference

A cross-reference refers you to another location in the same document—usually to a heading, a table, or a figure. When you create a cross-reference to a heading, the heading must be formatted with a style. When you create a cross-reference to a figure, table, or equation, you must use Word's caption feature. After you enter the cross-reference, though, the location of the heading or the number of the figure may change. If you create the cross-reference as a field, you can easily update the field and eliminate the need to manually edit the cross-reference.

The Cross-reference dialog box (see Figure 7-15) will guide you in specifying the type of reference (such as a table) and how you want the reference to be noted in the document (such as by the table caption number or by the page number). If you want to create a hyperlink for the cross-reference, make sure the Insert as hyperlink box is selected. When you point to the field result, a ScreenTip will display, prompting you to hold down Ctrl and click to follow the link.

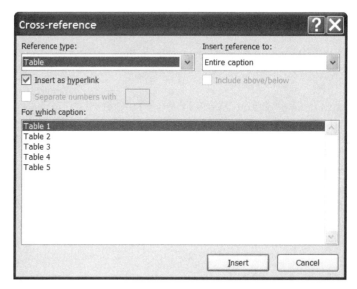

Figure 7-15 *The options in the Cross-reference dialog box will guide you in formatting a cross-reference to a figure, table, or equation.*

To create a cross-reference:

1. Position the insertion point in the document where you want to insert the cross-reference.

2. Enter the introductory text for the cross-reference—for example, "See Table 4." If at any time you want to change the introductory text, you can edit the text in the document.

3. Click the Cross-reference button in the Captions group on the References tab. The Cross-reference dialog box will display (see Figure 7-15).

4. In the Reference type box, select the type of item you want to refer to (for example, a table).

5. Under For which caption, select the caption (such as Table 4).

6. Click in the box under Insert reference to and select where you want the cross-reference to point to (such as Page number).

7. To include information about the relative position of the referenced item, turn on the option Include above/below. Word will automatically update the cross-reference to include whether the reference is above or below the cross-reference field.

8. Click Insert. The reference (such as the page number where the table is displayed) appears in place of the cross-reference field. If the field codes are displayed instead of the cross-reference text, press Alt+F9 to toggle the display to field results.

9. If you want to create additional cross-references, leave the dialog box open. Click in the document to reposition the insertion point, and repeat Steps 2 through 8.

Displaying Cross-Reference Field Codes

When you create a cross-reference field, Word inserts a Ref field or a PageRef field (if you reference a page number). By pressing Alt+F9, you can toggle between viewing the cross-reference and the field code.

The field code created for the examples suggested previously would look like the following:

{ *PAGEREF _Ref14696233 \p \h* }

- PAGEREF identifies the type of field. In the preceding example, the reference is to the page number where the figure is displayed.

- The backlash (\) is called a switch. The switch provides additional instructions.

- \p instructs the field to display the position relative to the source. For example, if the target of the reference (in this case, the figure) is on a different page than the field, "on page #" will display. If the target of the reference is on the same page as the field, only "above" or "below" will display.

- \h specifies that the cross-reference entry is formatted as a hyperlink.

Editing Cross-References

If you change your mind and want to change the options for a cross-reference, you just select new options in the Cross-reference dialog box.

1. Select the cross-reference field. (Drag the mouse pointer across the entire field name.)
2. Click the Cross-reference button in the Captions group on the References tab.
3. Select the new options.
4. Click Insert, and then click Close.

If the text or objects of your cross-reference are moved within the document, you can automatically update the cross-references by selecting a cross-reference (or selecting the entire document) and pressing F9. You can also right-click the selected text and choose Update Field in the shortcut menu.

Creating an Index

To create an index, you mark the text throughout the document that you want to appear in the index. Word creates a field when you click the Mark Entry button in the Index group (see Figure 7-16). The field includes information about the page number in the document where the marked text is located. For each entry, you can enter main text, subentry text, and third-level text. You can also format the index entry to include cross-reference information.

Figure 7-16 *Use the Mark Entry button to mark text to be included in an index.*

Marking Text for an Index Entry

You can create an index entry for a character or symbol, a word, or a group of words. To mark a text entry for the index,

1. Do one of the following:
   a. Position the insertion point following the text you want to index.
   b. Select the text you want to mark for the index entry.
2. Click Mark Entry in the Index group on the References tab. The Mark Index Entry dialog box is displayed.

3. If you selected text, that text is displayed in the Main entry box. If you did not select text, you can enter the text now.

4. If desired, create a subentry. For example, the Main entry is Styles and the subentry is Built-in. You can add a third-level index entry by entering a colon after the subentry text and then entering the third-level text.

5. Choose your preferences for the page number format.

6. Click Mark. (Click Mark All if you want to create index fields for all occurrences of the text throughout the document.) The index entry field will display next to the marked text. The field will not show when you print the document.

7. If you have additional index entries to mark, leave the dialog box open.

The index entry field is enclosed in curly brackets, and the field code begins with XE. Following is an example of an index entry field code:

{ *XE "Heading 1"* }

> **TIP** If necessary, click the Show/Hide button on the Home tab to display nonprinting characters. To delete an index entry, select the entire index entry field, including the braces ({}), and then press Delete.

Marking an Index Entry for a Range of Pages

The group of words for an index entry can spread across several pages. To mark the entire unit of text, create a bookmark as follows:

To mark a range of pages for an index entry:

1. Select the range of text.

2. Display the Insert tab.

3. Click Bookmark in the Links group.

4. Enter a name for the bookmark and click Add.

5. With the bookmarked text still selected, display the References tab, and click Mark Entry.

6. Under Options, click Page range.

7. In the Bookmark box, click the down arrow and select the bookmark name.

8. Click Mark.

Generating an Index

You generate an index just the same as you generate a TOC or a table of figures. The options for formatting the index are in the Index dialog box shown in Figure 7-17.

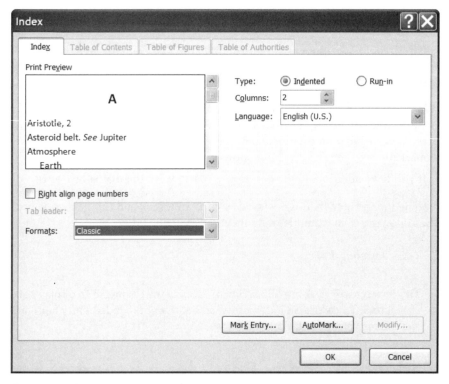

Figure 7-17 *Generating an index is similar to creating a TOC and a table of figures.*

1. Position the insertion point where you want the index to appear.
2. Click Insert Index in the Index group on the References tab.
3. Choose a design in the Formats box. The index design will display in the Print Preview box in the dialog box.

> **CAUTION** If you add any text or formatting to an index, all the changes will be lost when you update the index.

Updating an Index

If you change the pagination of the document, or if you add or delete index entries, you will want to update the index. To update the index, click Update Index in the Index group (or click anywhere inside the index and press F9). To edit or format an index entry, display the field code and change the text inside the quotation marks. Then, select the index field code or the index and press F9 to update the field.

> **TIP** To quickly navigate to the next XE field, press Ctrl+F, click Special, and then click Field. If you don't see the Special button, click More.

Creating a Table of Authorities

A *table of authorities* is commonly found in legal documents. Similar to a bibliography, the table of authorities compiles the document citations for cases, statutes, rules, or other sources.

Marking Citations for a Table of Authorities

A table of authorities groups the sources by categories based on the type of source, and then arranges them in alphabetical order within each group. Creating a table of authorities is parallel to creating a TOC. Instead of marking TC entry fields, you mark TA entry fields using the Mark Citation button in the Table of Authorities group (see Figure 7-18).

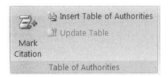

Figure 7-18 *Use the Mark Citation button to mark entries for a table of authorities.*

To mark citations for a table of authorities:

1. The citations must be displayed as field results (not field codes).
2. Select a citation by dragging the mouse pointer across the citation to select all the citation contents.
3. Click the Mark Citation button in the Table of Authorities group on the References tab. The Mark Citation dialog box will display.
4. If necessary, edit the citation in the Selected text box. Any edits you make, including formats, affect only the table of authorities. Your citation will not change.
5. If necessary, edit the text displayed in the Short citation box. This text is what Word will search for in the document. The text displayed in the Long Citation box is what will appear in the table of authorities.
6. Click the Category button (or the down arrow in the Category box) to change the category for grouping the sources.
7. Click Mark. Word inserts a TA entry field.
8. If you have more citations to mark, click Next Citation. The dialog box will remain open so you can format subsequent entries.
9. When you have marked all the citations, click Close.

The TA entry field is enclosed in curly brackets, and the field code begins with TA. Following is an example of an index entry field code:

{ *TA \I "Jones 42 \s "Jones42" \c 1* }

Generating a Table of Authorities

Once you have marked the citations, you can easily and quickly insert the table of authorities. Word will automatically arrange the sources in groups and create the table for you.

To insert a table of authorities:

1. Position the insertion point where you want to insert the table of authorities.
2. Click the Insert Table of Authorities button on the References tab. The Table of Authorities dialog box will display.
3. If necessary, under Category, change the category selection. And, if desired, click the down arrow in the Tab leader box and choose a different leader.
4. Click the down arrow in the Formats box to change the layout and click OK.

Updating a Table of Authorities

If you add, edit, or delete citations or move text around in a document, you need to update the table of authorities. To update a table of authorities, click in the table and then click the Update Table button on the References tab. If you edit text and change formats in the table of authorities, the edits will be lost when you choose the update command. You can also update the table of authorities by clicking in the table and pressing F9.

CHAPTER 8

Creating Envelopes, Labels, and Merge Documents

All the tools you need to create envelopes, labels, and mail merge documents can be found on the Mailings tab. In earlier versions of Word, many of these features are accessed using the Mail Merge toolbar. With the new user interface, the toolbar is no longer needed. The commands are much easier to find on the Mailings tab.

Creating Envelopes and Labels

Everyone knows it's important to make a good first impression. A letter recipient forms an opinion before opening the envelope. For business communications, you can usually make a better first impression if you print the address on the envelope (as opposed to handwriting the address). Furthermore, handwriting the address causes sorting delays, which can impede delivery. If you must use an oversize envelope that won't fit into your printer, or if you are doing a mass mailing, you can print the address(es) on labels. Instead of opening the Tools menu, you'll now find the options for creating envelopes and labels in the Create group on the Mailings tab (see Figure 8-1).

Figure 8-1 *The commands for creating envelopes, labels, and merge documents are easy to access on the Mailings tab*

Printing an Address on an Envelope

For faster delivery, the USPS offers several suggestions, including displaying all address text in capital letters and eliminating all punctuation except for the hyphen in the nine-digit ZIP code. The machines used for sorting mail for delivery read the address from the bottom up. The last two lines of the address must be reserved for the street address or the post office box number and the city, state, and ZIP code. If the apartment number or the suite number does not fit on the street address line, move the apartment number or the suite number to the line *above* the street address—*not* below. Tips in the steps that follow will help you format the address to meet these guidelines.

When you click the Envelopes button in the Create group (see Figure 8-2), the Envelopes tab in the Envelopes and Labels dialog box will display. The options have not changed, but the arrangement of the options in the dialog box is different.

Figure 8-2 *The Envelopes and Labels buttons display the Envelopes and Labels dialog box.*

To print an address on an envelope:

1. Open a document. If the envelope is for mailing a letter, open the letter. Or, you can copy the address from another document or application.

2. Click the Envelopes button. The Envelopes tab in the Envelopes and Labels dialog box will display.

3. Enter the address in the Delivery address box. If you opened a letter document, Word is intuitive on this point: it will display the inside address from the letter. You can, of course, replace the suggested address. If you copied the address from another document, hold down Ctrl and press V to paste the address in the box.

> **TIP** If you are logged on to Microsoft Exchange, click the Insert Address button ![icon] to select a contact from your Outlook address book.

4. If you accepted text automatically entered in the Delivery address box, or if you pasted an address in the Delivery address box, you will likely need to change the formats to meet the postal guidelines mentioned previously.

   a. To change the text to all caps, select the entire delivery address and press Ctrl+Shift+A.

   b. Remove periods after titles such as Mr. and Mrs., and remove the comma between the city and state.

   c. To change the font style or color, select the text and right-click in the Delivery address box and select Font in the shortcut menu (or press Ctrl+D) to display the Font dialog box. (For efficient processing, avoid script fonts and use black for the font color.)

5. If necessary, enter or edit the text in the Return address box. Word will automatically use this return address unless you turn on the Omit option. If you enable the Omit option, the return address will still display in the Return address box, but it will not print on the envelope.

6. Do one of the following:

   • If you want to print the envelope at a later time, click the Add to Document button. The formatted return and delivery addresses will be inserted in a new section at the beginning of the document. When you are ready to print the envelope, you can print the first page of the document. To edit the information on the envelope after it has been added to the document, make the changes in the document. Or, you can click the Envelope button in the Create group and then select Change Document on the Envelopes tab in the Envelope and Labels dialog box.

   • If you have installed software to print electronic postage, click the E-postage Properties button.

   • To print the envelope, insert the envelope in the printer document feeder and click the Print button.

Creating a Single Address Label

If you are using a large-size envelope that you cannot feed into your printer, you can create a single label for the envelope.

   To create a single label:

1. Open a document. If the envelope is for mailing a letter, open the letter. Or, you can copy the address from another document.

2. Click the Labels button. The Labels tab in the Envelopes and Labels dialog box will display.

3. Enter the address in the Address box. If you opened a letter document, Word is intuitive and will display the inside address from the letter. You can, of course, replace the suggested address. If you copied the address from another document, press Ctrl+V to paste the address in the box.

> **TIP** If you have a document containing multiple addresses, open the document and position the insertion point in the address for which you want to create an envelope or label. Or, select the lines of text that you want to display for the address. When you click the Envelopes or Labels button, the address where the insertion point is positioned (or the selected lines) will display in the address box.

4. Click the Options button to display the Label Options dialog box. Make sure the correct product number is selected. The printing area for the label will depend on the product selected.

5. If you accepted text automatically entered in the Address box, or if you pasted an address in the Address box, you will likely need to change the formats to meet the postal guidelines mentioned earlier.

   a. To change the text to all caps, select the entire delivery address and press Ctrl+Shift+A.

   b. Manually remove periods after titles such as Mr. and Mrs., and remove the comma between the city and state.

   c. To change the font style or color, select the text, right-click in the Address box, and select Font in the shortcut menu (or press Ctrl+D) to display the Font dialog box. (For efficient processing, avoid script fonts and use black for the font color.)

   d. To position the text vertically and horizontally on the label, right-click in the Address box, select Paragraph in the shortcut menu, and change the indentation and spacing settings.

6. Under Print, select Single label. Then, enter the row and column numbers that correspond to an available label on your sheet of labels (see Figure 8-3).

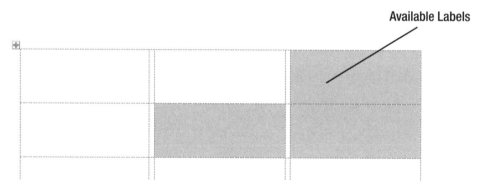

Figure 8-3 *The available labels on this sheet are Row 1–Column 3, Row 2–Column 2, and Row 2–Column 3.*

7. Do one of the following:

   • If you have installed software to print electronic postage, click the E-postage Properties button.

   • To print the label, insert the label sheet in the printer document feeder and click the Print button.

Creating a Full Page of the Same Label

If you do not use custom stationery with your return address already printed on the envelope, you can create a sheet of labels with your return address (see Figure 8-4). Or, if you routinely mail documents to the same address, you can create a sheet of labels with that same address. (To create labels for multiple addresses, see the section "Creating Mail Merge Documents.") You can also use labels to print text other than addresses.

Figure 8-4 *You can create a sheet of labels with your return address or other addresses that you use frequently.*

To create a full sheet with the same label:

1. Open a document.

2. Click the Labels button. The Labels tab in the Envelopes and Labels dialog box will display.

3. Click the Options button to display the Label Options dialog box. Make sure the correct product number is selected. The printing area for the label will depend on the label selected.

4. Enter the text in the Address box. (To add graphics, see the section "Updating Labels".) If you want to use the default return address, select Use return address.

    a. To change the font style or color, select the text, right-click in the Address box, and select Font (or press Ctrl+D) to display the Font dialog box. (For efficient processing, avoid script fonts and use black for the font color.)

    b. To position the text vertically and horizontally on the label, right-click in the Address box, select Paragraph in the shortcut menu, and change the indentation and spacing settings.

5. Under Print, select Full page of the same label.

6. Do one of the following:

    • To print the sheet of labels, insert the label sheet in the printer document feeder and click the Print button. The document will print based on your printer default settings. If you want to print more than one page, see the next bulleted item.

    • To preview the labels before you print, select New Document. Word will display the labels in a new document as shown previously in Figure 8-4. If necessary, you can edit the labels, and you can save the document for future use. When you print the document, you can choose the number of copies you want to print.

Creating Mail Merge Documents

When you are creating envelopes or labels for a group mailing, you can accomplish the task much more efficiently using the mail merge features. Merging documents involves two main parts: a main document and a data source. The main document provides the constant text and can be an envelope, a label, an e-mail message, an invitation, and so on. The data source contains the variable data and can be Outlook contacts, a table with product names and prices, an Excel spreadsheet with data about sales, and so on. The Mailings tab provides a visual guide for the merge process, beginning with the Start Mail Merge group (see Figure 8-5) and then following the sequence of groups to the right. The organization of the buttons in these groups is very similar to the Mail Merge toolbar in earlier versions of Word.

Figure 8-5 *Begin the merge process using the buttons in the Start Mail Merge group.*

If you prefer to be guided through the process, you can use the Mail Merge Wizard. Click the Start Mail Merge button and select Step-by-Step Mail Merge at the bottom of the menu. This option displays the Mail Merge task pane that is also available in previous versions of Word. Obviously, if you use the wizard, the instructions are already provided. Following is a description of the steps in the mail merge process, along with some tips for using the features.

Starting the Mail Merge Process

The Start Mail Merge button will help you begin the mail merge process. The first step is to identify the document to be used for the main document. You can use a document that already contains the constant text, or you can open a new blank document and enter the constant text during the process. The Start Mail Merge button displays options for the type of document (for example, Letters, E-Mail Messages, Envelopes, and so on). Choosing the document type is Step 1 and selecting the starting the document is Step 2 in the Mail Merge Wizard.

> **TIP** Choose the Directory option to create a catalog, a price list, or a list of names. Instead of merging the records to separate documents (envelopes, labels, or letters), the records are merged into the same document.

Selecting Recipients

The Select Recipients button displays commands so you can identify the data source you will use for the variable content in the merge. You can choose from three options:

- If the data does not already exist, you can select Type New List to create a new data source. The New Address List dialog box displays a table in which you can enter the data. If necessary, you can customize the column headings. When all the data is entered, click OK, and you will be prompted to save the data source.

- If the data source already exists, you can select Use Existing List to browse for the file. For example, you can access data from Word tables, Excel worksheets, and Access databases.

- You can choose the option Select from Outlook Contacts. You can then choose a subfolder from your Outlook Contacts folders.

Editing the Recipient List

Once a data source is identified, the Edit Recipient List button is enabled. The Edit Recipient List command enables you to edit the data in the data source that you selected. When you choose this command, the list of recipients is displayed in the Mail Merge Recipients dialog box.

There are several options available for sorting and filtering. Filtering options are especially useful when you are working with an extensive mailing list. It is common to have duplicate records in large mailing lists, so you can use this feature to help identify duplicate records. If you have installed add-in software for address verification services, you can select an option to validate the addresses in the data source. Editing the list of recipients is Step 3 in the Mail Merge Wizard; however, you can edit the data source at any time by clicking the Edit Recipient List button.

Writing and Inserting Fields

The Write & Insert Fields group shown in Figure 8-6 provides the tools you need to insert the fields for merging the variable data. At this stage in the merge process, you create your document by typing and formatting text that should remain static and inserting merge fields where you wish to customize. Writing and inserting fields is Step 4 in the Mail Merge Wizard.

Figure 8-6 *The Address Block and Greeting Line fields provide shortcuts for creating fields.*

Using the Address Block

The Address Block command opens a dialog box so you can identify the address elements you want to include. The Address Block pulls required data from fields in the data source, such as recipient's name, company name, postal address, and more (see Figure 8-7).

```
{ ADDRESSBLOCK \f "<< _TITLE0_ >><< _FIRST0_ >><< _LAST0_ >><< _SUFFIX0_ >>
<< _COMPANY_
>><< _STREET1_
>><< _STREET2_
>><< _CITY_ >><< , _STATE_ >><< _POSTAL_ >><<
_COUNTRY_ >>" \l 1033 \c 2 \e "United States" \d }
```

Figure 8-7 *The Address Block inserts several merge fields at once.*

To insert the Address Block:

1. Position the insertion point where you want the Address Block to display.

2. Click the Address Block button. The Insert Address Block dialog box displays.

3. Specify the elements you want to include in the address.

4. Click the Match Fields button to confirm that the field names in the recipient list correspond to the field names used in the Address Block.

5. Click OK twice to close both dialog boxes.

Inserting a Greeting Line

The Greeting Line command uses combined merge fields to create custom salutations for letters (see Figure 8-8). One of the options you can enable is to create a general salutation, such as "Dear Sir or Madam," when the data source does not include data in the name fields.

{ GREETINGLINE \f "<<_BEFORE_ Dear >><<_TITLE0_>><<_LAST0_>>⍰<<_AFTER_,>>" \l 1033 \e "Dear Sir or Madam," }

Figure 8-8 *The Greeting Line command also combines several merge fields.*

Inserting Individual Merge Fields

Use the Insert Merge Field command when you want to insert any other field besides the Address Block and the Greeting Line. When you click the Insert Merge Field button, you can choose from a list of all the fields that are available in the data source.

Adding Fields with Controls

The new Rules command provides access to additional Word fields. You can use these fields to control document content during the merge process. For example, you can insert a field to add an additional paragraph of text within the document. When the data records are merged, Word will compare the field criteria to the merged data. If the referenced merge field data meets the specified criteria, the additional paragraph will display in the merged document. If the record data for the next merged document does not meet the specified criteria, the additional paragraph will not display in the document.

To add a control, position the insertion point where you want the option to appear in the document. Click the Rules button and choose from the available fields. Many of the field options display dialog boxes so you can set the parameters for the fields. These Word fields are available for all Word documents. The following describes each of the fields:

- The *Ask field* will prompt you to respond so that you can enter text. For example, you can set a rule to prompt you when a name appears in a document for the second time, and then you can choose to use only the last name for all occurrences after the first occurrence.

- The *Fill in* field will also prompt you to insert information. Use this field when you want to insert information only once. For example, you can set the rule so that Word will prompt you to enter the quantity of an item ordered.

NOTE Each time you update the fields in your document, you will be prompted for a response for the Ask and Fill in fields.

- The *If . . . Else . . .* fields enable you to set conditions for the merge fields. For example, if the contact has a specified ZIP code, the letter will include a sentence about the location of the store.

- The *Merge Record #* field enables you to display the ordinal position of the current data record, which reflects any sorting or filtering before the merge. For example, you can assign registration numbers for each contact included in the merge.

- The *Merge Sequence #* field can be used to count the number of records in the merged document. The number is not visible until the merge is completed. For example, you can use this field to calculate the total number of discount coupons you mail.

- The *Next Record* field instructs Word to insert the next data record into the current document without starting a new document. This field is used when Word creates a full page of labels.

- The *Next Record If* field is used to determine whether the next data record should be merged into the current document or into a new document. For example, if two contacts have the same last name and address, both names can be inserted in the same document to eliminate mailing the same letter twice to the same address.

- The *Set Bookmark* field refers to specific information stored in a bookmark. For example, the date for an event may appear several times throughout the document. Insert the Set Bookmark field in the main document and assign the date as the value. Then cross-reference each occurrence of the date to the bookmark. When you want to change the date, you simply change the content in the bookmark field.

- The *Skip Record If* option enables you to set conditions for the merge fields. For example, if the contact has an out-of-state address, the contact is not included in the merge.

Highlighting Merge Fields

When turned on, the Highlight Merge Fields command identifies all the merge fields throughout the document (see Figure 8-9). This helps you quickly locate the areas in your document that will be replaced with variable information. The variable content is also highlighted when you preview the results (see the section "Previewing Results" later in this chapter).

Current date

«AddressBlock»

«GreetingLine»

Congratulations on your eligibility to particpate in the Merit Scholarship program! Your GPA of «GPA» ranks you among the best students in Union County. Applications for the Merit Scholarship are available online at www.meritscholarship@unioncounty.gov. The deadline for applications is «Deadline».

You will also find answers for frequently asked questions at the Merit Program website. If you don't find answers to all your questions, contact me at K.Rausch@unionscholarship.org.

The people of Union County support and fund this scholarship program because they believe in education and in they believe in you. On behalf of the scholarship board, I wish you great success in the years ahead.

Sincerely,

Tamara Goldberg
Merit Scholarship Board Director

aem

Figure 8-9 *You can quickly locate the merge fields or the variable text when the merge fields are highlighted in the document.*

Matching Fields to a Data Source

It is always a good idea to check to make sure that the fields in your data source correspond to merge fields you have selected. This feature is very useful when the field names in your database do not match the required fields included in the Address Block or the greeting line. The Match Fields command is also available in the dialog boxes when you choose the Address Block and Greeting Line commands.

To match the fields, click the Match Fields button to display the Match Fields dialog box. Required fields are listed on the left. For fields that do not match, click the down arrow and select the field from your data source that corresponds with the required field.

Updating Labels

The Update Labels button copies the fields and layout of the first label to all the other labels on the page. So, to create 30 labels on the page, you need to insert the Address Block only once for the first label on the page. Then you can use the Update Labels command to replicate the Address Block layout in the remaining 29 labels on the page.

Updating labels is sometimes referred to as *replicating labels*. In previous versions of Word, you use the Propagate Labels button on the Mail Merge toolbar. When you use the Mail Merge Wizard to create labels, after arranging the fields for the first label in Step 4, you will be prompted to update all labels.

You can update labels at any time. If the data source changes, click the Update Labels button to update the merged records. Or, you can change the format or even the layout for the label and then update all the labels. For example, after defining the fields for labels, you decide to customize the labels by adding a graphic. Figure 8-10 shows a graphic added to labels with the Address Block.

Figure 8-10 *Use graphics to customize your labels.*

You may need to adjust the font size and the spacing between paragraphs so that the entire address will display on the label.

To change the formats for the Address Block:

1. Select the Address Block field.

2. Use the formatting tools on the Mini toolbar or the Home tab, or press Ctrl+{ to decrease the font size.

3. Right-click the Address Block field, choose Paragraph, and change the paragraph settings in the Paragraph dialog box.

4. Click the Update Labels button. The new font size will be applied to the Address Block in all labels.

To add a graphic to the labels:

1. Position the insertion point in the first label where you want the graphic to display.

2. Insert the graphic. Resize and reposition the object as needed.

3. Click the Update Labels button. The graphic will be added to all the labels on the page.

To format the addresses as recommended in the postal guidelines:

1. Press Ctrl+A to select the entire document, and then press Ctrl+Shift+A to change all the text to all caps.

2. Use the Replace command to remove the punctuation. Enter the punctuation mark (such as a comma) in the Find box. Leave the Replace with box empty. Choose Replace All, and all occurrences of the punctuation will be removed.

Previewing Results

The Preview Results group (see Figure 8-11) provides commands for viewing the merged documents, locating recipients, and checking for errors.

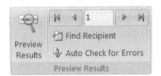

Figure 8-11 *You can preview results for specific records.*

Clicking the Preview Results button will toggle between displaying the merge fields and the merge field results in the open document (see Figure 8-12). To preview other merged records, click the Next Record or Previous Record buttons in the Preview Results group. Or, enter a record number in the Go to Record box. To find a specific record, click the Find Recipient command in the Preview Results group. The Find Entry dialog box will open, and you can enter the search criteria. Click the Auto Check for Errors command to choose options for checking and reporting errors.

Mrs. Georgia Bell HCR4 Box 2824A Branson, MO 65616	Ms. Rebecca Smith 647 Chestnut Street Marysville, OH 43040	Mr. Lou Kestella 1607 Sommers Lane Aston, PA 19014
Mrs. Erica Lopez 115 Yorkshire Road Lexington, OH 44904	Mr. Robert Vincent PO Box 111 Westwood, NJ 07675	Katrina Westfall 555 East Fifth Street Marysville, OH 43040

Figure 8-12 *The merge field results display the content exactly as it will appear when you print.*

Formatting Merge Fields

The merged data for the Address Block will most likely appear in initial caps and lowercase because that's how the data is entered in the data source. Usually, when you access information from databases, you get the raw data. Even if the data is formatted in the database, when it gets merged into the Word document, few if any of the formats are included. If you want the variable data to display with special formats, you can apply formats in the merge field in the main document, and then the new formats will be applied to the variable data when the data is merged. For example, you can format the merge field for address labels so the addresses print in all caps (see Figure 8-13). When you apply a font format to the first character in the field code, the format will apply to the entire field.

Figure 8-13 *You can format merge fields so that the variable data is formatted.*

To apply paragraph and font formats:

1. Display the merge fields.
2. Right-click the Address Block field in the first label.
3. Choose Paragraph in the shortcut menu to display the Paragraph dialog box.
4. Under Spacing, change the setting in the Before box to 0 and then click OK.
5. With the field code selected, press Alt+F9 to display the field codes.
6. Select the first character in the field code. (Select "A" in ADDRESSBLOCK.) Or, select the entire field code.
7. Press Ctrl+Shift+A to apply the all caps format. (Or, right-click and select the format in the Font dialog box.)
8. Press Alt+F9 to hide the field codes.
9. To add space above the first line in the Address Block, position the insertion point in front of the field code and press Enter.
10. Click the Update Labels button.
11. Click the Preview Results button to view the format changes.

To remove the punctuation marks on the labels:

1. With the results displayed, press Ctrl+A to select all of the labels.
2. Press Ctrl+H to display the Replace tab in the Find and Replace dialog box.
3. Enter a comma in the Find what box. Leave the Replace with box blank.
4. Click Replace All. All commas will be removed.
5. Click OK to confirm the number of replacements.
6. Enter a period in the Find what box and click Replace All.
7. Click OK to confirm the number of replacements, and then close the Find and Replace dialog box.

Adding a Switch to the Field Code

Another way to format merged data is to add switches to the field codes. For example, you create a catalog, using data from an existing source. The price in the data source shows only numbers (for example, 20), but when you merge the data into the catalog, you want the price to be formatted for currency (for example, $20.00). You can simply add a switch to apply a number format to the Balance merge field codes in the main document. The following illustrates a merge field with the switch for the dollar sign:

{ MERGEFIELD "Balance" \# $#,###.00 }

"Balance" is the name of the field referenced.

\# is the switch indicating to format numbers.

$ is the character to be included.

#,### indicates the maximum number of digits.

.00 indicates the decimal place and the number of digits following the decimal.

Completing the Merge

The final step in the merge process is to complete the merge. When you click the Finish & Merge command in the Finish group (see Figure 8-14), you have the option of printing the merged documents or editing the individual documents (letters, envelopes, and so forth).

Figure 8-14 *The Finish & Merge button completes the merge process.*

When you choose Print Documents, a dialog box will display so you can choose which records you want to print. When you choose Edit Individual Documents, you will also be prompted to choose records. Instead of printing, though, the merged results for the selected records will display in a new Word document. For example, if you are creating labels, the sheet(s) of labels will display. If your main document is a letter, each merged letter is displayed on a separate page in the document.

There are advantages to choosing the Edit Individual Documents option:

- You can preview the results before printing. If you notice errors, you can make the corrections in the main document.

- You can edit and format the merged document without affecting the main document or your data source. For example, you can add or delete a sentence to personalize one or more of the merged letters. Or, you can format some or all of the merge data.

- If there's a possibility you will use the merged document in the future (such as mailing labels), save the merged document. Then when you need to print more labels, you can skip the mail merge process, open the merged document, and print.

Merging to E-Mail

You can use Word's mail merge feature to create personalized e-mail messages. You can use your contact information in Outlook for your data source, or you can use a MAPI-compatible e-mail program. If you are using Outlook for your data source, the versions of Word and Outlook must be the same. The merge process is the same except that when you finish the document, instead of printing the document, you complete the e-mail header by entering a field for the e-mail address in the To box and entering text in the Subject Line box.

If you are using Outlook, before you begin, make sure you can identify the mail merge recipients. For example, the list of recipients may already be saved in a subfolder (such as a Christmas card list or a customer list). Or, if you assigned categories to the contacts, you can filter them by category.

To personalize an e-mail message directed to several recipients:

1. Open a new document.

2. Click the Start Mail Merge command in the Start Mail Merge group.

3. For the document type, select E-Mail Messages.

4. Click the Select Recipients button and either create a new data source or locate an existing data source.

5. Create the message and insert the merge field codes.

6. Preview the results.

7. Click the Finish & Merge command (or choose Electronic Mail in Step 6 of the Mail Merge Wizard).

8. Select Send E-mail Messages. The Merge to E-mail dialog box will display.

9. Make sure the e-mail address field is displayed in the To box.

10. Enter a subject in the Subject line box.

11. Select one of the options in the Mail format box:

- Select HTML or Plain text to send the document as the body of the e-mail message.

- Select Attachment to send the document as an attachment to the e-mail.

12. Select the records you want to merge and then click OK; the merged messages will go to the outbox in your default e-mail program.

> **NOTE** The Mail Merge Toolkit is an add-in that is available through Microsoft Office Marketplace. The toolkit enables you to customize e-mail messages by inserting data fields in e-mail subject fields and the contents of the e-mail message.

CHAPTER 9

Working with Others

I t's common to share documents with others and for collaborators to review documents, suggest revisions, and verify changes. The Review tab shown in Figure 9-1 organizes many of the tools for collaboration.

Figure 9-1 *The tools for collaborating on documents are on the Review tab.*

Proofing Documents

The Proofing group shown in Figure 9-2 includes several tools for making sure your document content is accurate. There are some familiar buttons and some new buttons in this group.

Figure 9-2 *The Proofing group displays some new buttons for proofing tools.*

Checking Spelling and Grammar

If you have turned off some of the check spelling and grammar options, the Spelling and Grammar dialog box may display when you click the Spelling & Grammar button. Instead, though, you may get a response that the spelling and grammar check is complete. If the settings to check spelling and mark grammar errors as you type are enabled, Word has already checked the document and flagged possible spelling or grammar errors. You can correct the errors as you create the document, which eliminates the need to display the Spelling and Grammar dialog box. You can customize the status bar to display an icon to show the status of the spelling and grammar checker. Right-click the status bar and select Spelling and Grammar check. As you edit the document, the proofing status will display on the status bar: 📖 will display when no errors are flagged. 📖 will display when errors have been flagged. When proofing errors are found, click the button to display a shortcut menu with options to correct the error.

A feature you should consider enabling is the new Contextual Spelling option. When this option is turned on, Word will identify errors like using the word "to" instead of "too." If you have enabled the options to mark grammar errors as you type, a wavy line displays below the possible error(s). You can right-click the word and select a correction from the shortcut menu. Otherwise, the possible grammar error will display in the Spelling and Grammar dialog box. Oddly, the Contextual Spelling option is not enabled in the default savings, so you may need to turn it on.

Another new option in the spelling and grammar checker is for ignoring repeated words. In previous versions of Word, repeated words were flagged as errors. If you intentionally repeat words, such as "boo boo," you can disable the option so that the repeated words will not be flagged.

To change the default spelling and grammar settings:

1. Click the Microsoft Office button.
2. Choose Word Options.
3. Select Proofing.
4. Turn on/off the options under When correcting spelling and grammar in Word.
5. Click OK.

> **TIP** If you frequently use a word that Word continues to flag as a possibly misspelled word, right-click the flagged word and select Add to Dictionary.

Setting AutoFormat and AutoCorrect Options

Because there is no longer a Tools menu, you may be wondering how you can change the AutoCorrect and AutoFormat options. You must open the Word Options menu.

To change AutoCorrect or AutoFormat settings:

1. Click the Microsoft Office button.
2. Choose Word Options.

3. Select Proofing.

4. Under AutoCorrect options, click the AutoCorrect Options button. The AutoCorrect dialog box will display.

5. Turn on/off the options under When correcting spelling and grammar in Word.

Searching Local and Internet Services

The Research command was first introduced in Word 2003, enabling users to search multiple resources without switching applications. For example, in earlier versions of Word, users can find synonyms for a word in the Word application, but if they want to use an online dictionary to look up a definition of a word, they must switch to a browser to access the Internet. The new Research feature enables you to search both local (installed on your computer) and Internet services without leaving the Word screen.

In Word 2003, you access the Research task pane by opening the Tools menu and choosing Research, or by opening the task pane and then choosing Research in the drop-down menu for the task pane. In Word 2007, the Research task pane displays when you click the Research button in the Proofing group.

The research services are very similar, including the Encarta dictionaries, thesauri in a variety of languages, and Encarta and MSN web sites. By default, a few of the many research services will already be activated for search and will display in the drop-down list under the Search for box. Here, you can choose to search local or Internet services. The service for All Reference Books will search the listed services installed on your computer. The service for All Research Sites will search all Internet services listed. The service for All Business and Financial Sites will search all Internet services listed.

There is more than one way to initiate a search:

- Right-click a word and select Look Up, Synonyms, or Translate in the shortcut menu. (Or, click anywhere within a word and press Shift+F7 to show Thesaurus options.)

- Click the Research button in the Proofing group to display the Research task pane. Enter the key words in the Search for box in the task pane, and then click the Start searching button.

- Hold down the Alt key and click anywhere within the document. The last service used will display results for the word you clicked. For example, if the last service you accessed was Thesaurus, then the Thesaurus options will display in the Research task pane.

When the Research task pane is displayed, the Research button in the Proofing group will have an orange fill color. To close the Research task pane, click the close button in the upper-right corner of the Research task pane, or click the Research button in the Proofing group. When the task pane is closed, the Research button will have a blue fill color just like all the other buttons on the ribbon. You can also display the Research task pane when the document is displayed in Full Screen Reading view. Click the Tools button at the top-left corner of the screen and select Research.

By default, several services are already installed. The Thesaurus and Translation services are installed locally and are available offline. The other services listed under

All Reference Books, All Research Sites, and All Business and Financial Sites are only available online (see Figure 9-3). If you want, you can modify this list of services.

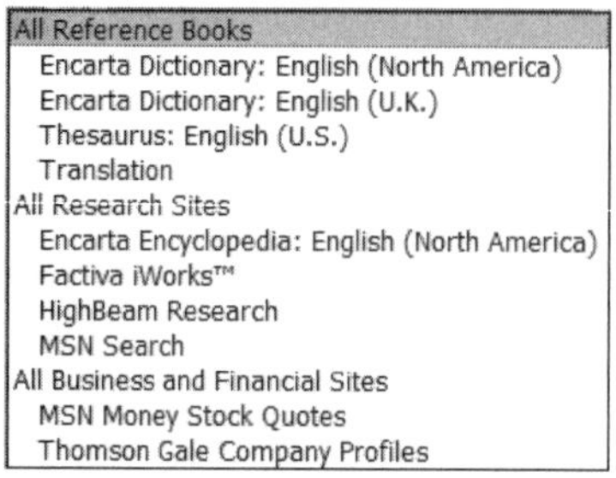

Figure 9-3 *Several of the research services are available online.*

To modify this list or expand it to include other services:

1. Click the Research button in the Proofing group.

2. Click Research options at the bottom of the Research task pane. The Research Options dialog box will display.

3. To activate or to deactivate services in the list, click in the box to the left of the listed resource. The service is activated when a checkmark is displayed.

Organizations can create their own resources or subscribe to services provided by third-party companies. You can refer to the Research and Reference Solution Developers Kit for information about building a custom service.

To add/remove services to the Research task pane:

4. To add services that are not included in the list, click the Add Services button in the dialog box. The Add Services dialog box will display. Enter the URL for the resource you wish to add and click the Add button. When you add a new service, the local or Internet information service must be compatible with Microsoft Office's Research task pane.

5. Click the Update/Remove button to display the Update or Remove Services dialog box. When you click the Update button, Word will automatically update or remove the services that are currently installed. Services are updated for the entire group of services. Click the Close button to close the dialog box.

6. Click the Parental Control button if you want to turn on controls to block offensive content. Not all services block offensive results, so you can choose to allow only those services that can block offensive content. If desired, you can add a password so that other users cannot change these settings. Click OK.

7. Click OK to close the dialog boxes and apply the settings.

Translating Text

The Translation feature is one of the built-in Reference Book services available in the Research task pane. The Translation feature should be used to put into words only the basic subject matter. The end translation does not necessarily convey the full meaning and tone of the text. When you click the Translate button in the Proofing group, the Translation service displays in the Research task pane (see Figure 9-4). If this is the first time you have used the Translation command, Word will download the bilingual dictionary. When translating text, Word may also access online resources if an Internet connection is available.

Click here to translate the whole document.

Figure 9-4 *The Research task pane includes the Translation feature.*

To translate all the text in a document:

1. Click the Translate button in the Proofing group. The Translation service in the Research task pane will display. If you have previously used this feature, a previous translation may display in the pane under WorldLingo.

2. In the Research task pane, choose the languages you want to translate *from* and *to*.

3. Click the right arrow under Translate the whole document. You may be prompted to accept that the document is being sent over the Internet to be translated by the WorldLingo service. All the words in the document are translated and display in a new Internet Explorer window (see Figure 9-5).

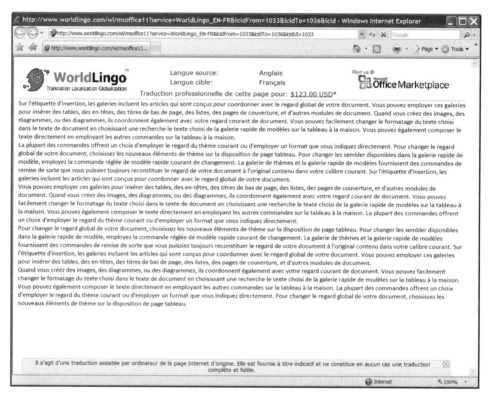

Figure 9-5 *When you translate an entire document, the translation displays in an Internet Explorer window.*

4. Copy and paste the translation.

To translate only a section of text in a document:

1. Select the text you want to translate.

2. Point to the selected text and right-click.

3. Choose Translate in the shortcut menu. If necessary, select a language. If you have previously created a translation, a language will already be selected. If you select a new language, right-click again and select Translate.

4. Select Translate in the drop-down menu. The Translation service in the Research pane will display (see Figure 9-6). If you have previously used this feature, a previous translation may display in the pane under WorldLingo.

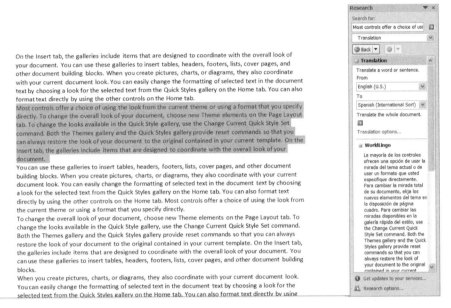

Figure 9-6 *When you translate selected text in the document, the translation displays in the Research task pane.*

5. Scroll down to view the entire translation. To select a paragraph in the translation, triple-click in the paragraph. To select all the paragraphs, click in a paragraph and press Ctrl+A.

6. Copy and paste the translation.

To translate a word or a group of words, you can enter the word(s) directly in the Research task pane.

1. Key the word(s) in the Search for box at the top of the task pane.

2. Click the Start searching button to the right. The translation will display in the task pane under WorldLingo.

Using Translation ScreenTips

Another way to translate specific words is to use the new feature Translation Screen-Tips. You can instantly translate document text in Arabic, English, French, or Spanish. (Other languages are available, depending on the Translation dictionary service that has been downloaded.) By default, this option is turned off. To turn this option on, click the Translate ScreenTip button in the Proofing group, and then select the desired language. When enabled, you can point to any word in the document, and Word will display the translation in a ScreenTip above the word (see Figure 9-7). Because Word is translating a single word, the tip will often include several options showing the translation for a noun, a verb, an adjective, and so forth.

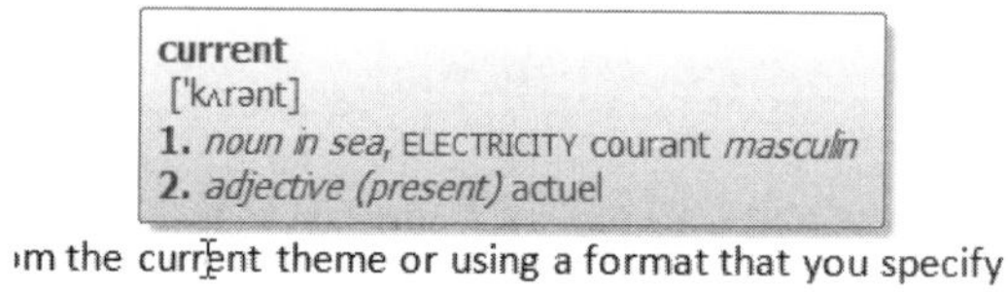

Figure 9-7 *The new Translation ScreenTip provides instant translation.*

Setting a Language for Proofing

If you use more than one language in a document, you can use proofing tools for all of the languages. Versions of Word purchased in the United States automatically proof for English, but you can identify other languages so that the foreign language in the document is also checked for spelling and grammar errors. You can also turn on the options to automatically detect the language and apply the same rules for checking spelling and grammar. When you add the language to the list for proofing, it remains selected for future documents. You can, of course, deselect the language at any time.

To proof the text written in a foreign language:

1. Click the Set Language button in the Proofing group. The Language dialog box will display.
2. Select the language you want to use. Notice that English (U.S.) is already selected.

   NOTE The available languages with proofing tools are identified with an ABC spelling check icon.

3. If desired, turn on the option Detect language automatically. If you have the option to check spelling as you type enabled, Word will identify any potential errors with wavy lines. You can use the shortcut menu to make corrections as shown in Figure 9-8.
4. Click OK.

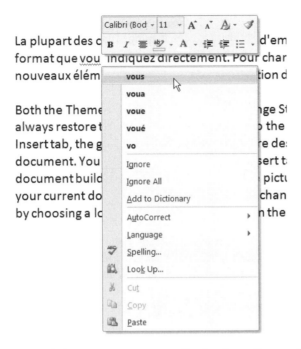

Figure 9-8 *You can automatically check spelling and grammar for foreign languages.*

Suppressing the Spelling and Grammar Check

You can also mark text so that Word does not check spelling and grammar. For example, if you write an article and quote someone, you want the quote to remain unchanged. You can suppress the display of possible spelling and grammar errors in the quoted text.

To mark text that you don't want proofed:

1. Select the text you want to mark.

2. Click the Set Language button in the Proofing group.

3. Turn on the option Do not check spelling or grammar.

4. Click OK.

Counting Words

The Word Count command is also available in the Proofing group. When you click the Word Count button, a summary displays showing the number of pages, words, characters, paragraphs, and lines in the entire document. If you want a count of only part of a document, select the portion of the document you want to include in the count, and then click the Word Count button. You can continually display the word count in the status bar (see Figure 9-9) by right-clicking the status bar and selecting Word Count in the shortcut menu. The word count is displayed next to the page number, and it is automatically updated as you edit the document.

Words: 304

Figure 9-9 *You can customize the status bar to display the current Word count.*

Making Comments

The Comments group provides options for creating and deleting comments, as well as navigating among the comments (see Figure 9-10). In previous versions of Word, you can find these commands on the Reviewing toolbar. Word 2007 organizes these features in the Comments group.

Figure 9-10 *The Comments group provides buttons for inserting and deleting comments.*

Adding Comments

When you add a comment to a document, the comment is connected to a word closest to the location of the insertion point. To identify a section of text related to the comment, select all of the text before inserting the comment. By default, the text will display in a balloon on the right side of the page in all views except Outline view. The size of the balloon will grow as needed to provide the necessary space for the text. Word automatically adjusts the zoom of the document so that you can see the document contents and the balloons. When there are multiple users adding comments to the document, you can quickly identify each user's comments by the color of the balloon. The comment data includes the initials of the author or reviewer, the date and time, and the comment text. The author's or reviewer's initials display in the balloon with the comment text (see Figure 9-11). When you position the mouse pointer over the balloon, a ScreenTip displays the name of the user and the date and time the comment was added.

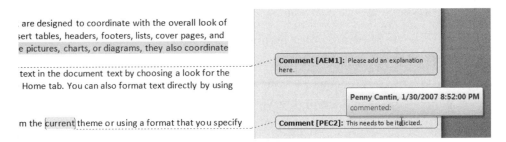

Figure 9-11 *The comments display in balloons and are connected to words in the document.*

> **NOTE** If the ScreenTip does not display, click the Microsoft Office button, choose Word Options, click Display, and under Page display options, make sure Show document tooltips on hover is turned on, and then click OK.

To insert a new comment:

1. Position the insertion point (or select the text to which the comment applies).

2. Click the New Comment button in the Comments group.

3. Enter the text for your comment.

The comments are numbered sequentially throughout the document. If the text gets moved, any the comments associated with that text move with it. You can quickly locate comments in the document using the Previous and Next buttons in the Comments group.

If you have a microphone built in or attached to your computer, or if you are using a Tablet PC, you can insert a voice comment. The comment is inserted as a sound object and displays as a sound object inside the balloon (see Figure 9-12). You can also insert the sound object inside an existing comment balloon. To listen to a voice comment, double-click the sound object. When you position the mouse pointer over the balloon, a ScreenTip will display the author's/reviewer's name and the date and time the voice comment was recorded.

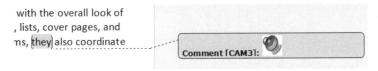

Figure 9-12 *Voice comments are indicated with a sound object in the balloon.*

To insert a voice comment:

1. Click the Microsoft Office button.
2. Click Word Options and then select Customize.
3. Under Choose commands from, select All Commands.
4. Scroll down and select Insert Voice in the list of commands.
5. Click Add and then click OK. The Insert Voice command is added to the Quick Access Toolbar.
6. Click the Insert Voice button. The Sound Object in *Document1* dialog box will display.
7. Click the Start button, record the comment, and press the Stop button.
8. Close the dialog box. If prompted to update the sound object, select Yes.

Also, if you are using a Tablet PC, you can add handwritten comments. Click the New Comment button. When the bubble displays, write your comment in the balloon.

Editing and Deleting Comments

After you insert a comment, you may change your mind and want to either change or delete the comment. You can select and format text in a comment just as you would select text in the document.

To edit a comment:

1. Click the comment to select it.
2. Position the insertion point in the comment text, and make the necessary changes.

To delete a comment:

1. Click the comment to select it.
2. To remove the selected comment, click the Delete button in the Comments group. (Or, right-click the comment and choose Delete Comment in the shortcut menu.)
3. To remove all the comments shown or to remove all the comments in the document, click the down arrow on the Delete button. For example, if you display only one reviewer's comments and you choose to remove all the comments shown, the comments from other reviewers will remain.

Tracking Changes

The Tracking group (see Figure 9-13) includes all the tools you need for tracking changes as you edit a document. Tracked changes are useful when individuals collaborate, because you can easily identify the edits and know who made them. And don't worry if you're sharing documents with someone who is using an older version of Word. The tracked changes also function in compatibility mode.

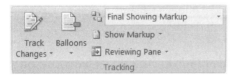

Figure 9-13 *Tracking changes helps you identify the edits and who made them.*

To turn the Track Changes feature on and off, click the Track Changes button in the Tracking group. As you insert, delete, and format text, the changes will be noted on the screen. It is obvious when the Track Changes feature is turned on because the Track Changes button is filled with an orange background. When the feature is turned off, the Track Changes button is filled with a blue background just like all the other buttons. When you stop tracking changes, new edits will not display on the screen; however, the existing tracked changes will remain intact and still display.

In previous versions of Word, the TRK button on the status bar can be used to toggle the tracking feature on and off. By default, the button does not display on the status bar in Word 2007, but you can customize the status bar to indicate whether the Track Changes feature is turned on or off (see Figure 9-14). And, you can also use this button to toggle Track Changes on and off.

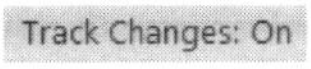

Track Changes: On

Figure 9-14 *When you customize the status bar to display a button for Track Changes, the button changes to indicate whether the feature is on or off.*

To customize the status bar:

1. Right-click the status bar. The Customize Status Bar menu will display.
2. Select Track Changes. The Track Changes button will always display on the status bar, and the button will change to indicate whether the feature is turned on or off.
3. Click the Track Changes button on the status bar to toggle the option on and off. (Or, you can press Ctrl+Shift+E.)

> **NOTE** If you cannot turn on Track Changes, the document may be protected. Click the Protect Document button in the Protect group and remove the restrictions for formatting and editing. You will need to enter the password.

Displaying Tracked Changes and Comments

By default, Word displays the tracked changes for insertions and deletions in the line of text, and format changes and comments are displayed in balloons on the right side of the document. You can make several adjustments to control what and how the tracked changes display on your screen.

- To change the colors and formats that display for tracked changes, click the down arrow on the Track Changes button and choose Change Tracking Options. The Track Changes Options dialog box will display, and you can change the formats for both comments and inserted, deleted, and moved text.

- To change the author/reviewer name or initials, click the down arrow on the Track Changes button and choose Change User Name. Enter a user name and initials under Personalize your copy of Microsoft Office, and then click OK.

- To change what displays in balloons, click the Balloons button in the Tracking group. If you choose to show all revisions inline, only the comment number will display. When you position the mouse pointer over the comment number in the line of text, the comment text will display in a ScreenTip.

- To distinguish which tracking changes display, click the button in the top right corner of the Tracking group. The default setting is Final Showing Markup. You can, however, choose to show the final image of the document, the original document with tracked changes, or the original document.

- You can choose to display or not display insertions, deletions, and format edits. Click the Show Markup button in the Tracking group and turn the options on or off. The ink option is for handwriting created on Tablet PCs. To display only the comments in the document, click the Show Markup button in the Tracking group and turn off all the other options.

NOTE Turning off all the options in the Show Markup command is the same as choosing Final in the Display for Review box.

- If you have multiple reviewers providing you feedback in a document, the tracked changes and comments can often be overwhelming. You can choose some options in the tracking settings to help you sort out all the comments and changes. For example, you receive an edited document with tracked changes and comments from four other members on your team. You want to review each team member's comments and edits separately. You can quickly sort out one team member's comments and edits. Click the Show Markup button, select Reviewers, and deselect the reviewers you do not want to include. Comments and tracked changes will display for only those reviewers with checkmarks.

- You can also make it easier to review the changes by focusing on one kind of change at a time. For example, when you first review the document, you can display only comments. Then, you can hide the comments and display only insertions and deletions. Then, hide those changes and display only the formatting. To choose the type of edit you want to review, click the Show Markup button in the Tracking group and turn on/off the options in the menu. The Markup Area Highlight toggles on and off a light gray shading behind the balloons.

Displaying the Reviewing Pane

The Reviewing pane is an alternative to displaying the changes in balloons. The Reviewing pane is similar to the task pane, and it displays a list of the edits and comments in the document. You can display the Reviewing pane in a vertical position (see Figure 9-15) or in a horizontal position (see Figure 9-16). Notice that the pane is divided into categories, including header and footer changes, text box changes, and footnote and endnote changes.

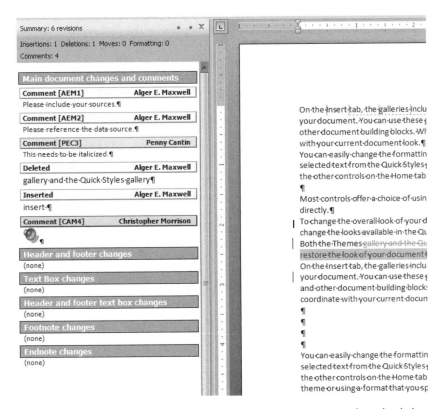

Figure 9-15 *The Reviewing pane displays the comments and tracked changes in categories.*

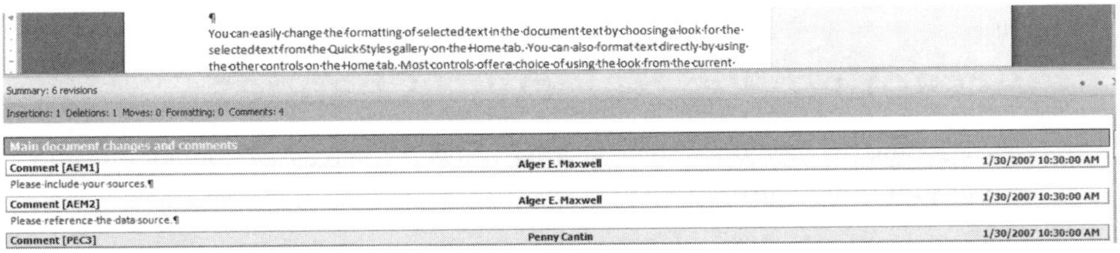

Figure 9-16 *The Reviewing pane includes a summary of the number of insertions, deletions, and so forth.*

To display and close the Reviewing pane:

1. Click the Reviewing Pane button in the Tracking group. (The pane will display in the same view it was last displayed—vertical or horizontal.)

2. To change the view, click the down arrow on the Reviewing Pane button.

3. To close the Reviewing pane, click the close button in the upper-right corner of the pane, or simply click the Reviewing Pane button again to toggle it off.

A summary of the number of insertions, deletions, moves, formatting, and comments is provided at the top of the Reviewing pane. When you display the Reviewing pane horizontally, you get more details about the change, because each entry includes the date and time. You can still access this information with the Reviewing pane displayed vertically. Double-click the comment or change in the Reviewing pane. The insertion point will be repositioned at the location of the change or comment in the document. Position the mouse pointer over the change or comment to display the details in a ScreenTip.

Printing Documents with Tracked Changes

By default, Word will print the document as it appears on the screen. Therefore, if you have some or all of the tracked changes displayed (Final Showing Markup or Original Showing Markup), those tracked edits will appear in the printed document. Comments and edits displayed in balloons will also appear in the printed document. If the Reviewing pane is displayed, the Reviewing pane does not appear in the printed document. However, you can choose to print the list of changes and comments from the Reviewing pane.

To print the Reviewing pane list on a separate page:

1. Click the Microsoft Office button, choose Print in the menu, and choose Print in the submenu. (Or, press Ctrl+P.) The Print dialog box will display.

2. In the Print what box, at the bottom-left corner, choose List of markup. Word will print only the Reviewing pane contents in a horizontal alignment, regardless of which alignment you chose when you displayed the Reviewing pane.

NOTE When you choose the option Document showing markup, the document prints exactly as it would display with the Final Showing Markup option selected in the Tracking group.

Accepting and Rejecting Changes

The buttons for accepting and rejecting tracked changes are included in the Changes group shown in Figure 9-17.

Figure 9-17 *You can accept or reject changes individually or as a group.*

When you click the down arrow for the Accept and the Reject buttons, you can choose to accept or reject a single change or multiple changes. To accept or reject all the changes for a portion of the document, select the parts of the document before clicking the Accept or Reject buttons. You can also accept or reject an individual change by pointing at the marked change, right-clicking, and choosing Accept Change or Reject Change in the shortcut menu.

Comparing and Merging Documents

What do you do when a reviewer edits a document for you, but he or she doesn't track the changes? Even though you can display the documents side by side and scroll synchronously, if the document is very long, comparing the two documents can be a tedious task.

Comparing Documents

The Compare Documents feature in the Compare group (see Figure 9-18) is useful when you want to compare the original version of a document with a revised document (sometimes referred to as *legal blackline*).

Figure 9-18 *Use the Compare command to compare the orginal version with a revised version of a document.*

Word displays the documents in a tri-pane view. In the pane on the left, a merged document labeled "Compared Document" is displayed. To the right, the original and the revised documents are displayed (see Figure 9-19). You can use the scroll bars in all three panes to navigate through the documents, or you can click inside each pane and use the arrow keys to move around. You can edit the compared document, but you cannot make any changes to the original document or the revised document.

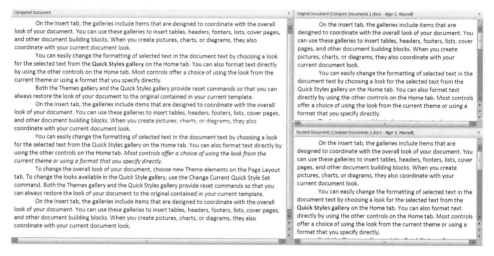

Figure 9-19 *When you compare documents, each version of the document is displayed in a separate pane*

To compare two documents:

1. Click the Compare button in the Compare group.

2. Select Compare. The Compare Documents dialog box will display.

3. Identify the original document and the revised document.

4. Click OK.

> **NOTE** If you do not see three panes, click the Show Source Documents button in the Compare group and select Show Both.

If you turn on the options Final Showing Markup or Original Showing Markup in the Tracking group, tracked changes will also display in the compared document. All differences in the revised document will become tracked changes in the compared document. If the Reviewing Pane option is turned on, the Reviewing pane will also display.

When you identify the two documents in the Compare Documents dialog box, you can also be specific about what you want to compare and how you want to show those changes. For example, you can choose the content in the document that you want to compare, or you may decide to compare only formatting. By default, Word compares all elements in the document, but you can turn off some of those options if you desire. Also by default, Word shows changes for whole words as opposed to showing changes for a single character in a word. In other words, if you add "ing" to the end of a word, the entire word will show the change instead of just the "ing." To change the default settings, click the More button in the Compare Documents dialog box to display the comparison settings as shown in Figure 9-20.

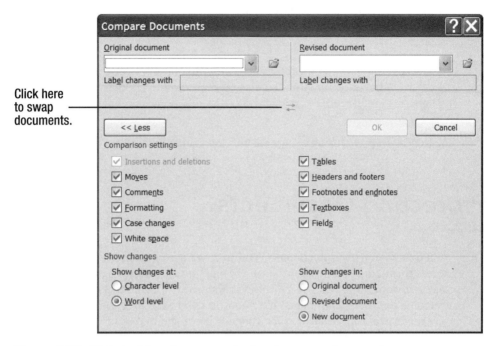

Figure 9-20 *Click the More button to display the comparison settings.*

To reverse the documents so that the revised document is considered to be the original document, click the Compare button, select Compare, and then click the Swap Documents arrows (double arrows) in the middle of the Compare Documents dialog box (see Figure 9-20), just to the left of the OK button.

Combining Documents

The task can be tedious when there are several reviewers providing edits and comments in separate documents. The Combine Documents feature is useful when you want to merge revisions from several reviewers into a single document. You can only merge two documents at a time, but in the long run, it will still make your task easier. All the comments and changes will be merged into a single document.

To combine documents:

1. Click the Compare button in the Compare group.

2. Choose Combine. The Combine Documents dialog box displays.

3. Identify the original document and one of the revised documents.

4. Click the More button. The comparison settings are same as those listed in the Compare Documents dialog box. If necessary, select the option Original document under Show changes in. Make any other desired changes to the settings.

5. Click OK. The combined document is displayed at the left, and the original and revised documents are displayed at the right.

If you want to show only the combined document, click the Show Source Documents button in the Compare group and choose Hide Source Documents.

> **NOTE** When there are differences in formatting, only one format can be used in the combined document. You may be prompted to choose which format to keep—the original document formatting or the revised document formatting.

6. Repeat Steps 1 through 4 for each of the remaining revised documents.

Protecting Documents

When you're sharing documents, you may want to be selective about who can have access to the documents. And, even though you're willing to share a document, you may not want other users to be able to change the document. For example, you might welcome the user's comments, but you don't want the user to make any changes. Or, you might want the user to track changes he or she makes in the document, but you don't want the user to be able to accept those changes. You can protect the document by restricting users from formatting and editing all or part of the document.

Restricting Access to Modify Documents

To be selective as to who can modify your document, you can add a password when you save the document. The user will need to enter the password to open the document and make edits. However, if the user does not know the password, the user can choose to open the document in Read-Only format. If you want to prohibit users from seeing your document, you need to encrypt the document. (See "Encrypting a Document" in Chapter 2.)

To restrict access with a password:

1. Click the Microsoft Office button and select Save As. The Save As dialog box will display.

2. Click the Tools button in the bottom-left corner of the dialog box and select General Options. The General Options dialog box will display.

3. Enter a password in the box for File sharing options for this document and click OK.

4. Enter the password again to confirm it, and then click OK to close the General Options dialog box.

5. Make any necessary changes in the Save As dialog box, and then click Save.

Restricting Formatting and Editing

To protect a document, you choose from options in the Restrict Formatting and Editing task pane. To display the task pane, you use the Protect Document button on the Developer tab (see Figure 9-21). You can restrict users from formatting and editing all or part of the document. If you want to allow the user to change formatting, you can limit the styles he or she can use, which will prevent him or her from applying direct formatting. When setting the editing restrictions, you can allow the user to track changes, add comments, or fill in forms. You can only select one of these options, but when you choose the option Tracked changes, the user can also add comments. However, if you select Filling in forms, the user cannot track changes or add comments. (Restricting access for filling in forms is also discussed in Chapter 11.)

Figure 9-21 *You can protect the document by controlling access and restricting formatting changes and editing.*

When you select the option Comments or No changes (Read only), you can make exceptions and allow some individuals to access all or part of the document. You must identify the users for whom you want to allow access. To identify an individual who logs in on the same PC that you are using, you can use that person's user name. If the individual uses a computer in your network domain, you can enter that individual's domain user name (that is, domain\user name). Or, you can use an individual's e-mail address.

After specifying the restrictions, you enter a password so other users cannot remove the restrictions. Be sure to remember your password. If necessary, write it down in a safe place. If you can't recall your password, you won't be able to access and/or edit the document. You may defeat your purpose if you enter a simple, easy password. Passwords should include letters, numbers, and symbols with a combination of uppercase and lowercase letters. The longer the password is, the better.

To restrict users from access and formatting and editing:

1. Click the Protect Document button on the Developer tab. The Restrict Formatting and Editing task pane will display.

2. To limit formatting to styles that you choose, turn on the option Limit formatting to a selection of styles. Click the link Settings, make any desired changes in the Formatting Restrictions dialog box, and then click OK.

3. Under Editing restrictions, turn on Allow only this type of editing in the document.

4. In the drop-down box, select the desired option. If you select Comments or No changes (Read only) exception options will display so you can identify those who are allowed to edit the document. If you select Tracked changes or Filling in forms, you cannot make any exceptions, so go to Step 10.

5. To identify users who can access the document, click the link More users. The Add Users dialog box will display.

6. Enter the user name, domain user name, or e-mail address for each individual you want to allow access. You can add multiple individuals by separating the entries with a semicolon.

7. Click OK to close the Add Users dialog box.

8. Select the portion of the document where you will permit access, and then select the user name under Groups in the Restrict Formatting and Editing task pane.

9. Repeat Step 8 to allow access to other portions of the document.

10. Under Start enforcement, click Yes, Start Enforcing Protection.

11. Enter a password twice and click OK.

When the user opens a protected document, the Restrict Formatting and Editing task pane may display; when the user attempts to enter new text in the document, many of the buttons on the Ribbon and shortcut commands may be disabled.

When only parts of the document are protected, the parts the user can edit will display with a yellow background shading. When the user tries to insert text in the protected areas, the Restrict Formatting and Editing task pane will display (if it wasn't already displayed) with a message noting that the document is protected. The user can choose options in the task pane to go to the next region or to show all regions that can be edited.

Removing Protection

If you restricted access to modify a document with a password, you have two options. You can open the document and remove the password, or you can save the document under a new file name. Either way, you must open the General Options dialog box. If you save the document under a new file name, the password settings will remain the same unless you remove them.

To remove a password from a document:

1. Open the document using the password.

2. Click the Microsoft Office button and choose the Save As command.

3. Click the Tools button and select General Options.

4. Delete the entry in the password box and click OK.

5. Enter a new file name if desired, as well as any other save options, and then click Save.

If you want to remove the protection from formatting and editing, you need to make the change in the Restrict Formatting and Editing task pane.

To remove the protection for formatting and editing:

1. Open the document that contains the restricted formatting and editing.

2. Click the Protect button on the Developer tab to display the Restrict Formatting and Editing task pane.

3. Click the Stop Protection button at the bottom of the pane. The Unprotect Document dialog box will display.

4. Enter the password and click OK.

Restricting Access for Opening or E-Mailing Documents

For restricted access, Word utilizes Information Rights Management (IRM), a service that provides a server to authenticate the credentials of people who create or receive documents or e-mail with restricted permission. Some organizations use their own rights management servers.

Microsoft offers a trial for their IRM service for users who have a Microsoft .NET Passport account. The service verifies the credentials of those who access your restricted access documents. Therefore, those with whom you share restricted access must also have .NET Passport accounts. The service maintains a record of each time credentials are verified. To use IRM, you must first install the Windows Rights Management client. Then, to restrict access to a document, you identify those who are permitted to read and/or change the document.

Sharing Documents

To share documents, you can save them on a server where your colleagues can have access to them. Or, you can attach documents to e-mails and distribute them that way. If you have a Microsoft SharePoint Services web site, you can create a document workspace to make the process of sharing documents even easier. Each time you edit a document, instead of e-mailing the new version to your colleagues, you can update the document in the document workspace. Your colleagues will be able to access all of your most recent changes and add their own edits to the document at the document workspace. Information about creating a document workspace is provided in Chapter 12.

To save the document to a server or document workspace:

1. Click the Microsoft Office button.

2. Choose Publish.

3. In the menu, choose one of the following:

- Document Management Server (The Save As dialog box will display.)
- Create Document Workspace (A task pane for Document Management will display.)

Removing Properties and Personal Information

Before you share a document electronically, you might want to remove document properties and personal information.

To remove properties and personal information:

1. Click the Microsoft Office button.
2. Choose Prepare.
3. Select Inspect Document.
4. Make sure Document Properties and Personal Information is selected.
5. Click Inspect. The Document Inspector dialog box will display.
6. Click Remove All to remove the document properties and personal information.

Converting to PDF or XPS Format

Another way to keep others from formatting and editing your document is to share the document in Portable Document Format (PDF) or XML Paper Specification (XPS) format. Both PDF and XPS formats preserve document formatting, which ensures that when others open or print the document, it will look exactly the same as it does on your computer. PDF and XPS formats are discussed in more detail in Chapter 12.

To save a document in PDF or XPS format:

1. Click the Microsoft Office button.
2. Click the arrow to the right of the Save As command.
3. Select PDF or XPS.

> **NOTE** If PDF or XPS is not an option in the menu, you must install an add-in. This is a free option from Microsoft. Once you install the add-in, the feature will always be available.

Sending a PDF or XPS Attachment in an E-Mail

The Send (formerly Send To) command options are different in Word 2007. You can choose to send a Word document as

- *An attachment to an e-mail message*: Word will automatically open a new document with an e-mail header. The document will already be attached to the e-mail document.

- *A PDF attachment to an e-mail message*: Word will automatically open a new document with an e-mail header. The document will already be converted to PDF format and attached to the e-mail document.

- *An XPS attachment to an e-mail*: Word will automatically open a new document with an e-mail header. The document will already be converted to XPS format and attached to the e-mail document.

To access the Send options, click the Microsoft Office button, select Send, and choose one of the options in the menu.

NOTE If you choose to e-mail the document as an attachment, you can choose to create a flag to the recipients to provide information about followup. Click the Follow Up button in the e-mail window and choose Flag for Recipients.

CHAPTER 10

Creating and Using Macros

Word 2007 offers many features that save you time, including building blocks, themes, and templates. These built-in features eliminate the need to perform numerous repetitive tasks. Some tasks, however, still require multiple commands. And sometimes, to complete a task, you need to click several buttons or open dialog boxes and select one or more options. These tasks, although not usually very complex, can be tedious, time-consuming, and prone to error. If you perform these tasks repetitively, you can save time using macros.

For example, consider this scenario. When you print a particular type of document, like invoices, you need to print four copies of page 3 in the document. You don't want to change the default settings for printing one copy, and it takes time to open the Print dialog box to change the setting for the number of copies to be printed. You can create a macro to do this for you. When you run the macro, four copies of page 3 in the document will print.

> **NOTE** Before creating a macro, make sure there isn't already a built-in Word command that you can use to complete the task. To see a list of built-in Word commands, click the Macros button in the Code group. In the Macros in box, select Word commands. The built-in macros will display in the Macro name box.

Displaying the Developer Tab

The tools you need to create a macro are found on the Developer tab, shown in Figure 10-1. By default, the Developer tab does not display.

Figure 10-1 *To create a macro, you must display the Developer tab.*

To display the Developer tab:

1. Click the Microsoft Office button.

2. Choose Word Options.

3. Select Popular.

4. Under Top options for working with Word, select Show Developer tab in the Ribbon.

Creating Macros

A *macro* is a series of commands grouped together so that a task can be performed with a single command. The macro commands and options can be found in the Code group on the Developer tab (see Figure 10-2).

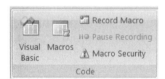

Figure 10-2 *You can record commands to create a macro.*

Macros are coded in Visual Basic for Applications (VBA). When you click the Visual Basic button in the Code group, the Visual Basic Editor displays. You use the Visual Basic Editor to create, modify, and manage macros. If you are proficient with VBA programming language, you can code your own macros or customize recorded ones. Using the Visual Basic Editor is addressed later in this chapter in the section "Editing a Macro."

Don't be concerned if you don't know how to write VBA codes. You can still create a macro. When you choose the Record Macro command in Word, you perform a series of tasks, and Word records your actions and creates the VBA codes for you. The following section provides guided steps for creating a macro using the Record Macro command.

Starting the Recording Process

You should plan your actions in advance, because once you start recording, every action you take is captured. If you stop to make corrections or undo commands, all of those actions are also recorded. Furthermore, some commands may trigger a prompt. For example, if the macro includes an action to close the document, a prompt may display asking whether you want to save the document before you close it. Such a prompt will interrupt the series of actions in the macro. The macro won't continue until you respond to the prompt. To avoid the prompt, include the action of saving the document in the macro.

To begin recording a macro:

1. Open a new document and save it as a macro-enabled document with a .docm extension to enable the functionality of the macro.

2. Click the Record Macro button in the Code group on the Developer tab. The Record Macro dialog box will display. Or, if the Macro Recording button is selected to display on the status bar, you can click the Record Macro button 🖫 in the status bar.

3. Leave the dialog box open.

Naming and Storing a Macro

When you start to record a macro, Word automatically assigns a macro name, such as Macro1 or Macro2. You should choose a name that will help you easily identify what the macro does, such as "Print4Copies." The macro name must begin with a letter, and it can contain up to 80 letters or digits. The name cannot contain spaces or symbols. If you enter a name that has already been assigned to another macro, Word will prompt you to replace the existing macro. You will also need to identify a place to store the macro. Where you choose to store a macro depends on when you want the macro to be available:

- Store the macro in the Normal.dot template, and the macro will be available in any Word document.

- Store the macro in the document's template, and the macro will be available in any document based on that template.

- Store the macro in the current document, and the macro will be available only in that document.

All the components for a macro are stored as a unit in a *module,* which is a collection of one or more macros. When you create the first macro, Word assigns the default name NewMacros to a new module. When you create additional macros, they are added to the NewMacros module. The module is stored in a *project,* which is a collection of one or more modules. The project is saved in a template. Information about changing the name of a module and copying projects is provided later in this chapter.

To name and store a macro:

1. Enter a new macro name in the Macro name box.
2. Click the down arrow in the Store macro in box and select an option.
3. Leave the dialog box open.

Assigning a Shortcut to a Macro

To save time in accessing and running the macro, you can assign a keyboard shortcut or create a toolbar button for it. You can choose to create one or the other, but you cannot create both shortcuts at the same time. After you finish recording the macro, you can assign the second shortcut. (See the section "Creating and Editing a Shortcut for an Existing Macro" later in this chapter.)

> **NOTE** Creating a shortcut is optional. If you choose to not create a shortcut, you will be able to access the macro by clicking the Macros button and displaying the Macros dialog box.

Creating a Keyboard Shortcut for a Macro

When you create a keyboard shortcut, you assign a key combination to the macro. You can use the Ctrl key, the Alt key, the Shift key, the function keys (F1 through F12), and all the alphabetic and number keys on the keyboard. If you choose a shortcut key combination that is not associated with any commands, an alert will display that the keys are unassigned. However, if you choose a key combination that is already associated with a command, Word will display an alert that the keys are currently assigned. For example, if you choose the key combination Ctrl+F2, Word will display that the keys are currently assigned to the File Print Preview command. You can still apply the shortcut keys, and the new macro shortcut will supersede previous keyboard shortcut assignments. If you saved the macro in the Normal template, pressing Ctrl+F2 will no longer work as a shortcut to display documents in Print Preview.

To create a keyboard shortcut:

1. Click the Keyboard option. The Customize Keyboard dialog box will display.
2. Enter the key combination in the box labeled Press new shortcut key. A prompt will display below the Current keys box indicating whether the keys are currently assigned or are unassigned. If necessary, enter a new key combination.
3. When you are satisfied with the shortcut key entry, click Assign. The shortcut key combination will display in the Current keys box.
4. Click Close to close the Customize Keyboard dialog box.
5. Leave the document open, and go to the section "Completing the Recording Process."

Creating a Toolbar Button for a Macro

Perhaps you don't like using shortcut keys. An alternative shortcut is to add a button to the Quick Access Toolbar. All macro buttons that you add will look the same and will display as ♣. If you have added multiple macro buttons to the toolbar, point to a button, and a ScreenTip will display the name of the macro. To remove the macro toolbar button from the Quick Access Toolbar, right-click the toolbar button and select Remove from Quick Access Toolbar.

To create a toolbar button for the macro:

1. Click the Button option. The Word Options dialog box will display. Macros will display in the Choose commands from box.

2. In the Separator list, select the macro name and click Add. The new macro will display in the list at the right.

3. Click OK. The new button will display on the Quick Access Toolbar.

4. Leave the document open and go to the next section, "Completing the Recording Process."

Completing the Recording Process

Note that a tape image displays with your mouse pointer. Also, note that the Record Macro button in the Code group is no longer visible; instead, the Stop Recording button is displayed in the Code group. You are in recording mode, and all actions you complete are being recorded for the macro.

Now that you have named and stored the macro, and assigned a shortcut, you are ready to perform the actions to complete the task. You can use the mouse or keystrokes to execute commands and choose options. However, you cannot use the mouse to scroll, to position the insertion point, or to select text. If you want to record any of these edits, you must use the keyboard to complete the action. Keep in mind as you record macros that many keyboard shortcuts function as formatting toggles. For example, Ctrl+B applies a bold format to selected text *unless* it is already bold, in which case it removes the bold format.

You can temporarily stop recording. For example, you may want to make some edits in the current document, or you may get interrupted and need to open and work with a different document. To pause recording, click the Pause Recording button in the Code group. When you're ready to continue recording, click the Resume Recording button in the Code group. When you've completed all the actions for the macro, click the Stop Recording button in the Code group.

To record a macro:

1. Perform the actions to complete the task. For example, press Ctrl+P to open the Print dialog box. Under Page range, select Pages and enter the number 3. Click the up arrow in the Number of copies box to change the setting to 4. Click OK. (Four copies of page 3 will print!)

2. When you have completed all the actions, click the Stop Recording button in the Code group. If you have the Macro Recording button selected to display in the status bar, you can click the Stop Recording button ▣.

3. Test the macro. If it doesn't work correctly, evaluate the actions, repeat the process, and assign the same macro name so the original macro will be replaced.

Creating and Editing a Shortcut for an Existing Macro

You can assign or edit a keyboard shortcut at any time after the macro has been created. If the macro has already been assigned a keyboard shortcut, you can assign a toolbar button, and vice versa.

To assign or edit a keyboard shortcut to an existing macro:

1. Click the Microsoft Office button and choose Word Options.

2. Select Customize. A dialog box will display popular commands.

3. Click the Customize button at the bottom of the dialog box. The Customize Keyboard dialog box will display.

4. Under Categories, scroll down and select Macros.

5. In the Save changes in box, select the location where you saved the macro.

6. Under Macros, select the macro name.

7. Enter the new shortcut in the Press new shortcut key box, click Assign, and then click Close.

To assign a toolbar button to an existing macro:

1. Click the Microsoft Office button and choose Word Options.

2. Select Customize. A dialog box will display popular commands.

3. Under Choose commands from, select Macros. A list of the available macros will display.

4. Select a macro and click the Add button.

5. Click OK. The new button will display on the Quick Access Toolbar.

Running a Macro

Before you execute a macro, position the insertion point at the correct place in the document. For example, if the macro replaces special characters throughout the document, you want to position the insertion point at the beginning of the document.

If you create a keyboard or toolbar shortcut for your macro, you can use either of them to run the macro. If you didn't create a shortcut, you can access the macro in the Macros dialog box. The Macros dialog box is very helpful if you want to test multiple macros.

To run a macro from the Macros dialog box:

1. Click the Macros button in the Code group (or press Alt+F8). The Macros dialog box will display.

2. Locate the macro. You may need to select the document or template name in the Macros in box.

3. Select the macro name in the Macro name list.

4. Click Run.

If a prompt displays indicating that the macro was not found or is unavailable, you may need to change the security settings for the document.

> **NOTE** If you stored the macro with a specific document, that document must be open in order to access that particular macro.

Editing a Macro

If a macro doesn't deliver the results you expect, you can modify it. If the macro is simple, with just a few actions, it may be easiest to just rerecord it. But if the macro is complex and you need to make just minor changes, you can edit the macro in the Visual Basic Editor. Don't worry if you don't know anything about VBA programming language. Give it a try. Chances are you'll be able to decipher the code that was generated for the captured action and change things appropriately.

To illustrate, let's continue with the scenario presented at the beginning of this chapter. You created a macro to print four copies of the current page. The name of the macro is Print4Copies. Instead of printing four copies of page 3 in the document, you only need to print two copies of page 2. To modify the macro, you want to change the number of copies to 2 and the print range from All to page 3.

To edit a macro in the Visual Basic Editor:

1. Click the Macros button in the Code group. The Macros dialog box will display.

2. In the Macro name list, select the macro name.

3. Click Edit. The Normal – NewMacros (Code) dialog box will display in the Visual Basic Editor. An example is shown in Figure 10-3.

4. Locate the code that specifies the number of copies. It currently displays as Copies:=4.

5. Change the 4 to 2.

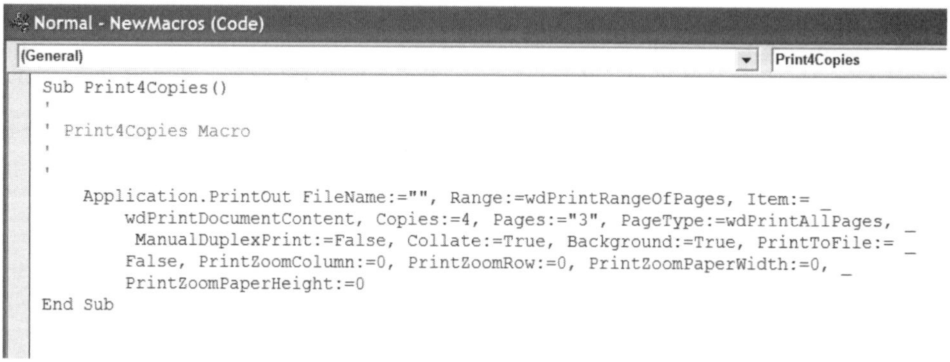

```
Normal - NewMacros (Code)
(General)                                                    ▼   Print4Copies
Sub Print4Copies()
'
' Print4Copies Macro
'
'
    Application.PrintOut FileName:="", Range:=wdPrintRangeOfPages, Item:= _
        wdPrintDocumentContent, Copies:=4, Pages:="3", PageType:=wdPrintAllPages, _
        ManualDuplexPrint:=False, Collate:=True, Background:=True, PrintToFile:= _
        False, PrintZoomColumn:=0, PrintZoomRow:=0, PrintZoomPaperWidth:=0, _
        PrintZoomPaperHeight:=0
End Sub
```

Figure 10-3 *You can edit a macro in the Visual Basic Editor.*

6. Immediately following the number of copies is the reference to the pages. It currently displays as Pages:="3." Change 3 to 2.

7. Click the Word icon on the toolbar, or open the File menu and choose Close and Return to Microsoft Word. The code changes will be saved.

8. Leave the document open.

Renaming a Macro

As mentioned earlier, a macro is saved within a collection of components that is referred to as a module. Renaming an individual macro is different from renaming a macro module. Later in the chapter, the section "Renaming a Macro Module" shows you how to do the latter. To rename an individual macro, you must first display the code in the Visual Basic Editor. But don't worry. Editing the macro name is easier than editing the macro commands and instructions. Remember, a macro name cannot include spaces and symbols, and the name cannot begin with a number.

To rename a macro:

1. Click the Macros button to display the Macros dialog box.

2. Select the macro and click Edit. The macro code will display in the Visual Basic Editor. The line in the code that begins with "Sub" includes the name of the macro. (In the print scenario, the name is Print4Copies, as shown in Figure 10-3.)

3. Edit the name by changing the 4 to a 2.

4. Click the Word icon on the toolbar, or open the File menu and choose Close and Return to Microsoft Word. The code change will be saved.

Undoing a Macro

If you are not satisfied with the results after you run a macro, you can reverse the actions. However, it's not a simple "undo." Remember that the macro is a recording of a series of actions. If you choose to undo the macro, you must reverse *all* of the actions. The best way to do this is to display the drop-down list for the Undo button, and select multiple actions.

If you didn't create the macro, it may be difficult to discern where in the list the macro actions end. Therefore, if you're trying a macro for the first time, and you're not confident it will deliver the results you want, save the document before you run the macro. Then, if you don't like the results, you can begin over by closing the current document and reopening the saved version.

Deleting a Macro

When you no longer need a macro, you can delete it from the macro list. Remember that Word has several built-in macros, such as F1 for displaying the Help dialog box.

To delete a macro:

1. Click the Macros button. The Macros dialog box will display.
2. Click the down arrow in the Macros in box and select where the macro is stored. The available macros will display above under Macro name.
3. Select the macro to be deleted.
4. Click the Delete button in the dialog box, and then confirm the deletion.

Organizing Macros

The Organizer dialog box helps you organize your macro modules. By using the Organizer, you can delete, rename, and copy macro modules.

Renaming a Macro Module

Renaming the macro module can help you keep your macros organized. The default name for a macro module is NewMacros, but it is easy to change that name. Like macro names, the macro module name cannot begin with numbers, and it cannot have spaces or symbols. When you rename a macro module, all the macros will remain within that module. However, when you create another new macro, Word will save the new macro in a new module named NewMacros. Therefore, if you intend to group several macros in one module, create all the macros before you rename the module.

> **CAUTION** When you rename a module, you will need to reassign keyboard or toolbar shortcuts, because the full name of the macro includes the name of the module where it is stored. To reassign a shortcut, see the section "Creating and Editing a Shortcut for an Existing Macro" earlier in this chapter.

To rename a macro module:

1. Click the Macros button in the Code group. The Macros dialog box will display.
2. Select Organizer. The Organizer dialog box will display.
3. If necessary, click the Macro Project Items tab. The macro modules saved to the active document display on the left. All macro modules saved to the Normal template display on the right. New macros are stored in the project named NewMacros.
4. Select the macro module to be renamed. If necessary, select a different option in the drop-down list for Macro Project Items available in.
5. Click Rename.
6. Enter a new name and click OK.

Copying a Macro Module

Macro modules are stored in a project, which is saved to a template. When you create a macro, you designate the document or template where you want to store it. At a later date, you may want to make the macro available in other documents and templates. You can use the Organizer to copy the macro module to other documents or templates. You cannot copy a module if the destination already lists a module with the same name. If necessary, rename the macro module before you copy it.

To copy a macro module:

1. Click the Macros button in the Code group (or press Alt+F8). The Macros dialog box will display.
2. Click the Organizer button in the dialog box. The Organizer dialog box will display.
3. If necessary, click the Macro Project Items tab. Two lists of macros will display. You can display available macro modules from two different templates or documents. If necessary, click the down arrow in the box labeled Macro Project Items available in, and choose a different document or template. If you don't see the document or template where the macro is stored, click Close File and then click Open File and browse for the document or template.
4. Select the macro module to be copied.

5. In the list opposite of where you have selected a macro name, click the down arrow in the box labeled Macro Project Items available in and select the document or template to which you want to copy.

6. Click Copy and then click Close.

Deleting a Macro Module

The Organizer also provides an option for removing macro modules. Remember, a module can contain multiple macros. You can remove the macro module from the current active document and/or from the Normal template.

To delete a macro project:

1. Click the Macros button in the Code group. The Macros dialog box will display.

2. Select Organizer. The Organizer dialog box will display.

3. If necessary, click the Macro Project Items tab. Two lists of macros will display. You can display available macro projects from two different templates or documents. If necessary, click the down arrow in the box labeled Macro Project Items available in, and choose a different document or template. If you don't see the document or template where the macro is stored, click Close File and then click Open File and browse for the document or template.

4. Select the macro project to be deleted. You can delete projects from either list.

5. Click Delete, and then confirm the deletion.

Locking a Macro Project

Just as you can lock documents, you can also lock macro projects. By locking a macro project, you can prevent users from making intentional or accidental changes to the macro. When you lock a project, you must save the project and close it before the changes take effect. When a user attempts to view the macros, he or she must enter a password. You should lock the macro project before you add your digital signature.

To lock a macro project:

1. Open the document containing the macro project.

2. Click the Visual Basic button in the Code group. The Visual Basic Editor will display.

3. Open the View menu and select Project Explorer (or press Ctrl+R).

4. Select the macro project to be locked.

5. Open the Tools menu and select Project Properties. The Project Properties dialog box will display.

6. Click the Protection tab. Under Lock project, turn on the option Lock project for viewing.

7. Enter a password, confirm the password, and then click OK.

8. Click the Save button in the Visual Basic Editor to save the changes.

9. Click the Word button or click the File menu and choose Close and Return to Microsoft Word, and then close the active document.

To unlock a project, repeat Steps 1 through 5 to display the Project Properties dialog box. Turn off the option Lock project for viewing, and remove the password. Then, save the project, return to the Word document, and close the document for the changes to take effect.

Digitally Signing a Macro Project

If you plan to share your macros with others, you can add a digital signature to a macro project, and those you share the macros with can add you as a trusted source (see "Adding Signatures to the Trusted Publishers List" later in this chapter). A digital signature will also confirm the authenticity of the macro and that the macro has not been altered since the signature was added. If you are widely distributing your macros publicly, you should sign them with a certified digital ID certificate (see "Obtaining a Digital Certificate" later in this chapter). However, if you are sharing your macros personally or within a small group of recipients, you can use a self-signed certificate.

Creating a Self-Signed Certificate

You can create your own self-signing certificate, but this ID can only be validated on your own computer. When you sign a macro, you are considered the publisher.

To create a self-signed certificate:

1. Click the Start button.

2. Select All Programs.

3. Select Microsoft Office.

4. Select Microsoft Office Tools.

5. Select Digital Certificate for VBA Projects. The Create Digital Certificate dialog box will display.

6. Enter a name for the certificate.

7. Click OK, and then confirm the new certificate.

Signing a Macro Project

Your digital signature confirms that you verify the contents at the time you sign it. When you add a digital signature to a macro project, obtain a timestamp if possible. That way, users can verify your signature even after the certificate expires.

Make sure your macro is final before adding the digital signature. If you edit the macro after signing it, the digital signature will be removed. If you have a valid digital certificate on your computer, the digital signature will automatically be added to the macro project when you save it. To digitally sign a macro project:

1. Open the document containing the macro project.
2. Click the Visual Basic button in the Code group to display the Visual Basic Editor.
3. Open the View menu and select Project Explorer (or press Ctrl+R).
4. Select the macro project to be signed.
5. Open the Tools menu and select Digital Signature. The Digital Signature dialog box will display.
6. Click the Choose button, select a digital certificate, and click OK twice.
7. Click the Word button or click the File menu and choose Close and Return to Microsoft Word.

Users can view the digital certificate by displaying the Visual Basic Editor, choosing the Tools menu, and selecting Digital Signature.

Obtaining a Digital Certificate

You can purchase a digital certificate from third-party authorities that provide signature services. The costs for these services vary depending on the services provided. Some providers offer prices with volume discounts.

To learn more about signature services:

1. Click the Microsoft Office button.
2. Select Prepare.
3. Select Add a Digital Signature. A dialog box will display referencing the digital signature service providers.
4. Click the Signature Services from the Office Marketplace button. You will be connected to a web site for Office Marketplace, and you can read about the partner companies that work with Microsoft to provide signature services.

Setting Macro Security Options

Macros can contain powerful code with many commands and can be used to spread computer viruses. The *Trust Center* helps protect your computer against these potentially invasive macros by checking digital signatures and displaying security alerts when there are problems with the digital signature.

Because macros can contain viruses, Word offers security levels for running macros. The settings can be adjusted in the Trust Center. If you set the options for

Word to warn you about macros in documents without trusted sources, a security alert dialog box will display, listing the reason(s) for the security alert as well as advice about what you should do. Obviously, when you receive a security alert, you should only enable the macro if you trust the source.

Changing the Trust Center Settings

The default setting will disable all macros with notification. With this setting, you have the option of running all macros, but only after you have been notified that the document contains a macro. When you receive notification of a macro, a security warning in the Message Bar will display. You can then choose to enable the content. If you are confident that the document is from a trusted source, you can turn on the option Trust all documents from this publisher. Future macros from this source will automatically be enabled without checking for a valid signature and without notification.

When you select the option Disable all macros with notification, the warning shown in Figure 10-4 will display in the Message Bar, just below the Ribbon.

Figure 10-4 *You can choose a setting to receive a notification when a document includes macros.*

When you select the option to disable all macros without notification, the document will open without a security warning. If the user attempts to run a macro, a prompt will display that all macros have been disabled.

When you choose the option to enable all macros, the document will also open without a security warning, and the macros will be enabled.

To set the macro security options:

1. Click the Macro Security button in the Code group. The Trust Center dialog box will open.

> **NOTE** If the Developer tab is not displayed, you can open the Trust Center dialog box by clicking the Microsoft Office button, selecting Word Options, selecting Trust Center, and then clicking Trust Center Settings.

2. Under Macro Settings, select an option and click OK.

Adding Signatures to the Trusted Publishers List

The Trusted Publishers list includes the signatures that you trust for digitally signed macros. When you set the trust settings to disable macros with notification or to disable macros except those that are digitally signed, Word will check for a digital signature. If the macros are digitally signed, Word will verify that the signature is from a trusted source. If the signature is not in the Trusted Publishers list, the warning shown in Figure 10-5 will display. You can choose to enable or disable the macros in the document. If you know the person connected to the invisible digital signature, and you trust the document is safe to open, you can add the signature to your list of trusted publishers by selecting the option Trust all from publisher.

Figure 10-5 *Word will verify digital signatures and let you know if they are in your Trusted Publishers list.*

To add a source to the Trusted Publishers list:

1. Click the Options button in the alert that displays in the Message Bar. The Microsoft Office Security Options dialog box will display with information about the signature. If desired, you can click a link to show details about the signature.

2. Turn on the option Trust all documents from this publisher.

3. Click OK.

The commands in the remaining groups on the Developer tab are presented in Chapter 11.

CHAPTER 11

Using Templates, Form Controls, and XML

Forms are used to collect a variety of information. You can use Word features to create both printed forms and online forms. You can connect the data collected in online forms to an Access database or an XML data system. This chapter addresses the features for creating online forms and explores how you can use Word to build your own XML data and incorporate that data in other Word documents.

Displaying the Developer Tab

The tools and options you need to work with form controls, XML, and templates are all available on the Developer tab (see Figure 11-1). By default, the Developer tab does not display in the Ribbon.

Figure 11-1 *The Developer tab displays commands for working with form controls, XML, and templates.*

To display the Developer tab:

1. Click the Microsoft Office button.
2. Choose Word Options.
3. Select Popular.
4. Under Top options for working with Word, select Show Developer tab in the Ribbon.

Using Templates

Document templates save you time and effort, because much of the work is done. A template contains predefined fonts, margins, styles, and layouts. Templates also contain content controls.

Creating a New Document Based on a Template

When you open a new document, Word offers hundreds of templates for you to choose from. Several of the templates are already installed, and many more are available at Microsoft Office Online. You can also create your own templates to add to the list. If you don't specify a template and you choose the Blank document option, Word will attach the Normal template.

Attaching a Template to a Document

If you want to access macros, styles, and building blocks that are stored in a different template from the one attached to your document, you can attach another template. To attach another template, you need to display the Template and Add-ins dialog box by clicking the Document Template button in the Templates group (see Figure 11-2). To utilize the new template styles, the names of the styles applied in your document must match the names of the styles in the template. If the style names match, you can automatically update the document styles.

Figure 11-2 *Use the Document Template button to display the Templates and Add-ins dialog box.*

To attach a different template to a document:

1. Click the Document Template button in the Templates group. The Templates and Add-ins dialog box will display.

2. Click the Attach button to locate the template. Word 2007 templates have a .dotx or a .dotm file name extension. Templates with a .dotm extension contain enabled macros.

3. Click Open. The Templates and Add-ins dialog box is still displayed.

4. To apply the styles in the template, make sure the option Automatically update document styles is checked.

5. Click OK.

If the style names don't match, after attaching the new template, you can replace the original style names with the new template style names. The quickest and easiest way to replace the style names is to use the Replace feature.

To replace the style names:

1. Click Ctrl+H to display the Replace tab in the Find and Replace dialog box. Click the More button to display all the options.

2. Click in the Find what box, remove any text entry if necessary, and then click the Format button at the bottom of the dialog box. In the drop-down list, choose Style, select the style name you want to replace, and click OK.

3. Click in the Replace with box, remove any text entry if necessary, and then click the Format button. In the drop-down list, choose the new style name, and then click OK.

4. Click Replace All, and then click OK.

5. Repeat Steps 2 through 4 to replace other style names and then close the dialog box.

Making a Template Global

To make a template available for all documents, you can designate the template as a global template. For example, the Normal.dotm template is global.

To make a template global:

1. Click the Document Template button in the Templates group. The Templates and Add-ins dialog box will display.

2. Under Global templates and add-ins, click the Add button. The Add Template dialog box will display.

3. Locate and select the template file and click OK. The template will be added to the list of global templates in the Templates and Add-ins dialog box.

4. Click OK.

The template will be global throughout your Word session. However, after exiting Word and launching the application again, the template will still be listed as a global template, but you will need to check the template in the Templates and Add-ins dialog box to load it. You can make a template available whenever you start Word by saving (or copying) the template in the Startup folder. To locate or change your Startup folder in Windows, the path looks like this:

- *Windows Vista*: \Users\username\AppData\Roaming\Microsoft\Word\Startup
- *Windows XP*: \Documents and Settings\username\Application Data\Microsoft\Word\Startup
- *Windows 2000*: \Program Files\Microsoft Office\Office

Using a Document As a Template

If you have a document that you want to use as a base for creating other documents, you can base your new documents on that existing document. The existing document functions like a template, but it does not need to be saved in a template format.

To create a new document based on an existing document:

1. Click the Microsoft Office button.
2. Choose New.
3. Select New from Existing. The New from Existing Document dialog box will display.
4. Locate the document on which you want to base the new document.
5. Click Create New. The new document opens and is exactly the same as the document on which it is based.

Using Form Controls

Like printed forms, many online forms include text instructions and some blank areas for users to respond. One of the advantages to using an online form is that you can use form controls to dictate the format of the answers. For example, you can use a form control that requires users to respond with a Yes or No answer, or you can use a form control that requires the user to choose from a list of predefined options. By dictating the format, you get more consistency in the information gathered.

You can create a form in a Word document and attach the form to an e-mail or make the form available on a server. You can also publish the form on a web page. Once the information is collected, you can compile and analyze the data using programs like Microsoft Access, Microsoft Excel, or Microsoft InfoPath. The Word 2007 controls are XML compatible, which means they can be used in documents that are to be opened in Word 2007 and in documents that are to be accessed in a web browser. However, the Word 2007 content controls will be converted to static text and graphics when opened in previous versions of Word. If users will be viewing the document in earlier versions of Word, see the section on "Using Legacy Tools" later in this chapter.

Creating a Form with Content Controls

Content controls (also called *form controls* or *form fields*) are predesigned elements that make it easy for you to create a form for online use. Content controls are what make online documents interactive. Buttons for the content controls are displayed in the Controls group on the Developer tab (see Figure 11-3). You can set the control options to meet your needs, and you can prevent users from editing or deleting the controls.

Figure 11-3 *The content control buttons are displayed in the Controls group.*

Word 2007 offers several new content controls and the legacy tools from previous versions of Word. The following list describes the purpose of each control:

- *Rich Text*: Provides a block of rich text. Rich text cannot be mapped to data in a custom XML part. You would use this control to create text that you don't want changed or accessed. For example, you could provide a privacy notation.

- *Text*: Provides a block of plain text. Plain text can be mapped to data in a custom XML part.

- *Picture Content Control*: Enables the user to select an image and insert it in the document. You can map a picture for an XML part. The picture is stored in base-64 binary format.

- *Combo Box*: Works similar to the Drop-Down List control. The difference is that the Combo Box control allows the user to edit the text.

- *Drop-Down List*: Provides a list of options in a drop-down menu. The data can be mapped to a custom XML part.

- *Date Picker*: Displays an interactive calendar, and the user can choose a date on the calendar. You can choose the date format.

- *Building Block Gallery*: Creates a placeholder so the user can choose a building block. from a building block gallery, such as Quick Parts or equations. You cannot map building blocks to XML data, but you can add building blocks to a content control, and the content control can be mapped to XML data.

- *Legacy Tools*: Provides a menu of the controls available in previous versions of Word. You would use these controls when the user is filling out the form using an earlier version of Word.

Inserting Content Controls

You should plan the layout of your form before you begin. Usually, it's more expedient to enter the boilerplate text first and then insert the content controls where needed. The content controls vary in length, so if you want to align the controls, using a table to organize the text and controls can make the task of formatting the form much easier. Figure 11-4 illustrates an online form with a table to organize the layout of the text and the controls. The controls will be inserted in the blank table cells.

Subscription·Notice¶

¶

Our·records·show·your·subscription·will·expire·in·30·days.·You·can·renew·your·subscription·today·by·confirming·your·address.·Please·complete·the·form·below·and·email·it·back·to·us·within·the·next·14·days.¶

¶

Yes.·Please·renew·my·subscription!¶

¶

¶

¶

First·Name¤ ¤		Last·Name¤ ¤		¤
Address¤ ¤				¤
City¤ ¤				¤
State¤ ¤		ZIP¤ ¤		¤
Telephone¤ ¤		Email¤ ¤		¤

¶

Figure 11-4 *Inserting the content controls in the table cells will help to align all the controls.*

When creating an online form with content controls, begin by saving the document as a template so you can create new documents from the template. The users will fill in the form in the new documents based on the template; the template itself will remain unchanged. To insert a content control, switch to design mode. In design mode, you can add or modify form controls. When you exit design mode, the controls will work as intended. To toggle the design mode on/off, click the Design Mode button in the Controls group. The command is turned on when the button displays with an orange background. Position the insertion point where you want the control to display and then select a control button in the Controls group.

To insert a content control:

1. Open a new document, enter the boilerplate text, and save the document as a template using the Word Template format with the extension (*.dotx).

2. Position the insertion point in the document where you want to insert the first control. (Or, select text in the document where you want to insert the control.) If you are using a table for the form layout, position the insertion point in a table cell.

3. Click one of the content control buttons in the Controls group.

4. Leave the document open.

Setting the Properties for Content Controls

Properties vary among the content controls. For example, the Date Picker offers format options displaying the date in a control box, while the Rich Text and Text control properties include an option to use a style to format the contents. You can also select an option to lock the controls to keep others from intentionally or accidentally removing or editing the content of the control.

When establishing the properties for the control, you can add an optional title, which will display when the control is selected (see Figure 11-5). The title name is used to refer to a control in a macro or a program. You may think a title is not necessary, because when you insert the Date Picker control, the placeholder text in the field box reads "Click here to enter a date." However, once the user chooses a date, the field content changes to the date the user selected, and there is no title to provide information about the box.

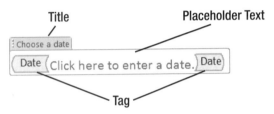

Figure 11-5 *You can establish a title and a tag name in the Content Controls Properties dialog box.*

Entering a tag name for the properties is also optional, and you can use the same name as the title. The tag name is visible only in design mode (see Figure 11-5), even when the control is not selected. The tag name is used to refer to the XML element. Whenever you add a tag name to a control, you create an XML element.

To enter or change the properties for a content control:

1. If necessary, turn on design mode and select the control in the document.

2. Click the Properties button in the Controls group (or right-click the control and choose Properties). The Content Control Properties dialog box will display.

3. In the Title box, enter the text you want to display as the title for the content control.

4. In the Tab box, enter the text to identify the XML element.

5. If you want the user's response to replace your instructions for the Rich Text and the Text controls, turn on the option Remove content control when contents are edited. Then, click OK.

6. Add some more controls to the document and leave the document open.

Figure 11-6 illustrates the online form with the content controls inserted in the table cells. The document is displayed in design mode. Notice that the tab names display for each control. Figure 11-7 illustrates the same online form with design mode turned off.

Figure 11-6 *The content controls in this document are displayed with design mode turned on.*

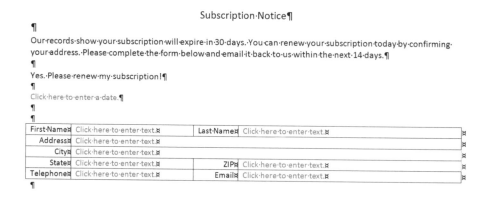

Figure 11-7 *The content controls in this document are displayed with design mode turned off.*

Adding Instructional Text

You can add instructional text to help the user complete the form. The instructional text is labeled as placeholder text (as shown earlier in Figure 11-5). Some controls already display default placeholder text, such as *Click here to enter text.*, but you can change that text if desired. You can even format the placeholder text with a style. The placeholder text will display only when the content control is empty.

To add instructional text:

1. If necessary, turn on design mode and select the control for which you want to add instructional text.
2. Select the existing placeholder text, and enter new text.
3. If desired, format the placeholder text. The revised placeholder text is saved when you exit design mode.

Grouping Content Controls

If you plan to use parts of the form again, you can group some of the controls. Then you can copy and paste them into a new document. All the property settings will stay with the controls.

When you select a control within a group, a border displays around all the controls in the group (see Figure 11-8). When you position the mouse pointer within a group, the background of the group shows a blue shading. You can position the insertion point inside the group and add more controls to the group.

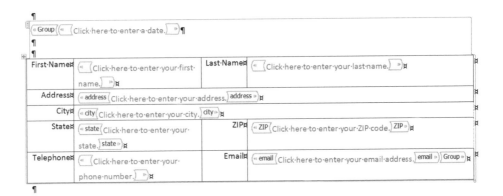

Figure 11-8 *When a group of controls is selected in design mode, a border displays around the group.*

To group multiple content controls:

1. Hold down Shift and click all the controls you want to include in the group. Text between the controls will also be selected. (If controls are inserted in table cells, you must select the entire table.)
2. Click the Group button in the Controls group.
3. Select the Group command. Tabs labeled "Group" will display at the beginning and end of the selected controls.

> **TIP** To lock multiple controls so they cannot be deleted, group the content controls, select the group, click Properties in the Controls group, and turn on Content control cannot be deleted.

Using Legacy Tools

If you open a document with the new Word 2007 content controls in an earlier version of Word, the controls will be converted to static text and will be unusable. Therefore, if you know the user of the form will be opening the document in a previous version of Word, you must use the Legacy Tools button options to create your form. The legacy tools include the basic form controls that are available on the Forms toolbar in previous versions of Word. Among the popular legacy tools is the Check Box control. The Legacy Tools button options also include the ActiveX Controls options, where you'll find another popular control, the Option button (often referred to as the radio button). All of these controls function well when the form is to be filled out in Word. However, the ActiveX controls do not function in many browsers.

When you insert an ActiveX control and click the Properties command, the control displays similarly to how it displays in earlier versions of Word. When you click the Properties command in the Properties group, instead of a dialog box displaying, the Properties task pane will display, just as it does in earlier versions of Word.

You can combine Word 2007 content controls and legacy tools in the same document. For example, if you want to limit the characters in a text content control, you will need to use the legacy Text Box form field. However, take caution when you combine the two types of controls. If you plan to create a database with the information you collect from the form, using the two types of controls may make the programming for the database complicated, and the database may not be able to read data from both types of controls.

Converting Controls to Word 2007

If you open a document with controls created in an earlier version of Word, you may need to convert the controls for Word 2007.

To convert legacy controls to Word 2007:

1. Open the document created in an earlier version of Word. A security alert may display because of the ActiveX controls.

2. Click the Microsoft Office button.

3. Click Convert. A prompt will display a warning that the layout of the document may change.

4. Click OK.

Restricting Users from Editing the Document

When you're preparing an online form, it sounds contradictory to say "restrict the user from editing the document" because you obviously expect users to change the document when they fill in the form. However, you don't want users to be able to edit the document because they could change the content and the overall layout of the form. They could even remove the content controls (either purposely or accidentally). So, it is important to protect the document by restricting the user from making changes to the document, except where there are content controls. To establish editing restrictions that allow users to only fill in forms, you use the Protect Document command in the Protect group (see Figure 11-9). More information about other formatting and editing restrictions is covered in Chapter 9.

Figure 11-9 *You can protect the document so the user can only make changes in the document by responding to the content controls.*

After specifying the restrictions, you enter a password so other users cannot remove the protection. Be sure to remember your password, or write it down and keep it in a safe place. If you can't recall your password, you won't be able to edit the document.

To protect the entire document and still allow users to fill in the form:

1. Click the Protect Document button in the Protect group. The Restrict Formatting and Editing task pane will display.

2. Under Editing restrictions, turn on Allow only this type of editing in the document.

3. In the drop-down box, select Filling in forms.

4. Under Start enforcement, click Yes, Start Enforcing Protection.

5. Enter a password twice and click OK.

If you attempt to delete or edit a content control in a protected document, the Restrict Formatting and Edits task pane will display, with a message noting that the document is protected. To remove the protection, click the Stop Protection button at the bottom of the pane. If the protection is password protected, you will need to enter the password before the protection is removed.

Understanding XML

The intent of this section is to provide a conceptual overview of XML so you can understand how XML can read tags created in Word. However, it is beyond the scope of this book to get into the details. To learn more about XML, you can refer to *Office 2003 XML for Power Users* by Matthew MacDonald (Apress, 2004) and *Beginning XML with DOM and Ajax: From Novice to Professional* by Sas Jacobs (Apress, 2006).

XML (Extensible Markup Language) is a data format that uses elements to describe the information contained in a document. Unlike HTML, which describes the look and feel of a document, XML describes the data structure of a document. You can use XML to mark information in a Word document so the data can be sorted, filtered, and manipulated for use in other applications. If the application supports XML, it can read, interpret, and process your XML data.

Word XML features were first introduced in the Office 2003 suite, allowing users to save XML elements with the document. If users move or delete some of the XML elements, the entire document is damaged. The new Word 2007 format stores pieces of document information into separate XML files. For example, information about the header and footer for a document would be stored in a separate file from information about the body of the document. This new format makes the information easier to recover and more secure. The XML commands are accessible in the XML group on the Developer tab (see Figure 11-10).

Figure 11-10 *The XML features provide a means for exchanging data between applications.*

To demonstrate how XML can be used in Word documents, consider the following scenario: every time a company receives referrals for a prospective customer, the company sends a letter of introduction. When the letter is created, the contact information is marked with XML tags. The tagged information can be used for several other purposes. For example, the company can extract the data and use it to create customized merge letters or mailing labels for promotions. When a prospective customer buys company goods, the data can be used for invoices.

You're probably thinking, "Why doesn't the company just create a database?" The answer is that XML data is not limited to the application that captured it. XML data can be manipulated with numerous applications and operating systems. If the company outsources its billing, as long as the billing service company uses software that is compatible with XML, the XML data can be easily transferred between databases. So what is XML, and how does it work? The following sections describe how to use XML features to capture the data for the scenario provided.

Using Schemas

If you are working with others and sharing documents, you want to be sure everyone is using the same rules for naming and structuring the elements. A *schema* specifies a set of rules for the XML elements. A portion of a schema is illustrated in Figure 11-11. These rules provide guidelines for structuring and validating the data. You can change these rules as needed. The plus side of using schemas is they help identify and evade corruptive data.

```
    targetNamespace="urn:schemas-Schema:word:xml">
 - <xsd:element name="contacts">
   - <xsd:complexType>
     - <xsd:sequence>
         <xsd:element name="contacts" type="cm:contacts" minOccurs="0" maxOccurs="unbounded" />
       </xsd:sequence>
     </xsd:complexType>
   </xsd:element>
 - <xsd:complexType name="contacts">
   - <xsd:all>
         <xsd:element name="title" type="xsd:string" />
         <xsd:element name="firstname" type="xsd:string" />
         <xsd:element name="lastname" type="xsd:string" />
         <xsd:element name="address" type="xsd:string" />
         <xsd:element name="city" type="xsd:string" />
         <xsd:element name="state" type="xsd:string" />
         <xsd:element name="ZIP" type="xsd:string" />
     </xsd:all>
   </xsd:complexType>
 </xsd:schema>
```

Figure 11-11 *A schema provides guidelines for structuring and validating the XML data.*

You can create your own schema with elements, formats, and document structure, but that is beyond the scope of this book. Custom schemas are generally created by developers. Once the schema is created, you must add it to the schema library. Schemas usually have an .xsd file name extension, while XML data files use the .xml extension.

To add a schema to the schema library:

1. Open the document to which you want to attach a schema.

2. Display the Developer tab.

3. Click the Schema button in the XML group. The XML Schema tab in the Templates and Add-ins dialog box will display.

4. Under Available XML schemas, select a schema. (You may see a built-in schema for contacts that you can select.) Make sure the box has a checkmark. If you want to select a custom schema that is not in the list, click Add Schema, browse for the file, and add the schema to the library.

5. Click OK. The schema is attached to the document.

Displaying XML Structure

The XML structure provides a map of the relationship of all the document pieces stored in the separate files. XML shows a hierarchical structure of the document by labeling all the elements in the document. You can view the XML structure at any time by clicking the Structure button in the XML group on the Developer tab.

The lower portion of the XML Structure task pane displays the available elements in the schema that is attached to the document. The upper portion of the task pane displays the elements, if any, that have been applied in the document (see Figure 11-12).

Figure 11-12 *The XML Structure pane displays the elements that are applied in a document.*

To view all the elements in the schema, turn off the option List only child elements of current element. The hierarchical structure is now evident (see Figure 11-13).

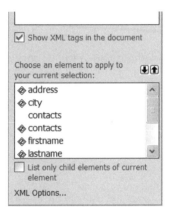

Figure 11-13 *To view all the elements in the structure of the schema, turn off the option List only child elements of current element.*

To identify data in the document:

1. If necessary, turn on the option List only child elements of current element.
2. Enter some contact information in the document (your name and address).
3. Select the contact information.
4. Click the contacts element in the XML Structure pane. A prompt will display.
5. Select Apply to Entire Document. Tags will be inserted at the beginning and the end of the selection.
6. Turn off the option List only child elements of current element.
7. Select the first name in the document and then select firstname in the XML Structure task pane. The selected text in the document will be marked with tags (see Figure 11-14). The element you applied to the text will be listed under Elements in the document at the top of the task pane (see Figure 11-15).

> **NOTE** When working with the document, you can hide the tags in the document by turning off the Show XML tags option in the XML Structure task pane.

8. Repeat Step 7 to tag the remaining contact data in the document.

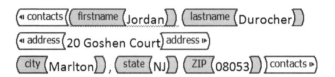

Figure 11-14 *Tags indicate where elements have been applied in the document.*

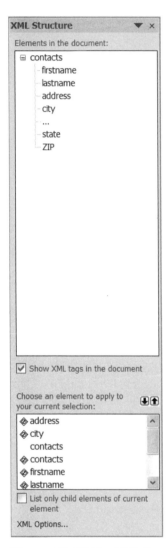

Figure 11-15 *The XML Structure pane illustrates the hierarchal structure of the schema.*

Setting XML Options

When you click the XML Options command at the bottom of the XML Structure task pane, the XML Options dialog box displays. The following explains the options available in this dialog box:

- *Save data only*: Only XML tags and contents from the attached schema are saved. Information about properties, formats, and layout settings is not saved.

- *Apply custom transform*: Extracts the elements you want and formats the information for another document. For example, you may want to use data from a newsletter document and apply a transform to create a web page.

- *Validate document against attached schemas*: Checks the validity of the document against the attached schema(s). Validation errors are noted with purple wavy lines.

- *Hide schema violations in this document*: Hides the purple wavy lines that indicate errors.

- *Ignore mixed content*: When turned off, entries of text outside of the XML elements are displayed as three dots in the XML Structure task pane. When turned on, the three dots will not display in the task pane.

- *Allow saving as XML even if not valid*: You can save the XML document, even if the document doesn't have all the required information for the attached schema.

- *Hide namespace alias in XML Structure task pane*: Alias names are displayed without the namespace identifiers. It may be easier to read the XML element hierarchy in the task pane.

- *Show advanced XML error messages*: Displays detailed error messages. When turned off, the messages are less informative.

- *Show placeholder text for all empty elements*: Alerts the user that there is an empty XML element in the document.

CHAPTER 12

Publishing Documents

You've completed a document, and you're ready to distribute it. Now, you need to decide whether you want others to access the document, and if so, how. Whether it's a draft or a final copy, you want to be sure the document is ready for others to review. Although it may sound rote, you need to proof all documents. Use the spelling and the grammar tools in the Proofing group on the Review tab. Then, preview the document using the different views. For example, display the document in Full Screen Reading view. If the document contains revisions marks and/or comments, choose the Final option in the Tracking group on the Review tab.

Now you're ready to publish, by printing, electronic distribution, or even on a web site. Lets' see how.

Printing a Document

We're not a paperless society yet. We still frequently depend on hard copies of documents. For many documents, especially long ones, duplex printing and booklet printing can save paper and even make reading easier.

Using Duplex Printing

Does your printer support duplex printing? To check, click the Microsoft Office button, select Print, and then select Properties in the Print dialog box. If you see any duplex printing or two-sided printing options, your printer offers that feature. Most Print dialog boxes will include an option for manual duplex. When you turn this option on, Word will print all the odd pages, and then prompt you to turn the pages over, insert them in the paper feeder again, and press OK to print on the other side. If you don't see any duplex printing options, you can still print the document on both sides of the paper. You simply print the odd and even pages separately.

To manually print the document on both sides of the paper:

1. Click the Microsoft Office button and choose Print to open the Print dialog box.

2. In the Print what box, select odd pages.

3. Put the pages back in the printer paper feeder.

4. In the Print what box, select even pages.

Printing a Booklet

If you are printing a program, invitation, or newsletter with a single centerfold, you can quickly format the margin settings to adjust for the centerfold.

To format the margins for printing a booklet:

1. Show the Page Layout tab.

2. Click the Margins button.

3. Select Custom Margins at the bottom of the menu. The Page Setup dialog box will display.

4. Under Pages, in the Multiple pages box, select Book fold.

Using Other Print Options

Even if you're not printing duplex pages or a booklet, you should consider some of the other print options that are available. The options vary, of course, depending on the printer you are using. Print options include print quality, paper quality, watermarks, document sizing, color management, and so forth. Many of the options are based on the printer and can be accessed in the Print dialog box. Several other print options can be accessed in Word. Generally, when you apply a Word print option, the Word option will override any options you select in the Print dialog box.

To view your printer options:

1. Click the Microsoft Office button.

2. Choose Print. The Print dialog box will display. If more than one printer is available, select the desired printer.

3. To view the available options for the selected printer, click the Properties button. See Table 12-1 for a description of some of the common printer options.

> **CAUTION** The setting for each of the options described in Table 12-1, and for those in Tables 12-2 and 12-3 a little later in this section, will remain enabled for printing all future documents. If you don't want a particular setting to apply to future printing, open the Print dialog box and turn the option off.

Table 12-1. Printer Options

Option	Description
Print to file	This feature is useful if the printer is not available. When you choose this option, you are prompted to save the file. To print the file, you must specify an LPT port (USB printers won't work).
Print quality	If you're going to use the printed pages to make multiple copies on a copier, you want high-quality printing. And, if you're printing a resume or a formal invitation or announcement, you will want high-quality printing. But if you are printing hard-copy drafts or documents that do not need to impress anyone, you can save ink or toner by choosing draft quality, and you will also save time because your document will print much faster.
Print color	You can choose to print in grayscale or black ink only. The grayscale option is useful when your document contains color graphics and you will be duplicating the document in black and white. The black ink only option is useful when you don't use colors in your document. Some computers use colors such as dark green to print black text. By choosing the black only option, you save your color ink, and you also save time because black-and-white printing is generally much faster than color printing.
Print in reverse order	When you're printing multiple page documents, it's convenient to use this option. Allow the pages to stack in the printer tray. When the last page is printed, you can pick up all the pages, and they are already in the correct sequence.
Mirror image	This feature is especially useful if you are printing iron-on transfers. When you create the transfer image, everything is backwards and presented in a mirror image. If you don't have this option on your printer, you can flip the text and images in the graphic before you print the transfer sheet.
Watermarks (or stamp background)	If you make a last-minute decision to add a watermark, you can choose from preformatted watermarks and apply them just before you click the Print button. The watermark will be added to all pages in the document. Be sure to turn this feature off so it won't print for all future printings.
Ink volume	When using an inkjet printer, you can adjust the amount of ink printed on a page. In addition to conserving the amount of ink you use, the printed pages will dry much quicker. On the other hand, if you choose to increase the ink volume, you can change the settings to slow down the process between pages to allow extra time for the ink on the pages to dry.

4. To set options for all Word documents, click the Options button in the Print dialog box to quickly display this dialog box. (Or, click the Microsoft Office button, choose Word Options, and then select Display.) The settings are listed under Printing options. See Table 12-2 for a description of the Word printing options.

Table 12-2. Word Printing Options

Option	Description
Print drawings created in Word	You can choose to not print drawings and floating text boxes, which will make the printing go much faster. A blank box is printed in place of each drawing.
Print background colors and images	When you format pages for others to view online, background colors and images can enhance the appearance of the document. When you print the pages, you can choose to print these enhancements.
Print document properties	The document and the document properties will print on separate pages.
Print hidden text	You can use the hidden text format (an option in the Font dialog box) to add text to a document that you don't want to appear in the printed document. If you decide to allow others to see this text in the printed document, you must turn this option on.
Update fields before printing	If you don't always remember to update fields, you can turn this option on to ensure that all printed documents will have updated field data.
Update linked data before printing	If you create a link to another document, such as an Excel spreadsheet chart, this option will ensure that the document will print the most recent data in the chart.

5. To view additional Word printing options, click the Microsoft Office button, choose Word Options, select Advanced, and scroll down to the Print section. See Table 12-3 for a description of additional Word printing options.

Table 12-3. Additional Word Printing Options

Option	Description
Use draft quality	If you are printing hard-copy drafts or documents that do not need to impress anyone, you can save ink or toner with this option, and you can save time because your document will print much faster.
Print in background	When enabled, this option allows you to continue working in Word while the document is printing. When this option is turned off, you will need to wait until the spooling to the printer is finished.
Print pages in reverse order	When you're printing multiple-page documents, it's convenient to use this option. Allow the pages to stack in the printer tray. When the last page is printed, you can pick up all the pages, and they are already in the correct sequence.
Print XML tags	The XML tags that display in your document do not print. If you want the XML tags to show on the printed document, you must turn on this option.

Table 12-3. Additional Word Printing Options

Option	Description
Print field codes instead of their values	By default, field codes do not print. Instead, the field values print. If you want field codes to print, you can turn on this option, which is useful if you want to review the fields inserted in a merge document.
Print on front of the sheet for duplex printing	If your printer supports duplex printing, you need to enable this option for the duplex printing feature to work correctly. Some printers guide you through the manual duplex printing steps. To follow these steps and successfully print on both sides of the paper, you must turn this option on.
Print on back of the sheet for duplex printing	If your printer supports duplex printing, you need to enable this option for the duplex printing feature to work correctly. Some printers guide you through the manual duplex printing steps. To follow these steps and successfully print on both sides of the paper, you must turn this option on.
Scale content for A4 or 8.5"×11" paper sizes	You may format some of your documents with page layout settings for a page size that is larger than the standard A4 or 8.5"×ll" paper size, When you enable this option, Word will automatically scale the document to make sure it fits on an 8.5"×11" sheet of paper.
Print PostScript over text	This option applies only to PostScript-compatible printers (usually laser printers). PostScript is a programming language that uses object-oriented (vector) graphics instead of bit-mapped graphics, which provides better print quality. Enable this option when printing a document that contains Print fields.
Print only the data from a form	When you're printing an online form, you can choose to print only the data from the form. This option is very useful if you are manually tabulating a set of surveys.

Preparing Documents for Electronic Distribution

If you're not printing the document, you're likely planning to electronically share the document file with others. When you permit others to access the file digitally, you become vulnerable. There are several options for formatting and distributing documents electronically, including a template format, PDF or XPS formats, or as a web page.

Saving a Documents As a Template

No doubt you've already saved the document several times, but now you need to determine the appropriate file format for those who will access the document. The format depends on how they'll use the document. If you want to use the document to create future documents, the template format is a good choice. Templates are discussed in more detail in Chapter 11.

To save a document as a template file:

1. Click the Microsoft Office button.

2. Click the arrow to the right of the Save As command.

3. Select Word Template. The Save As dialog box displays. Notice that Word Template (*.dotx) is already selected in the Save as type box.

4. Enter a name in the File name box and click Save.

Saving a Document in PDF or XPS Format

If you want others to be able to read or print, but not change, a document, save the document in a format so that it cannot be edited or modified. For example, newsletters, flyers, resumes, and press releases are commonly distributed and shared online. You want users to be able to open and read the documents, and possibly even print them, but you don't want them to be able to edit the documents. Even if users do not choose to print the document, the display of the document is affected by the type of printer installed on the computer. The difference in printers may change the wrapping of a single line in a paragraph, which may change the way all the text fits on a page.

There are options to protect you for all of these scenarios. If you want to be sure readers see a document just as you see it on your computer, save the document in PDF (Portable Document Format) or XPS (XML Paper Specification) format. You are most likely familiar with PDF, which was created by the Adobe Systems more than 15 years ago. Adobe offers free downloads, so many computer users are familiar with the application. Microsoft just introduced XPS and integrated the XPS technologies in Windows Vista and Office 2007 applications. PDF and XPS are very similar. They both use an open format so documents can be viewed and printed on all computers. When documents are saved in the PDF or XPS format, you can preserve the format settings, and users also won't be able to edit the document. The PDF and XPS formats are also good for commercial printing.

To open a document saved in PDF format, the user must have Adobe Reader installed. To open a document saved in XPS format, the user must have the XPS Document Reader, which is integrated in 2007 Microsoft Office applications and Windows Vista. Downloads are available at Microsoft.com so you can view XPS documents using Windows XP and Windows Server 2003.

To save a document in PDF or XPS format:

1. Click the Microsoft Office button.

2. Choose Save As.

3. Select PDF or XPS.

> **NOTE** If the PDF or XPS option is not available in the menu, you must install add-in software. You can find the add-in at the Microsoft Office web site: go to http://www.microsoft.com/downloads and enter **PDF** in the search box.

Saving a Document As a Web Page

All Word documents can be saved in a format to be published on the Web. You can publish reports, company information, and newsletters so the documents are available for others to view in a web browser. You can save the document directly to the web server, or you can save the document on your computer and upload the document later. To publish the documents on the Web, you need to save the document using a web page format. Word now offers three web page formats:

- *Web Page (*.htm; *.html)*: The web page and the initial files are saved in separate files. If you plan to reopen and edit the document in Word, you want to use this format because the HTML codes and Word codes are both saved. Hence, the file size is much larger.
- *Single File Web Page (*.mht; *.mhtml)*: The web page and the initial files are saved as a single document. This is convenient for finding and accessing all the files related to a web page (such as graphics). The drawback is that the file cannot be viewed in all browsers, especially browsers older than Internet Explorer 4.0.
- *Web Page, Filtered (*.htm; *.html)*: The Word codes are removed from the document and the format is entirely HTML code. Hence, the file size is significantly smaller, the page will open much faster in a browser, and it is much easier for someone who knows HTML code to edit the document. If you don't plan on reopening and editing the document in Word, you should use this format.

To save a document as a web page:

1. Click the Microsoft Office button and click Save As. The Save As dialog box will display.
2. In the Save as type box, select one of the three web page formats.
3. After selecting the file type, the Change Title button will display in the Save As dialog box. Click the Change Title button, enter a title, and click OK. The document will display in Web Layout view.
4. Click the Tools button in the bottom-left corner of the Save As dialog box. The Web Options dialog box will display, and you can change the several settings including the compatibility for browsers and the screen resolution (Picture tab).
5. If necessary, change the location of the file, and then click Save.

After you save the document in a web page format, the Document Information Panel will no longer display. Instead, when you choose the Properties command in the Prepare menu, the Properties dialog box will display. You also may lose some functionality in the Word features. For example, if you convert a newsletter to a web page format, the column formats and headers and footers may be removed.

Updating the Information in the Document Information Panel

Before you share a document, make sure the document includes all the information you want to share. For example, you may want users to be able to see who created a document. This information is stored in the Document Information Panel.

To edit the information in the Document Information Panel:

1. Click the Microsoft Office button.
2. Choose Prepare.
3. Select Properties. The Document Information Panel will display.
4. Enter information in the properties boxes. You can also add comments about the document.
5. To review more information about the document, click the down arrow next to Document Properties.
6. Select Advanced Properties. The Document Name Properties dialog box will display, and you can display each of the tabs to review and/or add information.

Inspecting a Document

If the recipients of your document aren't your coworkers, or if you're not collaborating with them on a document, you probably don't want to share hidden text, comments, or revision marks. Maybe you don't want users to see who created a document, when it was created, or how much time was spent editing it. You can remove this information from the document.

To remove sensitive information about the properties of a document:

1. Click the Microsoft Office button.
2. Choose Prepare.
3. Select Inspect Document. The Document Inspector dialog box will display. By default, all content areas are selected
4. Deselect the content areas you do not wish to inspect.
5. Click the Inspect button in the dialog box. The results of the inspection will display. If sensitive information is identified, a Remove All button will display in the inspection results.
6. Click Remove All to remove any content you do not want users to see.

Encrypting a Document

Encrypting a document prevents unauthorized users from opening your document. It also prevents others from accessing the document contents through other software. When you encrypt a document, you are prompted to add a password. When you reopen the document, you must know the password. (Be sure to keep the password in a secure place.) When the document is reopened with a password, it is decrypted.

To encrypt a document:

1. Click the Microsoft Office button.
2. Choose Prepare.
3. Select Encrypt Document. A prompt will display.
4. Enter a password and then confirm the password.

Adding a Digital Signature to a Document

A digital signature confirms the authenticity of the document. When you share your documents, those who access the document can trust that you were the person who created the document and that you were the last person to access the document. If you are sharing legal documents or contracts for large sums, you should consider subscribing to a third-party certification service. However, if you are sharing your documents personally within a small group of recipients, you can use a self-signed certificate.

Once you add a signature to a document, the View Signatures command is available when you click Prepare. If the document is edited after the signature is added, the signature is automatically removed. Thus, if you add a signature to a document and then make some changes in the document, you must add the signature again.

To add a digital signature to a document:

1. Click the Microsoft Office button.
2. Choose Prepare.
3. Select Add a Digital Signature. The Sign dialog box will display. (If you do not have a digital signature certificate from a service provider, you will likely see a message box with information about the benefits of acquiring a certificate. Click OK to create a self-signed certificate.)
4. If desired, enter information about the purpose of the signature. Users will see this information when they choose Signature Details under Valid Signatures in the task pane.
5. The signature last used will display. If necessary, click the Change button to select another name for the signer. (To add additional self-signed signatures, see "Creating a Self-Signed Certificate" in Chapter 10.)
6. Click Sign, and then click OK.

> **NOTE** If you don't have a digital ID, you can obtain a digital certificate from your internal security administrator or Information Technology (IT) professional. Or, you can purchase a digital certificate from third-party authorities. Click the Microsoft Office button, choose Prepare, and then select Add a Digital Signature. In the message box, click Signatures Services from the Office Marketplace. You will be connected to a web site with information about the services available through Microsoft partners.

Marking a Document As Final

When you mark a document as final, the user cannot enter new text or edit existing text. The proofing tools are also disabled. The Marked as Final button will display in the status bar. Users can access the document only as a read-only document. However, the user can make changes by saving the document under a new name. This option is not really a secure protection. If the user is familiar with this feature, he or she can choose the Mark as Final command to toggle the option off.

Remember, if you make any changes to a document after you add a digital signature, the signature will no longer be valid. Therefore, if you plan to add a digital signature to the document, the signature must be added after you mark the document as final.

To mark a document as final:

1. Click the Microsoft Office button.
2. Choose Prepare.
3. Select Mark as Final.
4. When prompted, click OK. The Marked as Final icon displays in the status bar.

Running the Compatibility Checker

Sometimes, elements and formatting, such as SmartArt, become static text when a document is converted so it can be opened in earlier versions of Word. When you run the compatibility checker, Word checks the content of a document to determine whether there will be any problems converting the document to earlier versions of Word. Any compatibility issues will be noted in the Microsoft Office Word Compatibility Checker dialog box (see Figure 12-1). Many of the known issues will include a Help link so you can search for related information about the issue. The Compatibility Checker is discussed in more detail in Chapter 2, and the topic includes information about a compatibility pack for users of Word 2003, Word 2002, and Word 2000.

To check the compatibility of a document:

1. Click the Microsoft Office button.
2. Choose Prepare.
3. Select Run Compatibility Checker.

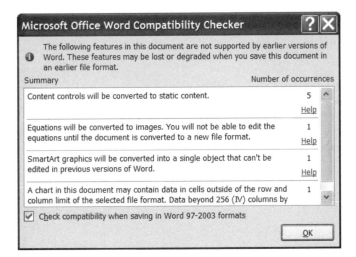

Figure 12-1 *The Compatibility Checker warns you of any problems converting the document for earlier versions of Word.*

Publishing to a Blog

Blogs are an open forum where users can express their opinions and post them on the Internet. Because they are posted on the Web, blogging services generally require that the content be created in HTML code. Word 2007 offers a new template that does all the coding for you. When you use the blog template, your documents can be published directly to blog sites. You can, of course, create your blog entry at your blog site. But if you prefer to take advantage of the proofing and editing tools in Word and create and edit the blog in Word first, you can easily post your blog from Word.

To post a blog, you must be a registered user with a Microsoft-enabled blog provider. The first time you try to create a blog post, you will be prompted to register your blog service. After you have completed the registration, you can begin creating blog posts. When you open a new blog post template, the Ribbon changes to display only two tabs. The first tab that displays is the Blog Post tab (see Figure 12-2).

Figure 12-2 *When you open a blog post document, the Blog Post tab displays.*

To create a new blog post:

1. Click the Microsoft Office button.

2. Choose Publish.

3. Select Blog. The Blog Post tab will display.

The groups on the tab should be very familiar, except for the first group. The Blog group shown in Figure 12-3 provides options for accessing and managing existing blogs and blog accounts.

Figure 12-3 *The commands in the Blog group help you access and manage your blogs and blog accounts.*

- The Publish button offers two options: to publish or to publish as a draft. If you choose Publish as a Draft, you can sign into the blog and review the entry.
- The Home Page button takes you to the home page of your blog site.
- The Insert Category button enables you to select a category where you want to post the blog entry.
- Use the Open Existing button to open an existing blog post.
- Click the Manage Accounts button to add and remove your blog accounts.

The Insert tab is also available for creating and formatting blogs (see Figure 12-4). The options available include tables, illustrations, links, WordArt, and symbols. The functionality for the graphics is gone, though, because the objects are converted to static graphics. Before you insert illustrations and WordArt, make sure your blog provider supports graphics.

Figure 12-4 *The Insert tab incudes buttons for inserting tables, graphics, and hyperlinks.*

When you are ready to publish your blog post, you have two options: you can publish it immediately, or you can publish it as a draft. The blog post will be saved to your blog server, but it will not be posted. When you log in to your blog server using your normal log on procedure, you can review and approve the blog post.

Publishing on a Document Management Server

To make a document easily accessible for many users, you can publish it on a document management server (such as SharePoint, shown in Figure 12-5 and also a little later in Figures 12-6 and 12-7). The document management server enables users to collaborate by sharing documents and information. Team members access the documents and information on a team web site. Businesses can choose from several sources for this service.

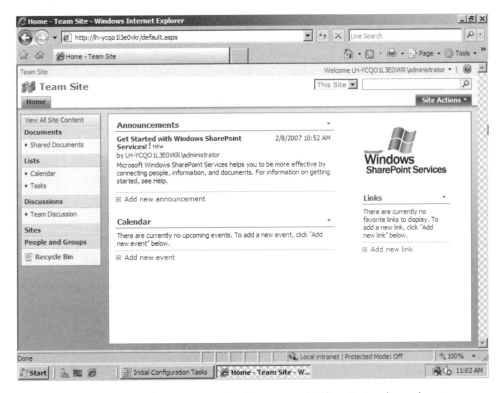

Figure 12-5 *Team members access the documents in SharePoint through a team web site.*

When you publish a Word document to SharePoint, the document is stored in a library. You can choose to store the document in the default Document Library, or you can create a new library. You can also post graphics in the Pictures Library (see Figure 12-6).

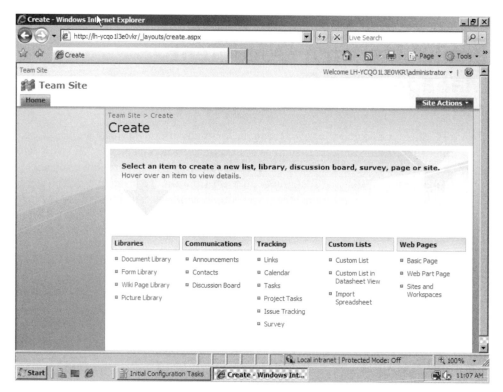

Figure 12-6 *When you post documents in SharePoint, they are added to the Document Library.*

To publish a document on a document management server:

1. Click the Microsoft Office button.

2. Choose Publish.

3. Select Document Manager Server. The Save As dialog box will display.

4. Browse and select the location where you want the document saved (the URL for the web site) and then click Save.

Creating a Document Workspace

A *document workspace* is a web site available within the SharePoint web site. You can create a document workspace to work with a document that is stored in a document library. The workspace web site is equipped with several management tools that enable you to share files, update files, and track and report the status of the files (see Figure 12-7).

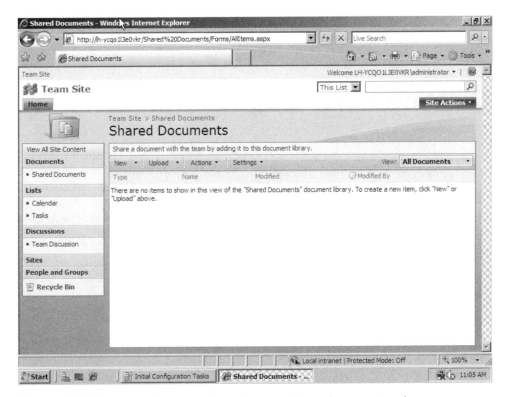

Figure 12-7 *Team members can share documents in a document workspace.*

When you post your Word document to the site, it is copied to the document library. You can work with Word or Word XML documents. You can work with your copy of the document directly in Word, or you can work with the file on the document workspace site. Then, you simply update your second copy. Team members can also access your document at the same time you are working with it. You can monitor changes to the document when others access and edit the copy you make available on the document workspace. You can also share the document with others and keep your own copy synchronized.

To create a document workspace:

1. Click the Microsoft Office button.
2. Choose Publish.
3. Select Create Document Workspace. The Document Workspace task pane will display.
4. Enter a document workspace name.
5. Enter a location for the new workspace (the URL for the document workspace web site).
6. Click Create.

Creating a Web Page

Creating a web page is the same as creating a typical Word document. If you are planning on developing a few basic pages, you can quickly create them in Word. However, if you plan to create a complex web site, you can work more efficiently using applications such as Microsoft FrontPage or Dreamweaver because these applications automate many of the formatting and design features that you would want to use. The following list provides some suggestions for creating a web page document:

- As you create the page, display it in Web Layout view so you know how it will appear in a browser. Click the Web Layout button in the Document Views group. Or, click the Web Layout view button ⬛ in the status bar.

- Use a table to create the layout for the web page. You can insert text and graphics in the table cells (see Figure 12-8).

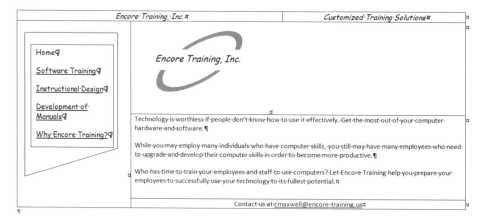

Figure 12-8 *Insert text and graphics in a table format to help organize the page content.*

- Create hyperlinks to other locations on the page, to other web pages, or to e-mail addresses.

- Apply a theme, choose a page color for the background, change font colors, add a background to table cells, and so forth. Be sure to remove table borders (see Figure 12-9).

Figure 12-9 *Apply themes and background colors to give the web page a professional look.*

Index

Numbers

3-D effects, using with AutoShapes, 105

8.5" × 11" paper sizes, scaling content for, 263

100% zoom level, specifying, 46

Symbols

... (ellipsis), meaning of, 22

/ (forward slash), separating table text with, 94–95

[] (brackets), displaying for bookmarks, 114

\ (backslash) switch

using with cross-reference field codes, 175

using with TOC field codes, 161

\# switch, using with merge field codes, 195

^ (caret), using with exponents, 124

=rand(), inserting random text with, 133

A

A4 paper sizes, scaling content for, 263

Access keys, using, 18

active window, maximizing, 45

ActiveX controls, relationship to Legacy Tools, 250

Add to Dictionary option, using with Spelling and Grammar feature, 200

Address Block, changing formats for, 192

Address Block command, using with mail merge, 188–189

Address Block layout, replicating with Update Labels command, 191–193

address labels

creating, 183–184

creating full pages of, 185–186

previewing before printing, 186

addresses

formatting per postal guidelines, 193

printing on envelopes, 182–183

Adjust group, using with picture settings, 98

adjustment handle, using with AutoShapes, 106

aligning text, tools for, 40–41

alignment

of pictures and objects, 99–100

of text within table cells, 89–91

vertical text alignment, 143

Alt key. *See* keyboard shortcuts

Arrange All button, using with multiple documents, 44

Ask field, description of, 190

AutoCorrect settings, changing, 200–201

AutoFit Contents option, using with tables, 87–88

AutoFormat settings

changing, 200–201

using, 66

automatic formatting, applying to styles, 66

Automatic Hyphenation feature, using, 141

AutoShapes. *See also* shapes

adding pictures to, 106

aligning objects for, 107

applying styles to, 104

copying text formatting to, 107

displaying, 100–101

formatting, 104–107

maintaining consistency of, 107

using adjustment handle with, 106

B

background color
adding to pages, 146–147
printing, 262
background printing, option for, 262
backslash (\) switch
using with cross-reference field codes, 175
using with TOC field codes, 161
badges, visibility of key tips in, 18
balloon displays, modifying for tracked changes, 212
Banded Columns table style, applying, 82
Banded Rows table style, applying, 82
bibliographies
creating, 11, 167–171
generating, 170
bibliography field codes, displaying, 171
Blank Page command, using with cover pages, 75
blog posts
creating, 270
template for, 6
body text
collapsing in Outline view, 38
customizing font styles for, 130
booklets
creating, 140
formatting margins for, 140–141
printing, 260
bookmarks
inserting, 114–115
using to create multiple TOCs, 163–164
border lines, customizing for tables, 82
borders
adding to pages, 147
changing, 120
brackets ([]), displaying for bookmarks, 114
brush strokes, making with Format Painter, 54
Building Block Gallery control, description of, 245

building blocks
accessing, 72
adding, 72–73, 117
changing content of, 73
changing properties of, 73
inserting, 72
sharing, 73–74
Building Blocks Organizer, features of, 8–9
built-in heading styles, including in TOC, 156–158
bullet formats, applying and removing, 60
buttons
adding toolbar buttons to Quick Access Toolbar, 20, 59
creating toolbar buttons for macros, 229
removing toolbar buttons from Quick Access Toolbar, 20

C

caps
changing delivery addresses to, 182, 184
formatting text in, 57
keyboard shortcut for, 194
caption styles, using with tables of figures, 172–173
captions
customizing labels for, 171–172
formatting, 171–172
caret (^), using with exponents, 124
case, changing for fonts, 57
cell margins, formatting for tables, 90–91
cell padding, explanation of, 89
Cell Size group, using options in, 87
cells
aligning text within, 89–91
changing width and height of, 87
removing from tables, 85
resizing in tables, 87–88
selecting, 85
undoing actions for, 86
using formulas in, 95–96
cells and tables, merging and splitting, 86

certificates, creating self-signed certificates for macro projects, 236

Change Chart Type option, using, 112

changes, tracking, 210–222

characters, showing and hiding nonprinting characters, 42

chart data, editing, 112

chart layouts and styles, changing, 112

chart styles, displaying, 112–113

Chart Tools Design tab, displaying, 111

charts, creating, 111

circles, creating, 104

citations
    creating, 11, 167–171
    inserting by adding sources, 167–168
    marking for tables of authorities, 179

Clear Formatting button, identifying, 58

Click-Shift-Click method, selecting text and objects with, 50

Clip Art, inserting, 100

clipart images, creating watermarks with, 145

Clipboard group, Format Painter button in, 53–54

Clipboard task pane
    moving and resizing, 52–53
    setting options for, 51–52

Close command, accessing in task pane, 52

collaboration, functionality for, 14

collapsed text, displaying in Outline view, 39

colors
    adding to pages, 147
    changing, 120
    changing for themes, 129–130
    modifying for tracked changes, 212

Colors options for themes, customizing, 130

columns. See also tables
    adding to and deleting from tables, 85–86
    distributing space among, 88
    formatting in tables, 81–82
    formatting text in, 141
    selecting in tables, 77

Combine Documents dialog box, displaying, 217

Command mode, switching from Text Entry mode to, 18

commands
    accessing with keystrokes, 18
    adding to Quick Access Toolbar, 20
    organization on Ribbon, 16

comments
    adding, 208–210
    displaying, 212
    displaying in Reviewing pane, 213–214
    displaying user information related to, 208
    editing and deleting, 210
    locating, 209
    reviewing summaries related to, 213

Comments or No changes option, selecting, 219

Compare Documents feature, using, 215–217

compared documents, reversing, 217

Compatibility Checker
    features of, 13–14
    running, 26–28, 268–269

compatibility mode, working in, 13

connector lines, joining shapes with, 102

content controls. See also controls; forms
    creating forms with, 245
    grouping, 249–250
    inserting, 246
    setting properties for, 247–248
    unlocking, 250

contextual options, explanation of, 3

Contextual Spelling option, using, 200

controls. See also content controls
    adding to fields, 189–190
    converting to Word 2007, 250

Convert Table To Text dialog box, displaying, 94

convertible document applications, list of, 28

cover pages
    creating, 74–75
    impact on watermarks, 144

cross-reference field codes, displaying, 175. See also field codes

cross-references
  creating, 174–175
  editing, 176
  inserting, 115–116
Ctrl key. *See* keyboard shortcuts
custom styles, using with TOCs, 159
custom watermarks, creating, 145
Customize Keyboard dialog box, displaying for macros, 228
customized themes
  deleting, 133
  saving, 132–133

D

data sources, matching fields to, 191
date and time fields, adding to headers and footers, 117
Date Picker control, description of, 245
delivery addresses, changing to caps for printing addresses on envelopes, 182, 184
design mode
  displaying documents in, 247–248
  toggling on and off, 246
Detect language automatically option, using with translations, 206
Developer tab
  displaying for use with form controls, XML, and templates, 241–242
  displaying for use with macros, 225–226
Dialog Box Launcher, using, 17–18
dialog boxes, using Help feature from, 32
dictionary, adding words to, 200
digital certificates
  obtaining for macro projects, 237
  purchasing, 268
digital signatures, adding, 26, 267–268
document conversion, checking compatibility of, 268–269
Document Information Panel
  displaying, 23
  editing information in, 266
  features of, 12

Document Inspector
  displaying, 24–25
  removing sensitive information with, 12–13
document management servers, publishing on, 271–272
document navigation, tools for, 40–41, 113
document pages. *See* pages
document properties
  setting, 23
  viewing and editing, 12
document protection
  from editing, 251
  removing, 220–221, 251
  restricting access for modifications, 218–219
  restricting access for opening e-mail documents, 221
  restricting formatting and editing, 219–220
document views, changing, 34, 44
document workspaces. *See also* workspaces
  creating, 273–274
  creating for publishing, 28
  saving documents to, 221–223
documentation style, choosing for citations and bibliographies, 167
documents. *See also* Word documents
  accessing recent documents, 28
  adding digital signatures to, 267–268
  arranging in Windows, 44–45
  attaching templates to, 242–243
  checking compatibility of, 268–269
  combining, 217–218
  combining to create master document, 40
  comparing, 215–217
  comparing side by side, 44–45
  converting, 22
  creating, 22
  creating subdocuments, 39–40
  decrypting, 26
  displaying text formats in, 54
  encrypting, 25, 267
  inspecting, 24, 266

jumping to beginning of, 35

jumping to end of, 35

jumping to pages in, 35

jumping to sections in, 35

marking as final, 26, 268

maximizing space in, 91

navigating in Full Screen Reading view, 34–35

navigating in Print Preview mode, 47

opening, 22

opening in other windows, 44

pinning, 28

preparing for distribution, 23–27

printing, 23

publishing, 28

reducing size of, 47

removing protection from, 220–221

removing sensitive information about properties of, 266

restricting access to, 218–219

saving, 23

saving as templates, 263–265

saving as web pages, 265–266

saving in PDF or XPS format, 264–265

selecting in entirety, 193

selecting text boxes in, 101

sharing, 221–223

using Arrange All feature with, 44

using as templates, 244

documents with equations, saving, 126

documents with tracked changes, printing, 214

double underline, formatting, 59

draft quality printing, option for, 262

Draft view

using with footnote and endnote continuation notices, 166

working in, 40

Draw Table tool, using, 78

Drawing Tools Format tab, using with shapes, 100–101

drawing canvas

changing settings in, 103

drawing shapes with, 103

toggling between text pane, 103

drawing mode, exiting, 79

drawings, preventing printing of, 262

drop cap feature, using, 120

Drop-Down List control, description of, 245

duplex printing

options for, 263

using, 259–260

E

Edit Data button, using with charts, 112

Edit Individual Documents option, using with mail merge, 196

Edit Points command, using with freeform shapes, 101–102

editing

protecting documents from, 251

restricting, 219–220

saving time during, 67–69

editing actions, repeating, 67

Editing group, selection commands in, 50

Effects options, applying to themes, 131

electronic distribution, preparing documents for, 263–268

ellipsis (...), meaning of, 22

e-mail

merging to, 196–197

personalizing with mail merge, 196–197

sending, 28

e-mail attachments, sending PDFs and XPS files as, 223

e-mail documents

preventing from opening in Full Screen Reading view, 37

restricting access to, 221

Encrypt Document option, using, 25

endnote continuation notice, creating, 166

endnote mark default, changing, 165

endnotes
    converting notes to, 166
    converting selected notes to, 166
    inserting and deleting, 164
    navigating, 165
enhanced ScreenTips, showing and hiding, 42
envelopes, printing addresses on, 182–183
Equation Builder, features of, 8–9
Equation Tools Design tab, displaying, 123
equations
    adding placeholders to, 125
    creating, 122–125
    displaying, 124
    editing, 124
    removing, 124
    saving documents with, 126
    using Structures with, 125
    viewing symbols for, 124–125
Excel spreadsheets, inserting in tables, 80
exponents, using caret (^) with, 124
EXT option, extending selections with, 50
Extensible Markup Language (XML)
    overview of, 252
    using schemas, 253

F

F keys. *See* keyboard shortcuts
facing pages, explanation of, 138
field codes, printing, 263. *See also* cross-reference field codes; TOC field codes
fields
    matching to data sources, 191
    updating before printing, 262
    using with cover pages, 75
    writing and inserting for mail merge, 188–193
fields with controls, adding to mail merge, 189–190
Figures, 119
    Address Block and Greeting Line fields for mail merge, 188
    Address Block command for mail merge, 188

Adjust group for picture settings, 98
adjustment handle used with AutoShape, 106
Alignment group options for text within table cells, 89
AutoShape consistency, 107
AutoShape styles, 104
AutoShapes, 101
AutoShapes with picture, 106
Blog group commands, 270
Blog post tab, 269
blog posts, 6
body text collapsed in Outline view, 38
bookmarks displayed in document, 114
building block options, 116
Building Blocks Organizer, 9
cell margin settings, 90
cell measurements for tables, 87
Change Chart Type option, 112
Chart Tools Design tab, 112
Citations & Bibliography group, 167
citations and bibliographies, 11
Colors options for themes, 129
comments displayed in balloons, 209
Comments group, 208
Compare command, 215
comparison settings, 217
Compatibility Checker, 14, 27, 269
content control buttons for forms, 245
content controls, 246
content controls grouped in design mode, 249
content controls in design mode, 248
contextual tabs, 3
Cover Page button, 74
Create Source dialog box, 168
Cross-reference dialog box, 174
cross-reference displayed as normal text, 116
Developer tab, 226
Dialog Box Launcher, 18
digital signature verification, 239
Document Information Panel, 23

Document Inspector, 13, 25

document protected from editing, 251

Document Template button, 242

Document Views group, 34

document workspace, 273

Draw Borders group, 79

Draw Table tool, 78

Drawing Tools Format tab used with shapes, 101

drop cap styles, 120

Edit Data button for charts, 112

Effects button in Themes group, 132

Envelopes and Labels buttons, 182

Equation Builder, 10

equation inserted, 123

Equation tools, 122

Equation Tools Design tab, 123

Eraser tool removes lines from table, 79

Excel spreadsheet inserted in table, 81

file extensions, 12

Finish & Merge button, 195

Font group, 3

Fonts button in Themes group, 131

Footnotes group, 164

foreign language checking for spelling and grammar errors, 207

formulas in tables, 95

full paragraph indents and paragraph spacing, 148

Full Screen Reading view, 34–35

graphics used to enhance text, 119

Greeting Line command for mail merge, 189

gridlines, 41

gutter added to document, 138

Header &Footer Tools Design tab, 117

header and footer formatting options, 119

Help windows revisited, 31

Illustrations group, 97

indent markers, 149

index generation, 178

Insert Caption feature, 171

Insert tab used with blog posts, 270

language selection for displaying translation, 37

layout options for SmartArt, 110

Line Spacing button, 62

Live Preview, 5, 57

macro edited in Visual Basic Editor, 232

Mailings tab, 181

margin settings, 135

Mark Citation button used with table of authorities, 179

Master Document group, 39

Merge Cells and Split Cells commands, 86

merge field results, 193

Merge group for tables, 86

merge process, 187

Mini toolbar, 55–56

mirror margins, 139

More button displaying more options, 17

nested tables, 80

new user interface, 2

Outline view, 38

Outlining tab, 38

Page Setup group commands, 134

Paragraph group, 152

picture styles, 98

Picture Tools Format contextual tab, 98

Preview group, 46

Print group Options button, 46

Print Preview tab, 45

Proofing group, 199

protecting documents, 218

Quick Access Toolbar, 2, 20

Quick Styles, 5

Quick Tables menu, 77

Repeat Header Rows feature for tables, 94

research services, 202

Research task pane, 203

Reviewing pane displays comments and tracked changes, 213

Ribbon, 3, 16

schema elements displayed, 255

schemas for XML, 253

section mark, 142

selection commands in Editing group, 50

SharePoint document posts, 272

signature line, 121

SmartArt graphics, 8, 108

SmartArt layout changes, 110

SmartArt styles, 110

SmartArt Tools Design tab, 108

sorting and calculating table data, 92

Source Manager for citations and
    bibliographies, 169

Styles task pane, 64

symbols for math equations, 125

Tab button, 151

Table button, 76

table cell margin settings, 90

table grid, 78

table move handle, 84

Table of Contents with built-in heading
    styles, 157

table of figures, 172

table split, 87

Table Style Options, 81

table styles, 83

Table Tools Layout tab, 84

tags related to schema elements, 256

task panes, 52

templates, 6

Text Direction button for table cells, 89

themes, 7

Themes gallery, 128

TOC (table of contents), 156

TOC entries marked manually, 161

Tools menu with options for Full Screen
    Reading view, 36

Track Changes button, 211

tracked changes accepted and rejected, 215

tracking changes, 211

translating documents, 204–205

Translation ScreenTips feature, 206

View tab, 33

views, 34

voice comments, 209

Watermark button, 144

white space hidden, 47

Window options, 44

word count, 208

Word settings, 29

XML features, 252

XML structure, 254

XML Structure pane, 256

zoom features, 43

Zoom Slider, 43

figures, creating table of, 172–173

file formats

    appearance of "m" in, 11, 30

    appearance of "x" in, 11, 30

    improvements in, 11–12

    using, 30

File menu. *See* Microsoft Office button

Fill in field, description of, 190

filler text, generating, 133

final, marking documents as, 268

Find entries, repeating, 68

finding text, 68

First Column table style, applying, 81

first line indents, formatting for paragraphs, 148

Fit Whole Page level, specifying, 46

floating text boxes, preventing printing of, 262

Font dialog box, displaying for delivery
    addresses, 183, 186

font formats, applying to merge fields, 194

Font group, location of, 2–3

font sizes, increasing and decreasing, 58

font styles

    customizing for headings and body text, 130

    previewing, 56

fonts. *See also* text formats

  applying subscript and superscript formats, 58

  changing case of, 57

  changing for themes, 130–131

  clearing formats for, 58

  formatting strikethrough marks, 59

  formatting with Mini toolbar, 55–56

  shrinking and growing, 58

  underlining text, 59

footer/header panes, placement of text in, 118–119

footers

  adding graphics to, 117

  creating in sections, 117–118

  location of, 116

footers and headers

  changing between, 118

  changing for first page and odd/even pages, 118–119

footnote continuation notice, creating, 166

footnote mark default, changing, 165

footnote reference marks, restarting, 165

footnote/endnote area, viewing, 165

footnotes

  converting notes to, 166

  converting selected notes to, 166

  inserting and deleting, 164

  navigating, 165

foreign-language text, proofing, 206–207

form controls. *See* content controls

form data, printing option for, 263

Format painter, using, 53–54

formats, modifying for tracked changes, 212

formatting, restricting, 219–220

formatting features

  Building Blocks Organizer, 8–9

  Equation Builder, 8–9

  Live Preview, 5

  Mini toolbar, 4

  Quick Styles, 4

  Reference Builder, 11

  SmartArt graphics, 8

  templates, 5–6

  themes, 7

forms. *See also* content controls

  adding instructional text to, 248–249

  filling in for protected documents, 251

formulas, using in tables, 95–96

forward slash (/), separating table text with, 94–95

fractions, indicating with x/y, 124

freeform shapes, using Edit Points command with, 101–102

Full Screen Reading view

  editing features for, 36

  exiting, 37

  preventing e-mail documents from opening in, 37

  using highlighter feature with, 37

  using Mini toolbar with, 36

  using Research option with, 36

  working in, 34–37

full-paragraph indents, formatting for paragraphs, 148

G

gallery, choosing list styles from, 61

global template, creating, 243–244

GOST style, using with sources, 170

grammar and spelling

  checking, 200

  suppressing checking of, 207

graphics

  adding to headers and footers, 117

  customizing labels with, 192

  enhancing text with, 119–120

  tools for alignment of, 40–41

Greeting Line command, using with mail merge, 189

gridlines

  displaying, 41

  viewing in tables, 84

Group command, using with content controls, 249

groups

accessing tabs in, 18

displaying more options in, 17

gutter margins, adding to mirror margins, 139

gutter settings, adding, 137–138

H

\h switch

using in TOC field codes, 161

using with cross-reference field codes, 175

hanging indents, formatting, 149–150

Header Row table style, applying, 81

header rows, repeating in tables, 93–94

header/footer designs, choosing, 116

header/footer panes, placement of text in, 118–119

headers

adding graphics to, 117

contents of, 116

creating, 116

creating in sections, 117–118

formatting for watermarks, 146

headers and footers

changing between, 118

changing for first page and odd/even pages, 118–119

heading levels, displaying in Outline view, 38

heading styles, including in TOC (table of contents), 156–158

headings

customizing font styles for, 130

selecting in Outline view, 39

Help button, identifying, 30

Help feature

using, 30–32

using from dialog boxes, 32

Help Viewer, opening, 30–31

Help window

displaying on top, 32

resizing, 32

hidden text, printing, 262

Highlight Merge Fields command, using, 190–191

highlighter feature, using with Full Screen Reading view, 37

*.htm and *.html formats, explanations of, 265

hyperlinks

creating, 113–114

formatting cross-reference entries as, 175

formatting TOC entries as, 161

hyphenating text automatically, 141–142

I

If...Else... fields, description of, 190

images, using with signature lines, 122

indents

adding to paragraphs, 148–150

first line indents, 148

full-paragraph indents, 148

hanging indents, 149–150

negative indents, 150

settings for, 151

index entries

deleting, 177

marking for range of pages, 177

marking text for, 176–177

indexes

advisory about updating of, 178

generating, 177–178

updating, 178

inkjet printers, using Ink volume option with, 261

Insert Chart dialog box, displaying, 111

Insert tab, using with blog posts, 270

insertion points, finding, 68

Inspect Document command, using, 24

instructional text, adding, 248–249

"Invalid signature" alert, troubleshooting, 122

IRM (Information Rights Management), implementing restricted access with, 221

ISO 690 style, using with sources, 170

K

key combinations, using, 19
key tips, visibility in badges, 18
keyboard
 navigating Ribbon with, 18–19
 selecting text and objects with, 50–51
Keyboard option, using with macros, 228
keyboard shortcut actions. *See also* shortcuts
 applying all caps, 194
 applying styles, 63
 brush strokes in Format Painter, 54
 changing case, 57
 changing delivery addresses to caps, 182
 copying text formatting to AutoShapes, 107
 creating and editing for macros, 230
 creating for macros, 228–229
 displaying bibliography field codes, 171
 displaying Font dialog box, 183, 186
 displaying Macros dialog box, 45
 displaying Replace tab, 195, 243
 displaying text formats in documents, 54
 displaying Thesaurus, 201
 displaying TOC field codes, 163
 double underlines, 59
 finding last insertion point, 68
 Help Viewer, 30–31
 hiding merge field codes, 194
 increasing and decreasing font sizes, 58
 inserting blank TC fields, 163–164
 inserting new cover pages, 75
 line spacing, 62, 153
 Macros dialog box, 234
 marking TOC entries, 160
 maximizing active window, 45
 navigating to XE fields in indexes, 178
 printing documents with tracked changes, 214
 Project Explorer, 235
 removing manual font formatting, 58

removing paragraph formats, 63
repeating editing actions, 67–68
repeating Find entries, 68
repeating last action, 68
selecting all paragraphs for translation, 205
selecting entire documents, 193
selecting mail-merge labels, 195
selecting text and objects, 51
small caps, 60
Subscript, 58
togging between text pane and drawing canvas, 103
toggling between cross-references and field codes, 175
Track Changes button, 211
using, 18
viewing TOC and TOC field codes, 161
keystrokes
 accessing commands with, 18
 for editing in SmartArt graphics, 109

L

labels
 creating full pages of, 185–186
 creating single address labels, 183–184
 customizing with graphics, 192
 customizing for captions, 171–172
 removing punctuation marks on, 195
 selecting, 195
 updating, 191–193
landscape orientation, using, 134, 140
languages, setting for proofing, 206–207
Last Column table style, applying, 82
layout options, using with SmartArt objects, 109–110
Layout tab, using with tables, 83
layouts, changing for charts, 112
Legacy Tools control
 description of, 245
 using, 250

line and paragraph spacing, adjusting, 152–153

line spacing

    changing, 62–63, 152–153

    keyboard shortcuts for, 153

Linear and Professional formats for equations, switching between, 124

Linear view, using with equations, 9–10

lines

    drawing for table grid, 78

    removing from tables, 79

Lines category of Shapes menu, using, 102

linked data, updating before printing, 262

links

    creating hyperlinks, 113–114

    inserting bookmarks, 114–115

    inserting cross-references, 115–116

list styles, modifying, 61–62

lists

    controlling numbers in, 61

    creating multiple levels of, 61–62

Live Preview feature

    description of, 5

    previewing fonts with, 56

    using with AutoShapes, 104–105

    using with picture styles, 98

    using with pictures and objects, 99–100

lowercase, formatting text in, 57

M

"m," appearance in file extensions, 11, 30

macro modules

    copying, 234–235

    renaming, 233–234

macro projects

    creating self-signed certificates for, 236

    deleting, 235

    digital signing of, 237

    locking, 235–236

    signing, 236–237

macros

    adding shortcuts to, 228–229

    completing recording process for, 229–230

    creating and editing keyboard shortcuts for, 230

    creating toolbar buttons for, 229

    deleting, 233

    displaying built-in macros, 225

    editing, 231–232

    naming and storing, 227–228

    organizing, 233–235

    planning, 227

    renaming, 232

    running, 230–231

    setting security options for, 237–239

    starting recording process for, 227

    undoing, 233

Macros dialog box

    displaying, 45

    keyboard shortcut for, 234

    running macros from, 231

Magnifier, using, 46–47

mail merge

    adding fields with controls to, 189–190

    completing, 195–196

    editing Recipient List for, 188

    inserting individual merge fields, 189

    printing records for, 196

    selecting recipients for, 187

    starting, 187–188

    using Address Block command with, 188–189

    using Greeting Line command with, 189

    writing and inserting fields for, 188–193

Mail Merge Toolkit, features of, 197

Mail Merge Wizard, starting, 187

margin settings

    changing defaults for, 136

    changing for entire document, 135–136

    changing for portions of documents, 137

    changing for sections of documents, 136–137

    displaying, 134

margins
    adding gutter settings to, 137–138
    changing, 46
    formatting for booklets, 140–141
    formatting for printing booklets, 260
    formatting for printing two pages on one sheet, 140
    formatting mirror margins, 137–138
Mark as Final option, using with documents, 26
master documents, creating, 39–40
Master List, selecting sources from, 169–170
Match Fields command, using, 191
math areas, changing to Normal text in, 124
Math AutoCorrect rules, using outside equations, 125
math equations. *See* equations
Merge Cells command, using with tables, 86
merge field codes
    adding switches to, 195
    hiding, 194
merge field results, displaying, 193
merge fields
    formatting, 194–195
    highlighting, 190–191
    inserting individually, 189
    locating, 190–191
    matching to data sources, 191
merge process. *See* mail merge
Merge Record# field, description of, 190
Merge Sequence# field, description of, 190
merged documents, previewing, 193–195
merging to e-mail, 196–197
Message Bar, disabling, 41
*.mht and *.mhtml formats, explanations of, 265
Microsoft Exchange, selecting Outlook contacts from, 182
Microsoft Office button
    features of, 2
    options associated with, 21
Microsoft support professionals, contacting, 32

Mini toolbar
    description of, 4
    formatting fonts with, 55–56
    Tools button for, 36
    using with Full Screen Reading view, 36
mirror image feature, printing option for, 261
mirror margins
    adding gutter margins to, 139
    formatting, 138–139
modules, storing macro components in, 227
More button, displaying options with, 17
mouse, navigating Ribbon with, 17–18
Move command, accessing in task pane, 52

N

navigation, tools for, 40–41, 113
negative indents, formatting, 150
nesting tables, 80
New Document dialog box, opening, 22
new user interface, 1
New Window button, using, 44
Next Record field, description of, 190
Next Record If field, description of, 190
nonprinting characters, showing and hiding, 42
Normal text style
    applying to math areas, 124
    restoring, 58
notes, converting to footnotes or endnotes, 166
NTFS system, encryption feature in, 26
Numbering feature, using with table rows, 96–97
numbering formats, applying and removing, 60
numbers, controlling in lists, 61

O

\o switch, using in TOC field codes, 161
objects. *See also* SmartArt objects
    aligning for AutoShapes, 107
    aligning with gridlines, 41
    positioning and aligning, 99–100
    resizing, 100
    resizing for AutoShapes, 105

resizing in drawing canvas, 103

restricting movement for AutoShapes, 105

objects and text. *See* text and objects

Office Online

connecting to, 31

searching document themes on, 132

online forms, including content controls in, 246

Open dialog box, displaying, 22

options

displaying with More button, 17

navigating with Tab key, 19

Organizer dialog box, using with macros, 233–235

orientation, changing, 46

Outline view

collapsing body text in, 38

displaying heading levels in, 38

selecting headings in, 39

working in, 37–39

Outlook address book, selecting contacts from, 182

Overtype mode, working in, 69

P

\p switch

using in TOC field codes, 161

using with cross-reference field codes, 175

Page Break command, using with cover pages, 75

page margins. *See* margins

page orientation, changing, 133–134

Page Setup dialog box, opening, 136

Page Setup group, options in, 46

PAGEREF field code, explanation of, 175

pages

adding background color to, 146–147

adding borders to, 147

jumping to, 35

paper, printing documents on both sides of, 260

paper size, changing, 133–134

paragraph and line spacing, adjusting, 152–153

Paragraph dialog box, creating hanging indent with, 150

paragraph formats

applying to merge fields, 194

bullets and numbering, 60

changing line spacing, 62–63

copying and pasting, 53–54

multilevel lists, 61–62

removing, 63

paragraphs

changing spacing before and after, 153

excluding for automatic hyphenation, 142

formatting first line indents for, 148

formatting full-paragraph indents for, 148

selecting, 205

passwords

removing from documents, 220–221

restricting document access with, 219

PDF attachments, sending in e-mail, 223

PDF format

converting documents to, 222

opening documents in, 264

saving documents in, 264–265

personal information, removing from documents, 222

Picture Content Control, description of, 245

picture settings, adjusting, 98

picture styles. *See also* styles

applying, 98–99

choosing shapes for, 98–99

customizing, 99

formatting, 99

pictures

adding to AutoShapes, 106

inserting, 97

positioning and aligning, 99–100

resizing, 100

pin icon, identifying, 28–29

placeholders, adding to equations, 125

portrait orientation, using, 134, 140

Position option, using with pictures and objects, 99–100

postal guidelines, following for addresses, 193

PostScript over text, printing option for, 263

Preview group, displaying Ruler from, 46

Preview Results feature, using with mail merge, 193

Print dialog box, opening, 45

Print Preview button, adding to Quick Access Toolbar, 47

Print Preview mode
editing documents in, 46
navigating documents in, 47
using, 45–47

printer options, viewing, 260–263

printing, 46
addresses on envelopes, 182–183
documents, 23
documents with tracked changes, 214
field codes, 263
keyboard shortcut for, 214
records for mail merge, 196
in reverse order, 261–262
sheets of address labels, 186
two pages per sheet, 140
using duplex printing, 259–260

Professional and Linear formats for equations, switching between, 124

Project Explorer, keyboard shortcut for, 235

projects, storing macro modules in, 227

proofing, setting languages for, 206–207

Proofing group, features of, 199

properties
removing from documents, 222
setting for content controls, 247–248

protected documents, disabling option for, 211

protecting documents, 218–220

Publish command
using, 28
using with blog posts, 270

punctuation marks, removing from labels, 195

Q

Quick Access Toolbar
adding commands to, 20
adding Print Preview button to, 47
adding text formats to, 59
features of, 2
using, 20

Quick Style Gallery, using, 63–64

Quick Styles feature, description of, 4

Quick Tables, creating tables with, 76–77. *See also* tables

R

=rand(), inserting random text with, 133

Read only option, selecting, 219

Reading Layout view. *See* Full Screen Reading view

Recipient List, editing for mail merge, 188

recipients, selecting for mail merge, 187–188

records, printing for mail merge, 196

Reference Builder, features of, 11

reference guide, accessing, 32

reference mark format, changing, 165

reference mark numbering, restarting, 165

Repeat command, using, 67–68

Repeat Header Rows feature, using with tables, 93–94

Replace button, using with text, 68

Replace tab, keyboard shortcut for display of, 195, 243

replacing text, 68

replicating labels, 192

Research option, using with Full Screen Reading view, 36

research services
customizing, 202
modifying and expanding list of, 202

Research task pane, opening and closing, 201

resolution, setting to display Ribbon, 16

reviewer details for tracked changes, managing, 212

Reviewing pane
  displaying and closing, 214
  displaying comments and tracked changes in, 213
Ribbon
  description of, 15–16
  displaying, 16
  displaying Text group on, 101
  features of, 2–3
  minimizing, 19
  navigating with keyboard, 18–19
  navigating with mouse, 17–18
  tabs, groups, and commands in, 16
Rich Text control, description of, 245
rows. *See also* tables
  adding to and deleting from tables, 85–86
  controlling breaks across pages, 93
  distributing space among, 88
  formatting in tables, 82
  numbering, 96–97
  selecting in tables, 77
Ruler
  creating hanging indents with, 149
  displaying, 46
  setting tabs with, 150–151
Rules command, using with mail merge, 189

S

schema elements, viewing, 255
schemas, adding to schema library, 253
screen space, saving, 47–48
screens, moving one at a time, 35
ScreenTips
  displaying text translations in, 36
  showing and hiding, 42
section breaks, editing, 142–143
sections
  creating, 142
  creating headers and footers in, 117–118
  deleting, 143
  setting margins for, 136–137

security options, setting for macros, 237–239
Select button, using with text, 68
Select command, options for, 49
selections, extending with EXT option, 50
self-signed certificates, creating for macro projects, 236
Send command, using with e-mail attachments, 223
sensitive information, checking for, 13
sentences, specifying spacing between, 67
separators, including in tables, 79–80
servers, saving documents to, 221–223
services, adding research services, 202
Set Bookmark field, description of, 190
settings for Word, locating, 29
shadow effects, using with AutoShapes, 105
shapes. *See also* AutoShapes
  adding text to, 101
  adding to SmartArt, 109
  choosing for pictures styles, 98–99
  joining with connector lines, 102
  using drawing canvas with, 103
SharePoint, publishing Word documents to, 271–272
sharing documents, 221–223
Shift key. *See* keyboard shortcuts
shortcut key combination. *See* keyboard shortcuts
shortcuts, creating for navigating documents, 113. *See also* keyboard shortcuts
Show Markup command, turning off options in, 212
Show Preview option, using with styles, 64
Show/Hide ¶ command, using with nonprinting characters, 42
Show/Hide groups, options in, 40–41
Shrink One Page feature, using, 47
Signature Details box, displaying, 122
signature lines
  adding, 121–122
  removing, 122
signatures, adding to Trusted Publishers list, 238–239

single spacing, keyboard shortcut for, 153

Size command, accessing in task pane, 52

Skip Record if field, description of, 190

small caps, formatting, 60

SmartArt graphics

    creating, 8

    description of, 107

    keystrokes for editing in, 109

SmartArt objects

    creating, 108–109

    layout options for, 110

    modifying, 109–111

    reverting to original design for, 111

    styles for, 110

sorting table data, 93

Source Manager, features of, 11

sources

    adding to insert citations, 167–168

    adding to Trusted Publishers list, 239

    managing for citations and bibliographies, 169–170

    selecting from Master List, 169–170

space

    distributing among table rows and columns, 88

    maximizing in documents, 91

spacing

    changing line spacing, 62–63

    changing before or after paragraphs, 153

    setting for lines and paragraphs, 152–153

    specifying between sentences, 67

spelling and grammar

    checking, 200

    suppressing checking of, 207

Split Cells command, using with tables, 86

Split option, using with windows, 44

Split Table command, using, 86

spreadsheets, inserting in tables, 80

squares, creating, 104

status bar

    adding Track Changes button to, 211

    changing options on, 44

strikethrough marks, formatting, 59

Structures group, using with equations, 125

style formats

    finding inconsistencies in, 66

    identifying errors related to, 66

    tracking, 65

    viewing details about, 66

Style Inspector task pane, opening, 64

style sets in Style Gallery, viewing, 63–64

styles. *See also* picture styles; table styles

    changing for charts, 112

    conversion of themes to, 133

    creating, 64–65

    displaying, 64

    formatting manually, 65–66

    formatting while typing, 66

    removing from Quick Style Gallery, 65

    using custom styles with TOCs (tables of contents), 159

    using format tracking list, 65

    using Quick Style Gallery, 63–64

subdocuments

    creating from existing documents, 39–40

    managing, 39

subscript format, applying, 58

summaries, displaying for tracked changes and comments, 213–214

superscript format, applying, 58

support professionals for Microsoft, contacting, 32

switches

    adding to merge field codes, 195

    using with cross-reference field codes, 175

    using with TOC field codes, 161

symbols
    using, 126
    viewing for math equations, 125
Synchronous Scrolling options, using with
    side-by-side documents, 44

T

TA entry fields, insertion of, 179–180
Tab key, navigating options with, 19
tab stops, setting precisely, 151–152
table borders, drawing, 78–79
table caption numbers, updating, 172
table cell margins, formatting, 90–91
table cells
    aligning text within, 89–91
    changing width and height of, 87
    removing from tables, 85
    resizing in tables, 87–88
    selecting, 85
    undoing actions for, 86
    using formulas in, 95–96
table columns
    adding to and deleting from tables, 85–86
    distributing space among, 88
    formatting in tables, 81–82
    formatting text in, 141
    selecting in tables, 77
table data, sorting, 93
Table Grid command, using, 77
table grid, drawing lines for, 78
table move handle, using, 84
table of authorities
    generating and updating, 180
    marking citations for, 179–180
table of contents (TOC)
    adding entries to, 159
    creating, 156
    creating using built-in heading styles, 156–158
    creating using custom styles, 159
    removing, 162
    updating, 162

Table of Contents dialog box, using, 159
table of figures, creating, 172–173
Table Properties dialog box, opening, 84
table rows
    adding to and deleting from tables, 85–86
    controlling breaks across pages, 93
    distributing space among, 88
    formatting in tables, 82
    numbering, 96–97
    selecting in tables, 77
table settings, changing, 91
table size, minimizing, 88
table styles. *See also* styles
    formatting, 81–83
    modifying, 82
    reusing, 82
Table Tools Design tab, displaying, 78
Table Tools tab, displaying, 3
tables. *See also* Quick Tables
    adding and deleting rows and columns in, 85–86
    aligning text within cells, 89–91
    converting text to, 79
    converting to text, 94–95
    creating with Quick Tables, 76–77
    creating with Table Grid command, 77
    customizing border lines for, 82
    including separators in, 79–80
    inserting Excel spreadsheets in, 80
    nesting, 80
    positioning, 91
    removing cells from, 85
    removing lines from, 79
    repeating header rows in, 93–94
    resizing cells in, 87–88
    selecting all or part of, 84
    selecting rows and columns in, 77
    using AutoFit option with, 87–88
    using Layout tab with, 83
    viewing gridlines in, 84
    wrapping text around, 79, 91–92

tables and cells, merging and splitting, 86

Tablet PCs, adding handwritten comments with, 210

tabs

  accessing in groups, 18

  separating table text with, 94–95

  setting with Ruler, 150–151

  settings for, 151

tags

  printing XML tags, 262

  using with schema elements, 255–256

task panes

  moving and resizing, 52–53

  moving and resizing Clipboard task pane, 52–53

  setting options for Clipboard task pane, 51–52

  for Styles Inspector, 64

  using with SmartArt objects, 109–110

TC fields

  creating manually for TOCs, 160

  creating multiple TOCs with, 163

  keyboard shortcut for insertion of, 163

templates

  attaching to documents, 242–243

  creating for sharing building blocks, 73–74

  creating new document based on, 242

  making global, 243–244

  saving documents as, 263–265

  types of, 5–6

  using documents as, 244

text

  adding to shapes, 101

  aligning vertically, 143

  aligning within table cells, 89–91

  animating, 60

  automatic hyphenation of, 141–142

  converting tables to, 94–95

  converting to tables, 79

  enhancing with graphics, 119–120

  finding and replacing, 68

  generating filler text, 133

  marking for index entries, 176–177

  placing in header/footer panes, 118–119

  restoring Normal style to, 58

  translating, 203–205

  underlining, 59

  wrapping around tables, 79, 91–92

text alignment tools, accessing, 40–41

text and objects

  selecting with Click-Shift-Click method, 50

  selecting with keyboard, 50–51

text boxes

  preventing printing of, 262

  selecting in documents, 101

Text control, description of, 245

text display, increasing by hiding white space, 47–48

Text Entry mode, switching to Command mode from, 18

text formats. *See also* fonts

  adding to Quick Access Toolbar, 59

  copying and pasting, 53–54

  displaying in documents, 54

Text group, displaying on Ribbon, 101

text in columns, formatting, 141

text pane, toggling between drawing canvas, 103

text translations, displaying in Screen Tips, 36

Text Wrapping feature, using with tables, 92

text written in foreign languages, proofing, 206–207

theme colors, changing, 129–130

theme effects, changing, 131

theme fonts, changing, 130–131

themes

  accessing, 7

  applying, 128–129

  conversion to styles, 133

  definition of, 127

  deleting customized themes, 133

  saving customized themes, 132–133

  searching on Office Online, 132

Thesaurus, displaying, 201

time and date fields, adding to headers and footers, 117

TOC (table of contents)

adding entries to, 159

creating, 156

creating multiples in same document, 162–164

creating using built-in heading styles, 156–158

creating using custom styles, 159

removing, 162

updating, 162

TOC entries

adding, 159

keyboard shortcut for, 160

marking manually, 160–161

TOC field codes. *See also* field codes

displaying, 161

editing, 162

including in tables of figures, 172

keyboard shortcut for display of, 163–164

TOC template styles, choosing, 157–158

toolbar buttons

adding to Quick Access Toolbar, 20

creating for macros, 229

removing from Quick Access Toolbar, 20

Total Row table style, applying, 82

Track Changes feature, turning on and off, 211

tracked changes

accepting and rejecting, 214–215

displaying in compared documents, 216

displaying and managing, 212

displaying in Reviewing pane, 213–214

printing documents with, 214

reviewing summaries related to, 213

Tracking group, monitoring changes with, 210–222

tracking options, turning off for manual styles, 65

Translation feature, using, 203–205

Translation ScreenTips, using, 206

translations of text, displaying in Screen Tips, 36

Trusted Publishers list

adding signatures to, 238–239

adding sources to, 239

U

underlining text, 59

undoing actions, for merged cells in tables, 86

Update Labels feature, using, 191–193

uppercase, formatting text in, 57

user information, displaying for comments, 208

users

accessing access privileges for, 220

restricting from editing documents, 251

V

versions, comparing, 215

vertical text alignment, changing, 143

View Side by Side option, using with documents, 44

View tab, groups in, 33

views

changing, 33–34

changing document views, 44

Draft view, 40

Full Screen Reading view, 34–37

Outline view, 37–39

Visual Basic Editor, editing macros in, 231–232

voice comments, inserting and listening to, 209–210

W

watermarks

adding predesigned watermarks, 144

creating with clipart images, 145

customizing, 145

editing, 145

formatting headers for, 146

printing, 261

removing, 146

using, 144

Web Layout view, displaying web pages in, 274

web pages
  creating, 274–275
  saving documents as, 265–266
Web Preview option, using with TOCs (tables of contents), 158
white space
  controlling around table cell margins, 89
  showing and hiding, 47–48
windows
  adjusting width for side-by-side documents, 45
  arranging documents in, 44–45
  maximizing active window, 45
  opening documents in, 44
  splitting, 44
Word, opening previous versions of, 27
Word 2007, converting controls to, 250
Word commands, displaying built-in commands, 225
Word Count command, using, 207–208
Word documents. *See also* documents
  converting to new file formats, 13–14
  using earlier versions of, 13–14
Word fields, accessing with Rules command, 189–190
Word settings, locating, 29
Word XML format, improvement of, 30
WordArt feature, using, 120
words, translating, 205
workspaces
  creating for documents, 273–274
  creating for publishing, 28
  saving documents to, 221–223

wrapping text around tables, 91–92
Write & Insert Fields group, using with mail merge, 188

X

"x," appearance in file extensions, 11, 30
XE fields for indexes
  explanation of, 177
  navigating to, 178
XML (Extensible Markup Language)
  overview of, 252
  setting options, 257
  using schemas, 253
XML format in Word, improvement of, 30
XML schemas, adding to schema library, 253
XML structure, displaying, 254–256
XML tags, printing, 262
XPS attachments, sending in e-mail, 223
XPS format, converting documents to, 222
XPS format
  opening documents in, 264
  saving documents in, 264–265
x/y, indicating fractions as, 124

Z

\z switch, using in TOC field codes, 161
zoom, setting, 43–44
Zoom dialog box, accessing, 43
zoom levels, specifying with Magnifier, 46

forums.apress.com

JOIN THE APRESS FORUMS AND BE PART OF OUR COMMUNITY. You'll find discussions that cover topics of interest to IT professionals, programmers, and enthusiasts just like you. If you post a query to one of our forums, you can expect that some of the best minds in the business—especially Apress authors, who all write with *The Expert's Voice*™—will chime in to help you. Why not aim to become one of our most valuable participants (MVPs) and win cool stuff? Here's a sampling of what you'll find:

DATABASES

Data drives everything.

Share information, exchange ideas, and discuss any database programming or administration issues.

INTERNET TECHNOLOGIES AND NETWORKING

Try living without plumbing (and eventually IPv6).

Talk about networking topics including protocols, design, administration, wireless, wired, storage, backup, certifications, trends, and new technologies.

JAVA

We've come a long way from the old Oak tree.

Hang out and discuss Java in whatever flavor you choose: J2SE, J2EE, J2ME, Jakarta, and so on.

MAC OS X

All about the Zen of OS X.

OS X is both the present and the future for Mac apps. Make suggestions, offer up ideas, or boast about your new hardware.

OPEN SOURCE

Source code is good; understanding (open) source is better.

Discuss open source technologies and related topics such as PHP, MySQL, Linux, Perl, Apache, Python, and more.

PROGRAMMING/BUSINESS

Unfortunately, it is.

Talk about the Apress line of books that cover software methodology, best practices, and how programmers interact with the "suits."

WEB DEVELOPMENT/DESIGN

Ugly doesn't cut it anymore, and CGI is absurd.

Help is in sight for your site. Find design solutions for your projects and get ideas for building an interactive Web site.

SECURITY

Lots of bad guys out there—the good guys need help.

Discuss computer and network security issues here. Just don't let anyone else know the answers!

TECHNOLOGY IN ACTION

Cool things. Fun things.

It's after hours. It's time to play. Whether you're into LEGO® MINDSTORMS™ or turning an old PC into a DVR, this is where technology turns into fun.

WINDOWS

No defenestration here.

Ask questions about all aspects of Windows programming, get help on Microsoft technologies covered in Apress books, or provide feedback on any Apress Windows book.

HOW TO PARTICIPATE:

Go to the Apress Forums site at **http://forums.apress.com/**.

Click the New User link.

You Need the Companion eBook

Your purchase of this book entitles you to buy the companion PDF-version eBook for only $10. Take the weightless companion with you anywhere.

We believe this Apress title will prove so indispensable that you'll want to carry it with you everywhere, which is why we are offering the companion eBook (in PDF format) for $10 to customers who purchase this book now. Convenient and fully searchable, the PDF version of any content-rich, page-heavy Apress book makes a valuable addition to your programming library. You can easily find and copy code—or perform examples by quickly toggling between instructions and the application. Even simultaneously tackling a donut, diet soda, and complex code becomes simplified with hands-free eBooks!

Once you purchase your book, getting the $10 companion eBook is simple:

❶ Visit **www.apress.com/promo/tendollars/**.

❷ Complete a basic registration form to receive a randomly generated question about this title.

❸ Answer the question correctly in 60 seconds, and you will receive a promotional code to redeem for the $10.00 eBook.

2560 Ninth Street • Suite 219 • Berkeley, CA 94710

eBookshop

THE EXPERT'S VOICE™